Moral Images of Freedom

New Critical Theory
General Editors: Patricia Huntington and Martin J. Beck Matuštík

The aim of *New Critical Theory* is to broaden the scope of critical theory beyond its two predominant strains, one generated by the research program of Jürgen Habermas and his students, the other by postmodern cultural studies. The series reinvigorates early critical theory—as developed by Theodor Adorno, Herbert Marcuse, Walter Benjamin, and others—but from more decisive postcolonial and post-patriarchal vantage points. *New Critical Theory* represents theoretical and activist concerns about class, gender, and race, seeking to learn from as well as nourish social liberation movements.

The radical project: Sartrean Investigations
   by Bill Martin
*Phenomenology of Chicana Experience and Identity: Communication and Transformation
   in Praxis*
   by Jacqueline M. Martinez
From Yugoslav Praxis to Global Pathos: Anti-Hegemonic Post-post-Marxist Essays
   by William L. McBride
Unjust Legality: A Critique of Habermas's Philosophy of Law
   by James L. Marsh
New Critical Theory: Essays on Liberation
   edited by William S. Wilkerson and Jeffrey Paris
The Quest for Community and Identity: Critical Essays in Africana Social Philosophy
   edited by Robert E. Birt
After Capitalism
   by David Schweickart
*The Adventures of Transcendental Philosophy: Karl-Otto Apel's Semiotics
   and Discourse Ethics*
   by Eduardo Mendieta
*Love and Revolution: A Political Memoir: People's History of the Greensboro Massacre,
   Its Setting and Aftermath*
   by Signe Waller
Beyond Philosophy: Ethics, History, and Liberation Theology
   by Enrique Dussel
   edited by Eduardo Mendieta
From Class to Race: Essays in White Marxism and Black Radicalism
   by Charles W. Mills
*Rights, Democracy, and Fulfillment in the Era of Identity Politics: Principled Compromises
   in a Compromised World*
   by David Ingram
Small Wonder: Global Power and Its Discontents
   by Fred Dallmayr
Globalizing Critical Theory
   by Max Pensky
Critical Social Theory in the Interests of Black Folks
   by Lucius T. Outlaw, Jr.
Moral Images of Freedom: A Future for Critical Theory
   by Drucilla Cornell

Moral Images of Freedom

A *Future for Critical Theory*

Drucilla Cornell

ROWMAN & LITTLEFIELD PUBLISHERS, INC.
Lanham • Boulder • New York • Toronto • Plymouth, UK

ROWMAN & LITTLEFIELD PUBLISHERS, INC.

Published in the United States of America
by Rowman & Littlefield Publishers, Inc.
A wholly owned subsidiary of The Rowman & Littlefield Publishing Group, Inc.
4501 Forbes Boulevard, Suite 200, Lanham, Maryland 20706
www.rowmanlittlefield.com

Estover Road, Plymouth PL6 7PY, United Kingdom

Copyright © 2008 by Rowman & Littlefield Publishers, Inc.

All rights reserved. No part of this publication may be reproduced, stored in a retrieval system, or transmitted in any form or by any means, electronic, mechanical, photocopying, recording, or otherwise, without the prior permission of the publisher.

British Library Cataloguing in Publication Information Available

Library of Congress Cataloging-in-Publication Data

Cornell, Drucilla.
  Moral images of freedom : a future for critical theory / Drucilla Cornell.
    p. cm. — (New critical theory)
  Includes bibliographical references and index.
  ISBN-13: 978-0-8476-9792-2 (cloth : alk. paper)
  ISBN-10: 0-8476-9792-4 (cloth : alk. paper)
  ISBN-13: 978-0-8476-9793-9 (pbk. : alk. paper)
  ISBN-10: 0-8476-9793-2 (pbk. : alk. paper)
  1. Social ethics. 2. Critical theory. 3. Liberty—Philosophy. 4. Civil rights—Philosophy. 5. Feminist ethics. I. Title.
  HM665.C674 2008
  172—dc22
                                                                               2007012385

Printed in the United States of America

∞™ The paper used in this publication meets the minimum requirements of American National Standard for Information Sciences—Permanence of Paper for Printed Library Materials, ANSI/NISO Z39.48-1992.

Contents

	Preface	vii
	Introduction: The Struggle for Redemptive Imagination	1
Chapter 1	Kantian Beginnings to the Legacy of Critical Theory: The Harmonious Play of Freedom	11
Chapter 2	Dignity in *Dasein*: Between Thrownness and Hospitality	39
Chapter 3	Symbolic Form as Other: Ethical Humanism and the Vivifying Power of Language	75
Chapter 4	Decolonizing Critical Theory: The Challenge of Black Existentialism	105
Chapter 5	Redemption in the Midst of Phantasmagoria: Dispelling the Fate of Socialism	137
	Conclusion: Heeding Piedade's Song—Toward a Transnational Feminist Solidarity	151
	Bibliography	165
	Index	169
	About the Author	177

Preface

The world seems to be in a dismal place and justice an ever-fading hope. How can anyone who has lived through the horrors of the twentieth and twenty-first centuries not sink into pessimism about the possibility of radical social transformation in the name of justice? This book deliberately runs against the grain of such pessimism without in any way denying the terrible, almost pathological, violence that has caused so much untold suffering for millions upon millions of human beings on this planet. But, we also cannot forgot the countervailing reality that during these past two centuries, millions upon millions of human beings also committed themselves to great ideals, particularly those of socialism and anticolonialism, and were willing to give up their lives in the name of freedom. Indeed, we might say that we owe those who died in pursuit of the dream of justice nothing less than the ongoing defense of the very ideals for which they fought to the very end of their lives.

As the thinker Walter Benjamin reminds us, "Hope is only for the hopeless." We are obliged, in a profound sense, to keep alive hope in the name of those who refused to give up their own faith for a better world even as they succumbed to death. New critical theory begins by taking that debt seriously, and taking that debt seriously means that we must begin to decolonize the critical project itself as a part of what is owed to the upheavals and revolutions that shook the foundations of what we have mistakenly reduced to the "Third World." Thus, the future of critical theory is itself integrally linked to the possibility of a future, just world. The impetus for this book is not only to revitalize many thinkers left outside narrow definitions limiting what is seen as the canon of critical theory itself, but also to open up the space for what such thinking should consider as the task of affirmative political philosophy. At the heart of this book is the argument that there can be no end of history, no death of the subject, and that the future is always open to the reimagining and reinvisioning of great ideals, even if we can no longer defend them through strong metaphysical arguments. But, defend these great ideals we must.

Similarly, this book is indebted to many special people. This manuscript could have never have been written without my research assistant and graduate student Kenneth Panfilio; he has partaken in every aspect of writing this book and has also been a major philosophical interlocutor with the heart of the arguments making up this text. While grappling with the deep complexities inherent to the thinkers wielded in this book could have easily been a burden, it was simply a pleasure due to Kenneth's poetic additions and brilliant insights. I am deeply in his debt, and there are simply no adequate words to thank him for the work he has put into all of the areas of my academic life.

At the last stages of revision, Kenneth Panfilio and Maureen MacGrogan helped by reading this text aloud with me to edit its content, with the goal of rendering complex philosophical ideas as readable and accessible as possible. Maureen MacGrogan was the editor of my first six books. After she left Routledge I followed her to Rowman & Littlefield. She has been an invaluable source of emotional support and intellectual engagement since the beginning of my academic career. Maureen has always been and even now in her retirement continues to be an editor with unmatched talent. But, she played an especially important role in this book due to the fact that she wrote her dissertation on *Being and Time* and is familiar with the work of Ernst Cassirer. Her dedication to critical theory and political philosophy was evident by her commitment to help me complete this book, and, as always, her friendship remains a gift beyond words.

Sara Murphy and Sally Ruddick have my deepest gratitude for their unwavering friendship and helpful comments on drafts of this book as they went through innumerable revisions. Sally Ruddick has become an indispensible critic, bringing analytic clarity and logical precision to my writing; her breadth of mind always carries with it a rigor, keeping my thoughts firmly grounded to the argument at hand. Lewis Gordon and Paget Henry gave me extensive and thoughtful comments on chapter 4, which were extremely valuable in helping me come to terms with the growing literature on black philosophies of existence to which this manuscript is hopefully faithful. Such careful reading is only further valued since both thinkers deserve our highest respect for the ways in which they have reworked and kept alive the meaning of critical theory in a thoroughly racialized world.

Laurie Ackermann, former constitutional judge in South Africa, is truly a moral exemplar of what it means to be an ethical person in an unjust world. Judge Ackermann played a major role in developing the dignity jurisprudence in the new South Africa, which explicitly addresses the critical tradition of Immanuel Kant. During the last two years we have become friends and began a Kant reading group in South Africa. Judge Ackermann's lifelong dedication to the tradition of transcendental idealism and well-crafted questions during our reading group led me to make significant changes to the first chapter. He deserves my deepest appreciation not only for his thoughtful comments but also for the inspiration drawn from his example. Martin Matustik and Patricia Huntington, both editors of this series, deserve all of our thanks and appreciation for having the broad vision to see the need for this series and for their tireless work to build such an excellent collection of manuscripts. They have read all of the chapters in this book and given thoughtful comments, which I hope I have faithfully addressed.

Of course, my daughter Serena is a constant source of inspiration as well as the deepest wellspring of hope for the future, something that I have fought for throughout all of my political and academic struggles. Her lyrical insight from one of my favorite songs that she has composed—"if you don't like memories, then forget who you are"—reminded me of the debt we owe to all generations if something like the idea of perpetual peace can even have meaning in our lives. My beloved friend Mary Elizabeth Bartholomew has been a constant source of support in every possible way for me during the last year, giving me nothing less than the very space and time to write this book. Without friends like Mary Elizabeth who are always there for you, it is perhaps impossible to even undertake a project as intellectually draining and emotionally overwhelming as writing a book. Irena Molitoris has helped me with childcare since I first became a mother and has provided my daughter with immeasurable love and friendship.

It is a deep honor to offer remembrance to one of our greatest political philosophers, Wilson Carey McWilliams, who tragically died in March 2004 and has played such an important role in keeping political theory alive in the world of political science. His passing has been an irreplaceable loss for the political theory faculty at Rutgers University, but in the last five years my colleagues—Gordon Schochet, Dennis Bathory, and Stephen Bronner—have been indispensible in supporting my varied research projects. Yearly, Gordon Schochet and I have held debates which have influenced me more than I will probably ever tell him, because the next debate is just around the corner. Both his wit and his erudition are almost unmatched in our field and he continues to teach me so very much. I also want to thank my colleagues working with me on the Ubuntu Project, particularly the young women who worked so tirelessly to conduct the interviews that first began that project and taught me so much about Africana philosophy as it survives on the ground.

Jaco Barnard and I first met when I was a member of his dissertation committee. I was so impressed with his dissertation that we have continued to correspond, building an intellectual community at the University of Cape Town, which is one of the central reasons that I am joining the faculty there. His brilliant readings of continental philosophy have influenced me profoundly, and you will find echoes of his insight in many of the chapters in this book, especially in my continuing reflections on Jacques Derrida. Jaco exemplifies the spirit of intellectual rigor and political and ethical passion so necessary for the next generation of scholars in the new South Africa. I am honored to know him and to call him a friend.

What strikes me the most about all of these people, even more than their intellectual insights, is their lasting commitment to intergenerational friendship.

Roger Berkowitz, who I first met in 1993 when he took a year off from his program at Berkeley to study Kant and Hegel with me, has since been a brilliant interlocutor and colleague. We have met nearly every week since that time to slowly and systematically work through the major texts of Kant, Hegel, and Heidegger. Roger Berkowitz is simply an outstanding translator, making sure that we remain faithful to all of the subtleties of the German language that are so often poorly translated into English. Roger is also one of our most careful and profound interpreters of Martin Heidegger, and he challenged me to take up these texts again from a fresh viewpoint. It is no exaggeration to say that every page in this book echoes with the full force of my ongoing study with Roger. Of course, full responsibility for all of the mistakes in what follows belongs to me, but to honor the years of intensive and invaluable study together, this book is dedicated to Roger Berkowitz.

DLC, New York, 2007

INTRODUCTION

∽

The Struggle for Redemptive Imagination

The New Critical Theory Series challenges us to think about nothing less than justice and what role theory can or should play in envisioning and actualizing a more just world. The critical theory of the Frankfurt School was inspired by Marxism and the effort to move beyond the inequalities of advanced capitalism to a socialist society. We often forget that in 1920s Europe lively debates about socialism as both a political reality and an ethical ideal were prominent, particularly in France and Germany. Throughout this book we will return, of course, to the moral image of the world that socialism offered so many progressives during the twentieth century; however, before uncovering such details we can move ahead by broadly construing socialism as the ideal that human beings can free themselves from the fundamental alienation imposed by class inequality so as to claim the truth of a grander world: humanity alone brings value into the world. It is humanity, both collectively and individually, that sets its own ends.

Within the ideal of socialism we are reminded that it is up to us to make our own history, no longer needing to project outward our own end-making capability as something that originated beyond us. But, of course the horror of World War II—the terrifying erasure of so many lives during the Holocaust—shook the optimism that socialism had sparked and made it seem like it was no longer a possibility.

Much to this point, some of the great thinkers of the Frankfurt School—such as Theodor Adorno, Max Horkheimer, and Herbert Marcuse—came to despair against the possibility of any moral image of the world that could claim even a small degree of freedom from within the virulent bombardment of the phantasmagoria of advanced capitalism. It seemed that the human subject was no longer simply exploited but also blinded by the dazzle of a consumer society that promises everything from perfect bodies made without flesh to the next wave of digital gadgetry giving us virtual reclusion in a space of the interior that has become wholly consumed by the expanse of capital. In this nightmare world of supposed glamour, the individual digs for the remnants of a subjectivity that can only find itself by holding tightly to its own despair and perhaps the thought that there once might have been a different passageway through this life. Even art, which Adorno hoped could hold on to the negativity that might fissure apart the totality of advanced capital, has become a commodity with managed artists whose bodies become a brand and whose talent is turned into a product label. We add to all this the enthusiastic celebration of the final defeat of socialism symbolized by the fall of the Berlin Wall in 1989 and we are left with renewed tales that celebrate capitalism as the only natural form of production and economic activity available to modern "man" during a time falsely labeled "the end of history."

As Sylvia Wynter has pointed out, "man" in this story is *homo economicus*, and all other aspects and conceptions of freedom are rendered irrelevant. Freedom becomes freedom of the consumer to "choose" from an endless array of products. It is an unfettered exercise of the will to partake in the full force of the cash nexus uninhibited that is now celebrated as the victory of democracy. Truly, it is "man" as this *homo economicus* that dominates the new trends in positive and social political science, where the human subject is atomized into abstraction and categorically defined as simply an economic exchanger and wealth maximizer. Yet, we do not even use big words like *man* or *humanity*, not for feminist purposes to remind ourselves that one gender has always stood in for the whole, but because we are intellectually predisposed as individuals in an endless scramble against other individuals, something like a caravan of rats crawling all over each other fighting over a mere crumb of bread in the worst sorts of nightmares ever imagined even by Nietzsche.

Those who hold on to the old ideas of freedom, equality, and justice—ideals, as we shall see throughout this book, that have origins reaching far into the world beyond Europe—are mocked as out of step with the time. After 9/11 those of us who stood by those ideals were even denounced as anti-American and out of touch with the needs of national security. We have now even gone so far that constitutional democracy, particularly as it ensured limits on executive power, seems to be out of sync with the so-called post-9/11 reality. Such security rhetoric bandied about in perfunctory speeches about looming "axes of evil" or invisible terrorist cells constitutes nothing more than a grand metanarrative, one that speaks in sweeping terms of clashes of civilization where the West is identified as the civilization against all others who never made it to our enlightened capitalist reality.[1] But, this metanarrative is not only the reigning story of right-wing conservatives, unfortunately those who hold power currently in the United States, but it has regrettably also been taken up in some of what has been called "postmodernism."[2]

We are faced with a similar pessimistic affront to the grand ideals of socialism that inspired the Frankfurt School, as we ourselves confront stifling academic reductionism mixed with dangerous relativity and a world of political machinations whose power through capital smacks of the sort of looming populism not itself dissimilar from the fascism that brought about World War II. What follows in this introduction is both an overview of some of the central ideas constituting this book and more importantly a rereading of my work in the *Philosophy of the Limit* meant to counter incapacitating intellectual and political pessimism, pointing instead to the hopeful future offered by moral images of freedom.

Moving from the Philosophy of the Limit

In my earlier work I renamed deconstruction the *philosophy of the limit* in order to read Jacques Derrida against a certain reception to postmodernism in the United States which put deconstruction paradoxically on the side of the disillusionment of the possibility of practical philosophy and thus in alliance with the metanarrative of advanced capitalism as the true end of history. Throughout this book we will return to the theme of limitation, as this is crucial to the good news that the future, as what is *other* to our present social reality, cannot be known in advance and already foreclosed by some grand theory. It simply cannot be known that humanity is fated to live out its relations as *homo economicus*, that politics is grounded in some iron casting of our historical situation, destining us to the oblivion of being under the victory of technology and the imprisonment of the spirit of justice in local struggles of resistance. Instead, the critical philosophy of Immanuel Kant begins with a more humble understanding of the notion of the limit of theoretical knowledge, suggesting to us that the world as we know it is the world as we have represented it to ourselves; there is no beyond that the mind can reach out and grasp, and, as Kant famously tells us, what we know in reality as scientific law is what we have put there.

Many Anglo-American commentators on Kant have focused on how his work effectively justifies scientific validity. Indeed, this is part of the critical project for Kant, but it is merely a small part of a larger architectonic. Kant himself reminds us of the three great questions of philosophy: What can I know? What am I to do? and What can I hope for? Critical philosophy begins with this first understanding of the limit of theoretical reason in that we can never get beyond our own representations and the world as it is given to us by the imagination. It is precisely this critical insight about how the world is knowable to us at all through a *secret in the soul* that Heidegger argued made Kantian philosophy a radical shift, or a Copernican revolution, in how human beings approach their world.

Indeed, given trends in the history of philosophy it is often forgotten that Heidegger began his own endeavors with a thorough engagement with Kant and a reworking of the concept of the transcendental imagination. One aspect of this book is to recover Heidegger's ultimate rejection of Kantian practical philosophy as this came to be thought by him as inseparable from the technological domination of a subject-centered universe, a subject-centered universe which for Heidegger eclipsed the true meaning of our freedom by separating us from the unconcealment of Being behind a veil of scientific objectification. For Heidegger, we can think this oblivion, and in a certain sense that is all that we can do without risk of reinforcing the veil that keeps us from our true dignity as the being to whom Being makes itself present. Heideggerian pessimism, in the terms used here, refuses what I am calling the critical insight into the limitation of theoretical reason, and replaces it with a pessimism that forbiddingly resists reform efforts as simply digging us deeper into the grave of a seemingly technocratic destiny in which humanity itself becomes one more project for engineering, social or otherwise.

Yet, Heidegger also opens up the phenomenological tradition of embodiment and fragility as itself a limitation on what can be known. Indeed, this is the second sense of limitation returned to throughout this book. Human beings are not only embodied but also come into ourselves in and through the language and other symbolic forms used to shape our world. Our knowledge is inevitably connected to both our place in the world and to the symbolic forms in which we know it. Both embodiment and the inevitability that our world comes to us in symbolic forms already represented are conceptual facilitators and limitations of how we know and relate to the world. Neither force denies aspirations to universal ideals, but both recognize that we have to proceed through some sort of acknowledgement of how we are to get to those ideals. In the world of Edmund Husserl, the great predecessor of Heidegger, we bracket aspects of our perspectives in order to open them up to other possibilities by seeing them as contingent and limited. In the case of Ernst Cassirer, the human being is in a sense transcendentally limited by a mark of ideality in which the world comes to us in the symbolic forms in which it is both presented (*darstellen*) and represented (*vorstellen*). Both the phenomenological and the Cassirerian insight into limitation will resound throughout this book, as such complex understandings can help us come to terms with what limitation means for new critical theory.

But, these limitations are not simply abstract philosophical ruminations. The recognition that the fate of Europe is not the fate of humanity or that the ends of the European white "man" do not represent the ends of humanity gives us a meaningful political, ethical, and deeply philosophical challenge about the future possibility of our shared being in the world. These fissures break open the canonical foundation of how we see the world in an empire, as such challenges were brought on by the actual struggle against colonialism. Of course, there have been good reasons for feminists to celebrate the death of such patriarchal, phallogocentric theoretical traditions since, for as Simone de Beauvoir pointed out to us long ago, such images of "man" eclipsed the feminine "other" as less than a human being. However, if feminism is to offer any meaningful counterperspective, then it must itself return to the critical insight offered by the critique of Eurocentrism, which forces all of us who are Anglo-American and European to come to terms with our own historical situation as exactly what it is: a historical situation, and not the destiny of all of humanity. Otherwise, we are left with mimetic second-wave feminist alternatives harkening back to the very grand narrative presented by Hegel that posited the European "man" as the culmination of the ideal of humanity finally capable of realizing the truth of its freedom within the context of the modern nation state; and such a vision was always conveniently made inseparable from the long and brutal history legitimating the domination of other people who were violently thrown out of this grand narrative of history. What is emerging here is a third sense of limitation where we must knowingly confront the limits of what European philosophy has to offer us without falling back into a self-contradictory relativism; that is, we need to understand the complex relationship of a plurality of symbolic forms and our aspiration to universal ideals in issues such as human rights, and even more broadly construed in the very struggle for liberation.

The fourth iteration of limitation was a deliberate attempt to provide a strong reinterpretation of the significance of certain strands of practical philosophy found throughout the work of Jacques Derrida. Here, the philosophy of the limit meant to turn around the idea put forward by Derrida that the limit of what can be known is also a condition of knowability. Derrida is, of course, engaging most specifically with Heidegger but also with other thinkers like Wittgenstein. Often, this reflection on the constitutive aspect of knowability has been used to reinstate a dangerous positive understanding of the unknowable that gets translated into a strong notion of what this means for practical political philosophy in that it provides some kind of normative limit on what we can hope for in the future. But, this goes exactly in the opposite direction of my own reading of the philosophy of the limit which argues strongly against naturalistic or positivistic reductions of either social or psychic life that would give us a strong theory of the subject capable of limiting our aspirations to justice. In other words, I argued that the unknowable, or what Derrida often refers to as the beyond, renders a certain kind of pessimism, at least theoretically unjustifiable, because this beyond cannot be shown to be either illusory or fully accessible to us in the present. Limitation, then, actually keeps open the impossibility of knowing what is impossible, leaving certain positivistic or naturalistic conceptions of humanity incapable of concretely postulating what we cannot hope to achieve. Much of the academic shifts across disciplines to rational-choice theories and risk-management calculations turn us back to "naturalistic" conceptions of human beings that are purportedly knowable and by allusion suppose to tell us what we can hope to aspire to in the big ideas of justice and freedom. Ultimately, I suggested that Derrida, and the experience of deconstruction, undermines this appeal to strong notions of human nature claiming to stand in as the truth of what we can expect from each other and society at large.

In my continued defense of the philosophy of the limit as a defense of the possibility of our increasingly ethical being in the world, the heart of this book contains a steadfast defense of the role of aesthetic ideas in political theory. Such a work is in no way meant to undermine the importance of critiquing hegemonic meanings and symbols that dominate our life. But, as Nietzsche tells us repeatedly, the idea of genealogy originates in an act of imagination or fabrication. A Nietzschean genealogy, in other words, is not a positivist account that ever reaches beyond the fundamental Kantian insight that the world is given to us in the reproductive imagination and then received and reworked by us in the productive imagination. Heidegger's critique of Nietzsche is that he remained too Kantian in his acceptance of the will and of the imagination as being at the very heart of the transvaluation of all values. However, to argue for the place of aesthetic ideas does change some of the claims and justifications that can be made for such ideas and ideals.

Once deconstruction and some major texts of Derrida are read in the ethical light I advocated in *The Philosophy of the Limit*, we are left with our responsibility to not only critique the status quo but also practically and theoretically reconfigure the great ideals of justice, freedom, and equality. Of course, this works against scientific notions of Marx that argued that we must stay within an analysis of the primary contradiction and develop social movements based on an articulation of what reality offers to us and not on idealistic or ethical hopes for a future. And yet, the irony is that many great thinkers were still imaginatively writing for liberation throughout what has now become known as the Third World, and the reality of socialism—no matter how corrupt—is still a force in the world. There was, in other words, an alternative to capitalism that was almost assumed as something that could be reconfigured and reworked by the new Left of my generation. I should say, from the beginning of my own activism, which included membership in several Marxist-Leninist organizations, I strongly opposed the view of Marx that reduced the aspiration for a just world to the scientific necessity of collapsed capitalism. Much ink has been spilled as to whether Marx ever gave up his ethical aspirations and the influence of both Kant and Hegel on his work which he returns to in *Capital*. But, there is a tenor of thought in the young Marx which speaks to the larger project of German idealism as one trying desperately to call forth a moral image of the world, especially when he suggests, "The criticism of religion ends with the teaching that *man is the highest being for man*, hence with the *categorical imperative* to *overthrow all relations* in which man is a debased, enslaved, forsaken, despicable being."[3] Although German idealism is clearly a Eurocentric tradition, it is perhaps time for us to reconsider the moral image of humanity that its great thinkers defended as we try to reassess what European philosophy has to offer as well as its limits in the larger discourse of how we come to know ourselves in our world.

Some critics have questioned the relationship between my first two books, *Beyond Accommodation* and *The Philosophy of the Limit*, and my explicit defense of an aesthetic idea in the *imaginary domain* throughout my later work. There is, in my opinion, a misunderstanding among such critics on the role of aesthetic ideas in political philosophy that turns me now to offer a fuller justification. My project in those early works was to pave a way for the defense of aesthetic ideas, by arguing against what is now called postmodernism as it is often situated in contrast to the possibility of affirmative political philosophy. Some of the resistance to any kind of affirmative political philosophy stems in its most significant form from a pessimism brought about through Heidegger, which in my reading was certainly taken seriously yet ultimately challenged in the work of Derrida. Simply said, it is up to us to accept our responsibility, knowing that in a deep sense we cannot theoretically justify an escape from such responsibility by reliance on a theorist like Derrida, who at times has been read to undermine moral agency. For example, the structure of such an understanding of *différance* would be that the moment we pose ourselves to an "other," what we are proposing cannot be communicated because in this very moment of posing, the self as an "other" is already ensnared in an explicit appeal through which it communicates. Thus, *différance* on this reading undermines any theory of the subject including moral subjectivity.

But this, of course, would imply that moral and ethical responsibility stands and falls with the theory of the subject. Indeed, my argument has been that Kant already argued against the possibility of such a theory of the subject. It is Kant who first introduces the conception that the "I" is an "other." For Kant, it is always a question of the form of time in general which distinguishes between the act of an "I" and the ego to which the act is attributed: an infinite modulation, no longer a mode. The form of interiority for a subject necessarily "in time" means not only that time is internal to us but also that our interiority constantly divides us from ourselves; in this sense, it splits us in two, which is a splitting in two that never runs its course since time has no end for us as finite human beings. We cannot know ourselves as free subjects in the sense of a theoretical knowledge. Although Kant changes his position in his justification of the force of practical reason, it is always the case that the faculty of desire is not and cannot be rooted in any theoretical ground of the subject as one that is so definitively constitutive of it that the possibility of the practical point of view, and with it the standpoint of practical reason, is obliterated.

The mere glimmer that remains in a moral image of justice shows us both how grim the world appears for a moment and how much it can itself become "other" from that moment. We can certainly heed Adorno's warning with all of its passion that any aesthetic idea or configuration of justice will risk the distortion and indigence it seeks to escape. At times, Adorno himself undoubtedly stepped back from affirmative, practical, political philosophy, seeing it as impossible to reconcile in the glaring phantasmagoria of advanced capitalism. But, he also stood against a universalization, or globalization, of pessimism as a philosophical truth, and as such suggests to us, "It is the simplest of all things, because the situation calls imperatively for such knowledge, indeed because consummate negativity, once squarely faced, delineates the mirror-image of its opposite."[4] So, even in Adorno the insistence that we must come to terms with the full force of the internalization of how we have become subjected and the objects of a society of total commodification, we do so not merely by holding on to consummate negativity because in a sense that negativity can never be grasped or configured without another standpoint.

We need to distinguish more carefully, then, the double message of searing critics suggesting that advanced capitalism eats up the remnants of our subjectivity as it not only gets into our heads but also renders us simply momentarily knocked down. There is a difference between the critiques of life under advanced capitalism from more sweeping forms of philosophical pessimism such as those put forth by Heidegger, which would swiftly reject the possibility of practical philosophy as only some sort of optimistic window dressing ultimately infected with the sort of ensnarement that keeps us concealed from our being in the world. Such a message of pessimism has its momentary place in the perpetuation of a world dominated by a barrage of technology and the worst forms of naturalized positivism that deny any remaining dignity to human beings and their aspirations. However, despite the bold banner of such pessimism claiming that the world of advanced capitalism has eaten up the ideal of freedom itself, we must remember the lessons of limitation and realize that what else but this grand ideal of freedom could lead us out of such a labyrinth of wayward capitalist distractions and leave us ever still with the possibility of generating moral images of our freedom in the world.

Notes

1. See, generally, Amartya Sen, *Identity and Violence: The Illusion of Destiny* (New York: W. W. Norton, 2006).

2. I have argued elsewhere against the designation of an identifiable period such as the "postmodern"; see, for instance, *Philosophy of the Limit* (New York: Routledge, 1992), "Introduction: What is Postmodernism Anyway?"

3. Karl Marx, "A Contribution to the Critique of Hegel's Philosophy of Law: Introduction" [1844], in *Collected Works*, vol. 3, Karl Marx and Fredrich Engels, 182 (New York: International Publishers, 1976), cited from Kojin Karatani, *Transcritique: On Kant and Marx*, trans. Sabu Kohso (Cambridge, MA: MIT Press, 2005), xi–xii.

4. Theodor Adorno, *Minima Moralia: Reflections on a Damaged Life* (New York: Verso, 1978), 247.

CHAPTER ONE

∼

Kantian Beginnings to the Legacy of Critical Theory: The Harmonious Play of Freedom

In this chapter I will strongly defend the role of the imagination and, more specifically, aesthetic ideas in political philosophy. In order to explore more deeply the philosophical significance of aesthetic ideas, we need to look more closely at the writings of Immanuel Kant and his work in the *Critique of Judgment*. To open this discussion of aesthetic ideas and their importance in political philosophy, we begin with the example of the *imaginary domain*, an aesthetic idea I developed to resolve a seeming paradox in feminist jurisprudence. Before turning to Kant's complex relationship to the imagination and his elaboration of what constitutes an aesthetic idea, we must begin with that debate.

In the mid-1990s the feminist movement in the United States fell upon a quandary. On the one hand, feminist activists and lawyers had very effectively used the word *sex* in the Civil Rights Act of 1965 to argue for equal rights for women. *Sex* became *gender*, and the legal standard for discrimination was to compare whether or not a differential treatment between men and women was fair. This logic was meant to determine if there was an actual difference, or discrimination, meaning there was no actual difference in terms of the category of adjudication. In other words, on the level of social life it became literalized that if a woman was to be enough like a man in order to get a job, she should indeed have the lifestyle of a man, that is, not bother a company with pregnancies or the complexities of raising children. However, the terms of the debate mistakenly framed our ideas of sex and gender with a myopic narrowness such that the rights of gays, lesbians, and transgendered people were excluded from the reach of civil rights law.¹ Still, despite this dire effect, the achievements of early feminist lawyers must be noted. The bringing down of the barriers for the participation of women in the workforce should never be denied as an achievement even though it was a limited one, especially considering that neither of the two women who have been on the U.S. Supreme Court—Ruth Bader Ginsburg and Sandra Day O'Connor—could get jobs as lawyers after graduating at the top of their classes in law school. However, while recognizing this achievement we must also take serious notice of why gay and lesbian theorists question the category of woman as being inseparable from the heterosexual norms that made up what femininity was supposed to be as an ideal. It was not a coincidence that the reigning notion of femininity that rendered gays and lesbians beyond the reach of law and outside the success of civil rights actions carried within it the danger of a reinforced femininity that ultimately made the actual achievement of what law opened up a difficult possibility for many women to realize.

This critique of femininity as inhering in genderized norms led many to be suspicious of any use of law or idea of rights as an avenue in the struggle for truer equality, as this would be applied to sexual life. Indeed, this led some feminists to question whether feminists should fight for civil rights or an idea of gender equality even if it was expanded to include gays, lesbians, and the transgendered.² Legalization then became a foe because it implied a concept of right that no matter how it was articulated would reinstate universalizable sexual norms, and it was just such universalizable sexual norms that queer theory set itself against. These norms were thought to not only undermine sexual enjoyment but also impose a trauma by closeting forms of sexuality outside stated norms.

For many involved in recent literary and cultural theory, it has become customary to turn to psychoanalysis for a radical critique of sexual norms. The idea of a bisexual unconscious can serve nicely to upset the stifling language of heterosexual normality which does service for virtue in the bankrupt discourse of family values. Jacqueline Rose has nicely summarized this paradox that seemed to arise in the dispute between queer theory and some feminists. It might be, however, that those who welcome attention to the question of our sexuate being without considering it a matter of justice will soon find the entire matter unexamined and unexposed:

> "The requirement... that there shall be a single kind of sexual life for everyone," writes Freud in *Civilization and its Discontents*, "cuts off a fair number from sexual enjoyment, and so becomes the course of serious *injustice*" ("*Ungerechtigkeit*").

And yet, as he himself puts it only a few pages earlier, for a law to be just ("*Gerechtigkeit*") it *must* be universal, that is, broken in no-one's favour; although this tells us nothing, he adds, about the ethical value of such a law.³

Rose has eloquently summarized the dilemma in Freud when he demands that there be a universalizable right and that any such universalizable right would seem to go against what it would seek to protect, that is, the right to what I am going to call somatic freedom. Rose concludes that this paradox is not simply internal to a universalizable right of sexual or somatic freedom but to the concept of justice itself.

My solution to this paradox was to develop or defend the aesthetic idea of the imaginary domain. The idea of a domain returned to Virginia Woolf's call for a room of one's own. But now not as a literal reality—although, of course, we may need that, too—but a domain that allows the imagination to roam freely in the safety provided by the acceptance of play as crucial to sexual pleasure. The domain is only bound by our respect for others as also in need for the space of play and for somatic freedom. Hence, the degradation prohibition. By the degradation prohibition I meant to indicate that not one of us could fall below the register of humanity and the respect for that humanity because of our sexual practices. The imaginary domain would resolve this paradox in two ways. First, the right is universalizable as the moral and psychic space necessary for each one of us to come to terms with who we are as a sexuate being. *Sexuate being* broadly defined means nothing more than who we are as embodied finite creatures, and always involves some necessary confrontation with sexual differentiation and pleasure. The space of the imaginary domain is limited only by what I defended as the degradation principle, but degradation was not meant to be used in a flowery or imprecise way. Degradation was meant to forbid only those social practices, whether legalized or not, which actually took away from someone their equal standing as a person because of their expressed sexuality. In other words, two gay men sitting together in a restaurant in no way degrades the experience of heterosexuals sitting at a nearby table who might happen to harbor a prejudiced disdain for homosexuality, for those heterosexuals are still able to claim their personhood. But, if gays and lesbians are not allowed equal rights as persons, then they are degraded, and the same would apply to transgendered identity and any other form of sexuality anyone chooses to develop and articulate in the imaginary domain. What degrades is precisely what Freud worried about: norms that regulate sexuality as good or bad. Yet, it would still be a configuration of an ideal of somatic freedom which was necessary for feminism when it was trying to argue not only for the equal standing of women as persons both in the law and society but also for other forms of lived sexuality and lived sexual difference.

I have already written that the imaginary domain is an aesthetic idea and borrowed the notion of an aesthetic idea from Immanuel Kant. When Kant wrote of aesthetic ideas, he wrote of the great works of art created by genius. And, of course, no aesthetic idea, including the imaginary domain, can ever achieve the same power or spirit as a work of art that can animate our own reaction to it by bringing into life a fuller configuration offered by this more minimalist view of the aesthetic idea. This being said, it is still, to my mind, best to allow a place and an understanding for aesthetic ideas as hypothetical experiments in the imagination in political philosophy. To begin to unpack this argument, we need to return to why Kant refers to these aesthetic ideas as ideas. Of course, Kant did not speak of somatic freedom, but he did speak of the need to represent the great ideas of reason, including freedom, which could never yield a strictly logical presentation. Therefore, the representation of such freedom will always occur through analogy or indirectly through symbolization since there could be no concept adequate to the great ideas of reason. That being said, Kant was well aware that as phenomenal beings we need to have aesthetic ideas which present to our sensibility the force of these great ideas. To quote Kant:

> Now I maintain that this principle is nothing other than the faculty for the presentation of **aesthetic ideas**; by an aesthetic idea, however, I mean that representation of the imagination that occasions much thinking though without it being possible for any determinate thought, i.e., **concept**, to be adequate to it, which, consequently, no language fully attains or can make intelligible.— One readily sees that it is the counterpart (pendant) of an **idea of reason**, which is, conversely, a concept to which no **intuition** (representation of the imagination) can be adequate.[4]

For Kant, the powerful role of an aesthetic idea is that it activates the spirit and so as to make these great ideas come alive, irreducible to empty abstraction. Again, to quote Kant:

> **Spirit**, in an aesthetic significance, means the animating principle in the mind. That, however, by which this principle animates the soul, the material which it uses for this purpose, is that which purposively sets the mental powers into motion, i.e., into a play that is self-maintaining and even strengthens the powers to that end.[5]

The imaginary domain was meant to be an answer to the spirit of the seeming paradox that Rose argued Freud noticed and never resolved. But how do we understand the spirit of somatic freedom and the militant critique of gender norms that seem to constrain it? Is it the case that somehow or another sex and gender have become a serious business, something we can fail at if we do not live up to the ideas of what it means to be a good man or woman?

Indeed, so much of morality for women, as Rose also points out, is tied to restrictive notions of feminine sexuality. Rose remarks that she, like so many others of our generation, rebelled against this moral stricture that labeled many of us who sought sexual pleasure as "bad girls." So, how do we break up the norm of sexuality while providing people the space to play with their own sexual being in a way that undermines the moral seriousness of such endeavors and at least allows the playfulness of sexuality to be recognized? To answer this question, the word *imaginary* was chosen for two reasons. First, to recognize the psychoanalytic insight that who we are and even our most primordial sexual formations take place through the imaginary images that others have of us and that these imaginary images themselves can always be morally loaded. But, even if we begin our own struggle to become who we are as sexuate beings through an imaginary that is always already imposed, and indeed symbolized, we still can at least as a matter of possibility rework those symbolizations. Is this not what Judith Butler so brilliantly showed us in her book *Gender Trouble* in terms of the performative aspect of language, especially in terms of gender and sex? Second, I choose the word *imaginary* to emphasize the playful role of the imaginary in the affirmative aesthetic play of our own bodies and sexuate being that allows us to reenvision and act out ever increasing differentiation in our sexuality. In this way if we are fated to be a sexuate being we are not destined to a deadening sexuality that moralizes what is proper and imprisons us in rigid gender norms. Here the imaginary was meant to emphasize the possible field of play within sexual difference. Jacques Derrida liked to configure that play as a new choreography shared as a dance is shared, rooted in known dances and yet always offering the possibility of creative innovation.[6]

Schiller's Insight into Aesthetic Play

The paradox of sexual freedom is that it demands moral space that does not normalize the content of sexuality itself. One aspect of the imaginary domain is to remember Friedrich Schiller's lesson of the importance of aesthetic play more generally in freeing us from the overseriousness of revolutionary politics that can easily degenerate into a self-righteousness justifying the worst kind of violence. Schiller famously sought a balance that he believed we would only find in the realm of the aesthetic between the demands of sensibility and the demands of Kantian moral philosophy. It was in Kant's own aesthetics that Schiller found an effort to achieve such a balance, and we will return to Kant's discussion of harmonious play in the judgment of beautiful objects shortly. For now, I want to remain focused on the imaginary domain as it attempted to incorporate Schiller's insight into the need for a balance between sensibility and morality, as this particularly relates to the notion of somatic freedom. To this end, Schiller suggests to us:

> But the relaxing of the sense drive must in no wise be the result of physical importance or blunted feeling, which never merits anything but contempt. It must be an act of free choice, an activity of the person that, by its moral intensity, moderates that of the senses and, by mastering impressions, robs them of their depth only in order to give them increased surface. It is character that must set bounds to temperament, for it is *only to profit the mind* that sense may go short. In the same way the relaxing of the formal drive must not be the result of spiritual impotence or flabbiness of thought or will; for this would only degrade man. It must, if it is to be at all praiseworthy, spring from abundance of feeling and sensation. Sense herself must, with triumphant power, remain mistress of her own domain, and resist the violence of the mind, by its usurping tactics, would fain inflict upon her. In a single word: personality must keep the sensuous drive within its proper bounds, and receptivity, or nature, must do the same with the formal drive.[7]

There is a certain sense in which what is protected as a moral and psychic right is precisely the space for play with sexuality that, although not aesthetic in any strict Kantian sense, is itself aesthetic in the more common sense of the word in that it involves the play of personas and dressing up of ourselves as sexuate beings.

Schiller reemphasized the Kantian lesson that any blunt subjugation of the aesthetic realm to morality, such as in socialist realism, would undermine the experience of freedom that allows aesthetic feeling to promote a sense of a graceful ease with who we are as creatures of both sensibility and reason. It is the experience of freedom that reinforces who we are as moral creatures, yet as an experience it cannot be constrained in advance by either reason or understanding, even though, as we will see, it is enhanced by both. Schiller suggests:

> In the midst of the fearful kingdom of forces, and in the midst of the sacred kingdom of laws, the aesthetic impulse to form is at work, unnoticed, on the

building of a third joyous kingdom of play and of semblance, in which man is relieved of the shackles of circumstance, and released from all that might be called constraint, alike in the physical and in the moral sphere.

If in the *dynamic* state of rights it is as force that one man encounters another, and imposes limits upon his activities; if in the *ethical* state of duties man sets himself over against man with all the majesty of law, and puts a curb upon his desires: in those circles where conduct is governed by beauty, in the *aesthetic* state, none may appear to the other except as form, or confront him except as an object of play. To *bestow freedom by means of freedom* is the fundamental law of this kingdom.[8]

In Schiller's own terms the imaginary domain is accorded to us as a matter of respect for our dignity, as our dignity, in turn, demands the physic space we need for what Schiller calls grace and the experience of freedom. But we need to ask ourselves now what precisely an aesthetic idea is and how aesthetic ideas are more generally related to Kant's own notion of reflective judgment, as reflective judgment, in turn, is the basis for judgments about the beautiful and the sublime. First, we should turn to Kant and his understanding of how we can judge an object as beautiful because it ignites in us a certain feeling, a certain feeling that is life enhancing as we experience the harmonious play of the faculties of the imagination, understanding, and reason.

Kant on the Beautiful

Kant famously argues that what we experience when we judge an object as beautiful is not simply a feeling, although it is rooted in feeling, but one that turns on an experience of the purposelessness purpose of such a judgment; it is feeling in that we have no interest in the beautiful object in either moral or conceptual terms. What exactly is this play of our faculties that as we take note of it gives us such pleasure in the sense of animating the mind and heart while also allowing us to defend our judgment as one universally communicable and ideally agreed upon by everyone else? Famously, in the first *Critique* Kant introduces his notion of *darstellen*, which in loose translation means something like the exhibition or presentation of an object. To quote Kant:

> To every empirical concept, namely, there belong three actions of the self-active faculty of cognition: 1. the **apprehension** (*apprehensio*) of the manifold of intuition; 2. the **comprehension**, i.e., the synthetic unity of the consciousness of this manifold in the concept of an object (*apperceptio comprehensiva*); 3. the **presentation** (*exhibitio*) of the object corresponding to this concept in

intuition. For the first action imagination is required, for the second understanding, for the third the power of judgment, which, if it is an empirical concept that is at issue, would be the determining power of judgment.[9]

In the first *Critique*, to exhibit a concept means to associate with it an intuition, a manifold of distinctive unity, temporal and/or spatial, which gives every object a distinctive shape. The imagination in the first *Critique* is famously subject to the understanding; all form is only given to us as a determinate object through judgment in the first *Critique*. Judgment, then, proceeds through a schematization which allows for the categories, or concepts a priori, to be exhibited. In the case of a determinate judgment the imagination is always subordinate to its service of schematizing the categories so that we are able to judge a particular object as being what it is for all of our conceptual purposes.

In like manner, Kant speaks of *darstellen* in the first introduction of the *Critique of the Power of Judgment*, but here the power of reflective judgment holds up the imagination as it apprehends the mere form of the object to the understanding, not as it schematizes for the purpose of exhibiting concepts, but to the understanding as the active form-giving faculty. And, as such, the imagination must play its role here only in that it gives form in general. The mere form of a beautiful object, of which Kant so often speaks, is that this form is other than a predicative or objective condition of all objectification. The imagination can only play with form if the understanding is in league with it in that it gives form to the manifold in the first place, and yet it is the singularity of the object that commands of us that it is beautiful. It is this object here before us in all of its particularity.

Yet, what gives pleasure is never an aspect that is directly attributable to the object but to our subjective feeling of life-enhancing pleasure as we take note of the free alliance of understanding and imagination, which gives us a sense of the animation of the powers of the human mind; it is in the subject, not in the object, in which we locate the reflective judgment of the beautiful. Kant confirms this relationship between the subject and the object when he suggests to us:

> If, then, the form of a given object in empirical intuition is so constituted that the **apprehension** of its manifold in the imagination agrees with the **presentation** of a concept of the understanding (though which concept be undetermined), then in the mere reflection understanding and imagination mutually agree for the advancement of their business, and the object will be perceived as purposive merely for the power of judgment, hence the purposiveness itself

will be considered as merely subjective; for which, further, no determinate concept of the object at all is required nor is one thereby generated, and the judgment itself is not a cognitive judgment.—Such a judgment is called an **aesthetic judgment of reflection**.[10]

Throughout this book we will be dealing with only aesthetic judgments of reflection because these are the ones that are relevant to aesthetic ideas, even though Kant also uses reflective judgment when we attribute to nature either a teleological form of life or, alternatively, a system in which all natural laws cohere into a form. The later judgments are teleological and reflective, but they are also ultimately cognitive judgments about the objects of nature. It is important to note here that, for Kant, the determining ground remains sensation and must in that sense remain merely subjective. But, it is a sensation that is not related to the object but to the harmonious play of the imagination and understanding. If this were not the case it would be impossible for an aesthetic judgment based in feeling to be communicated to others. Again, to quote Kant on the matter:

> Thus an aesthetic judgment is that whose determining ground lies in a sensation that is immediately connected with the feeling of pleasure and displeasure. In the aesthetic judgment of sense it is that sensation which is immediately produced by the empirical intuition of the object, in the aesthetic judgment of reflection, however, it is that sensation which the harmonious play of the two faculties of cognition in the power of judgment, imagination and understanding, produces in the subject insofar as in the given representation of the faculty of the apprehension of the one and the faculty of presentation of the other are reciprocally expeditious, which relation in such a case produces through this mere form a sensation that is the determining ground of a judgment which for that reason is called aesthetic and as subject purposiveness (without a concept) is combined with the feeling of pleasure.[11]

Thus, in Kant there can be no rules for taste since there can be no schematization through concepts; indeed, aesthetic judgments freeze the imagination from its service to conceptualization. And, yet, Kant calls us to form a universalizable ideal of beauty in each one of us as a guidepost for taste even as this ideal must be developed in each one of us independently.

Kant's use of ideals in the first *Critique* diverges from that of his use of ideals in the third *Critique* in an important way. In the *Critique of Pure Reason*, to quote Kant, "just as the idea gives the **rule**, so the ideal in such a case serves as the **original image** for the thoroughgoing determination of the copy."[12] An ideal in the *Critique of Pure Reason* is archetypal in that it represents an ideal of reason in its most perfect form. An ideal is an object completely adequate to an idea. Thus, for example, the ideal of a stoic person of virtue is one that is completely adequate to the virtues of stoicism. Obviously, such a perfect individual can only be present in thought. At least in the first *Critique* Kant is extremely skeptical about ideals of the imagination. In the first *Critique* Kant dismisses the ideals of the imagination as incommunicable, shadowy images.[13] Yet, in the *Critique of Judgment* the ideal of beauty is identified as an ideal of the imagination. This ideal is no longer simply condemned as shadowy and incommunicable and is connected to rational ideas in the sense that such ideas project a necessary maximum standard of perfection. Models and archetypes which serve the ideal of beauty are no longer rigidly distinguished as they are in the *Critique of Pure Reason*. But, the highest ideal of beauty can only be found in the example of the human being. Kant comments on how different cultures diverge on what they distinguish as the normal ideals of human beauty; however, what they share in common is the projection of reason and its aspiration to a maximum. The universal communicable ideal of beauty, then, is seemingly ironic in that this is supposed to be an ideal for aesthetic and not moral judgment only to be found in the moral example of a human being who aspires to realize the moral law in her or his life. There is, then, a distinction in Kant between the ideal of beauty as it serves as a guidepost for all aesthetic judgments and that which is connected in its highest form given the aspiration to perfection with the human figure, since this figure, in turn, represents the aspiration of reason to unite with the imagination in bringing into our experience the ultimate purpose of our humanity. Even if the ideal of beauty is to be developed in all of us in all judgments of taste, it is only ultimately applicable to the human figure. This is because for Kant the ultimate application of any ideal, including that of perfection, pertains only to those things whose purpose can be traced conceptually. Such a purpose cannot be found in a beautiful flower, but it can be found in the moral aspiration of humanity.

Rudolf Makkreel argues that Kant does make a distinction between the free beauty of a flower and a dependant beauty of the human figure,[14] and I agree with him that this distinction explains why it is only the human figure in its aspirations to express the moral that we can find a universal archetype that would move beyond cultural norms of what is humanly beautiful. The ideal of the beautiful also plays another role in Kant other than that of the exemplar. A classic example of the exemplar disclosing to us the ideal of beauty in the expression of an aspiration to live by the moral law is Nelson Mandela, former president of South Africa. But, the ideal of beauty is also something that each one of us must develop in ourselves since it is only in relationship to such an ideal that we are able to develop our own sense of taste without reference to any pre-given rule or concept. Judgments of taste for Kant are judgments we should share as human beings who have certain cognitive powers in common.

We need to emphasize the "should be" because if it were an actual public to which Kant appealed in his *sensus communis*, then there would be shared conventional rules that would allow us to reach a natural agreement in a given community at a given time and place. But remember, for Kant the feeling of the harmonization of the imagination in understanding judgments of taste has to be rooted in the judgment of a singular object and indeed in a subjectively felt moment of pleasure. This is why Kant argues:

> The judgment of taste ascribes assent to everyone, and whoever declares something to be beautiful wishes that everyone **should** approve of the object in question and similarly declare it to be beautiful. The **should** in aesthetic judgments of taste is thus pronounced only conditionally even given all the data that are required for the judging. One solicits assent from everyone else because one has a ground for it that is common to all; one could even count on this assent if only one were always sure that the case were correctly subsumed under that ground as the rule of approval.[15]

We will return to a longer discussion of the *sensus communis* when we later turn to the role of the sublime in feminist theory. For now, I simply want to underscore that if the *sensus communis*, or common sense, was an actual community and it was this actual community that gave conventional standards for judgment, then the root of aesthetic judgment in subjectivity and feeling would be undermined. It has to be a unique judgment about a unique object that is actually felt and that could be communicated precisely so that others are able to experience pleasure in the free play of the imagination and its alliance with understanding.

In a sense, we are all called to develop in ourselves something like an archetype or ideal of beauty that would allow us to be in touch with this pleasure. But, here Kant is speaking more of an ideal in the sense of a regulative ideal in that it could never be reduced to a rigid set of rules, let alone a determinative concept. The enlarged community, as large as that of humanity itself, is related to this development, or perhaps more precisely a continual striving toward the attunement of an ideal. Kant follows these remarks when he suggests:

> By "*sensus communis*," however, must be understood the idea of a **communal** sense, i.e., a faculty for judging that in its reflection takes account (*a priori*) of

everyone else's way of representing in thought, in order **as it were** to hold its judgment up to human reason as a whole and thereby avoid the illusion which, from subjective private conditions that could easily be held to be objective, would have a detrimental influence on the judgment. Now this happens by one holding his judgment up not so much to the actual as to the merely possible judgments of others, and putting himself into the position of everyone else, merely by abstracting from the limitations that contingently attach to our own judging; which is in turn accomplished by leaving out as far as possible everything in one's representational state that is matter, i.e., sensation, and attending solely to the formal peculiarities of his representation or his representational state. Now perhaps this operation of reflection seems much too artificial to be attributed to the faculty we call the **common** sense; but it only appears thus if we express it in abstract formulas; in itself, nothing is more natural than to abstract from charm and emotion if one is seeking a judgment that is to serve as a universal rule.[16]

Thus, the *sensus communis* is a community of the "ought to be." Kant himself never completely decides whether this common sense is a constitutive principle or only a higher principle of reason such as a regulative ideal. However, his vacillation on the matter can be given sufficient texture when he says:

> This indeterminate norm of a common sense is really presupposed by us: our presumption in making judgments of taste proves that. Whether there is in fact such a common sense, as a constitutive principle of the possibility of experience, or whether a yet higher principle of reason only makes it into a regulative principle for us first to produce a common sense in ourselves for higher ends, thus whether taste is an original and natural faculty, or only the idea of one that is yet to be acquired and is artificial, so that a judgment of taste, with its expectation of a universal assent, is in fact only a demand of reason to produce such a unanimity in the manner of sensing, and whether the "should," i.e., the objective necessity of the confluence of the feeling of everyone with that of each, signifies only the possibility of coming to agreement about this, and the judgment of taste only provides an example of the application of this principle—this we would not and cannot yet investigate here; for now we have only to resolve the faculty of taste into its elements and to untie them ultimately in the idea of a common sense.[17]

Kirk Pillow has argued that the form of an object is what is subjectively felt as pleasure in a judgment of the beautiful and that an interpretation of thematic content of an aesthetic idea should be seen as involving the interpretative action of the sublime.[18] Yet, Kant explicitly says that beautiful objects are themselves an expression of aesthetic ideas. So, at least for Kant, we cannot make the sharp distinction that Pillow makes. However, I believe that Pillow is right to distinguish between what he calls the strong judgments of world-making in metaphoric transfer implicit in certain judgments of the sublime, particularly the mathematical sublime, from weaker versions, as he would put it, of the symbolic transference in which the imagination seeks an intuition adequate to the great ideas of reason, even knowing the symbolization will never achieve its aspiration. Again, we will return to the stronger world-making potential of the metaphoric transfers Pillow attributes to sublime judgment when we discuss questions of feminist theory and multiculturalism in the concluding chapter. For now, we need to note that in the judgment about the mere form of an object theoretical and practical reason are present only in the shape of the concept of the general and/or the mere idea. For this reason, a judgment of taste involves an elementary intertwining of theoretical and practical reason in advance of their ordinary and mutually exclusive employment in critical philosophy.

In judgments of the beautiful a strict distinction no longer remains between sensible intuition and the ideas that exceed the limits of all intuition, even though in the first *Critique* Kant requires intuitable schematizations of the categories in all theoretical cognition and determinate judgment. In the third *Critique*, sensible intuition in the shape of the mere form of the object and ideas in the shape of mere ideas appear intimately interconnected in judgments of taste. In a pure judgment upon the beautiful, the imagination gathers a manifold into the presentation of a form of this object here which enlivens the mind as it gives pleasure in the aspiration now connected to reason to achieve a maximum of perfection. Thus, understanding and reason, even in a judgment of taste, interplay, but differently so in the free play of the imagination as it interfaces and yet is never determined by the archetype or the ideal of beauty. Again, to quote Kant:

> Hence some products of taste are regarded as **exemplary**—not as if taste could be acquired by imitating others. For taste must be a faculty of one's own; however, whoever imitates a model certainly shows, so far as he gets it right, a skill, but he shows taste only insofar as he can judge this model himself. From this, however, it follows that the highest model, the archetype of taste, is a mere idea, which everyone must produce in himself, and in accordance with which he must judge everything that is an object of taste, or that is an example of judging through taste, even the taste of everyone. **Idea** signifies, strictly speaking, a concept of reason, and **ideal** the representation of an individual being as adequate to an idea. Hence that archetype of taste,

which indeed rests on reason's indeterminate idea of a maximum, but cannot be represented through concepts, but only in an individual presentation, would better be called the ideal of the beautiful, something that we strive to produce in ourselves even if we are not in possession of it. But it will be merely an ideal of the imagination, precisely because it does not rest on concepts but on presentation, and the faculty of presentation is the imagination.—Now how do we attain such an ideal of beauty? A *priori* or empirically? Likewise, what species of beauty admits of an ideal?[19]

Even if this archetype is to be brought forward uniquely in each being to the degree that it interfaces with the maxim of reason as an idea, it must be understood as connected with the ideas of reason. In this case, reason, then, must have a central role to play in judgments about the mere form of beautiful things, even if only in the sense that it only presents the maxim as an aspiration in the ideal of beauty. To put it somewhat differently, in such judgments the imagined must relate in some way to reason as the faculty of ideas, in addition to freely relating to the understanding.

In a pure judgment about the beautiful, the imagination gathers the manifold, deploying, if not determinately, the mere idea of a maxim of reason as a standard of gathering even as it comes to us as "this beautiful red rose." This interfacing between the ideal of beauty as a mere idea deepens our understanding of why beauty might become the symbol of morality. In a certain sense, a judgment on a beautiful object is expressive then of aesthetic ideas because of this interfacing of reason seeking after its own maxim as an ideal with the reliance of understanding in the imagination. Thus, reason informs judgments of beauty in a reflective judgment, even if indirectly, by setting the maximum of reason. I stress this because the role of reason is always emphasized in judgments of the sublime and it is right to do so, for without the maxim of reason judgments of taste would not have any reference to the indeterminate role of beauty:

> Just as the ideality of the objects of the senses as appearances is the only way to explain the possibility that their forms can be determined *a priori*, likewise the idealism of the purposiveness in judging of the beautiful in nature and in art is the only presupposition under which the critique can explain the possibility of a judgment of taste, which demands *a priori* validity for everyone (yet without basing the purposiveness that is represented in the object of the concepts).[20]

Beauty, then, is able to symbolize morality because it appeals to an experience of freedom that is common both to practical reason and to reflective judgment. But as already suggested, it can also do so because the ideal of beauty itself appeals to a maxim that inheres in the aspiration of reason.

Kant on the Sublime

In both the dynamical and mathematical, sublime reason, of course, plays a more direct role. The imagination collapses before the aspiration of reason to reach mathematical infinity. The mind can mathematically figure out what no intuition can adequately imagine. Thus, reason falters, as Makkreel has argued, before the supersensible strata which underlie the ideality of all objects in the critical philosophy of Kant.[21] In the dynamical sublime we experience not pleasure as in a judgment of the beautiful, but a combination of pain and animation as we see our smallness against the mighty tides of the ocean, the vastness of the starry heavens, or the fury of a violent storm. The instant of fear, or even tension, yields to an animation of a moral feeling of respect we have for ourselves, small though we may be, before the might of nature in light of our own moral freedom.

As Kant reminds us, we need to have at least have two conditions for being able to judge the power of nature through a sublime judgment. The first is that we must be relatively safe for otherwise we would be overwhelmed by terror and unable to be mindful of the moral feeling generated by our understanding of our freedom as creatures capable of putting ourselves under the moral law. Second, Kant explicitly argues that there must be not only an ideal of beauty or its cultivation but also actual cultural development in order for human beings not to tremble before the surrounding physical world. The feeling of sublimity, then, is integrally connected to our lives as moral creatures; although I agree with Makkreel that the mathematical sublime is best thought through the transcendental ideality of the supersensible world that underlies all of our experience,[22] still there is a moral dimension present in both, in that reason is returned to its fullest aspiration to come to terms with our freedom in the world. This is confirmed by Kant in his own reworking of the sublime:

> For just as we found our own limitation in the immeasurability of nature and the insufficiency of our capacity to adopt a standard proportionate to the aesthetic estimation of the magnitude of its **domain**, but nevertheless at the same time found in our own faculty of reason another, nonsensible standard, which has that very infinity under itself as a unit against which everything in nature is small, and thus found in our own mind a superiority over nature itself even in its immeasurability: likewise the irresistibility of its power certainly makes

us, considered as natural beings, recognize our physical powerlessness, but at the same time it reveals a capacity for judging ourselves as independent of it and a superiority over nature on which is grounded a self-preservation of quite another kind than that which can be threatened and endangered by nature outside of us, whereby the humanity in our person remains undemeaned even though the human being must submit to that domination. In this way, in our aesthetic judgment nature is judged as sublime not insofar as it arouses fear, but rather because it calls forth our power (which is not part of nature) to regard those things about which we are concerned (goods, health, and life) as trivial, and hence to regard its power (to which we are, to be sure, subjected in regard to these things) as not the sort of domination over ourselves and our authority to which we would have to bow if it came down to our highest principles and their affirmation or abandonment. Thus nature is here called sublime merely because it raises the imagination to the point of presenting those cases in which the mind can make palatable to itself the sublimity of its own vocation even over nature.[23]

One of Kant's most original uses of *darstellen* is his notion of hypotyposis. As Kant explains:

> All **hypotyposis** (presentation, *subjecto sub adspectum*), as making something sensible, is of one of two kinds: either **schematic**, where to a concept grasped by the understanding the corresponding intuition is given *a priori*; or **symbolic**, where to a concept which only reason can think, and to which no sensible intuition can be adequate, an intuition is attributed with which the power of judgment proceeds in a way merely analogous to that which it observes in schematization, i.e., it is merely the rule of this procedure, not of the intuition itself, and thus merely the form of the reflection, not the content, which corresponds to the concept.[24]

Symbolic formation proceeds, according to Kant, usually through an analogue of the imagination (*gegenbildung*) and seeks to form an intuitive counterpart (*gegenstuck*) in which the idea of reason aspired to is specified or made more vivid to our sense through a symbolic analogue. As Kant tells us, in a symbolic presentation:

> One can call such representations of the imagination **ideas**: on the one hand because they at least strive toward something lying beyond the bounds of experience, and thus seek to approximate a presentation of concepts of reason (of intellectual ideas), which gives them the appearance of an objective reality; on the other hand, and indeed principally, because no concept can be fully adequate to them, as inner intuitions. The poet ventures to make sensible rational

ideas of invisible beings, the kingdom of the blessed, the kingdom of hell, eternity, creation, etc., as well as to make that of which there are examples in experience, e.g., death, envy, and all sorts of vices, as well as love, fame, etc., sensible beyond the limits of experience, with a completeness that goes beyond anything of which there is an example in nature, by means of an imagination that emulates the precedent of reason in attaining to a maximum; and it is really the art of poetry in which the faculty of aesthetic ideas can reveal itself in its full measure. This faculty, however, considered by itself alone, is really only a talent (of the imagination).[25]

The Hypothetical Imagination

Famously, John Rawls sought to specify the idea of a noumenal self by postulating an experiment in the imagination in which we might seek to specify such a concept of the self for political philosophy. Rawls figures the noumenal self as someone who would put themselves behind the *veil of ignorance,* a position where one does not have any information about his or her actual social status in terms of factors such as class or gender and is able to reflect from the standpoint of what morally motivated free persons would legislate to themselves as principles of justice. Rawls expressly defends his idea of the *original position* as a representational device when he suggests the following:

> Here we face a second difficulty, which is, however, only apparent. To explain: from what we have said it is clear that the original position is to be seen as a device of representation and hence any agreement reached by the parties must be regarded as both hypothetical and nonhistorical. But if so, since hypothetical agreements cannot bind, what is the significance of the original position? The answer is implicit in what has already been said: it is given by the role of the various features of the original position as a device of representation.[26]

Rawls defends the original position as a representational device to answer his critics who have argued that none of us are ever actually disembodied, ahistorical human beings who are capable of reaching beyond their own self-interest to make moral judgments. Yet, the entire Kantian moral edifice turns on the idea that even though we cannot do so in a theoretical sense, we are indeed capable of such judgments and can very much postulate a standpoint in which moral freedom is a possible mode of action.

In his original work, *A Theory of Justice,* Rawls does not use the language of the third *Critique;* however, his concern is to bring the categorical imperative and its demands on us as moral person into empirical theory so that we can understand ourselves through our desire to act justly, because by acting justly we promote among ourselves an ethic of mutual respect and self-esteem. Rawls wants to make an addition to Kant in that he seeks to show us why acting justly is actually an expression of our desire for a particular kind of self-fulfillment, a self-fulfillment only open to those who are able to postulate themselves as free beings among other free beings who can harmonize their own ends through the regulative ideal of the kingdom of ends. To quote Rawls:

> The original position may be viewed, then, as a procedural interpretation of Kant's conception of autonomy and the categorical imperative within the framework of empirical theory. The principles regulative of the kingdom of ends are those that would be chosen in this position, and the description of this situation enables us to explain the sense in which acting from these principles expresses our nature as free and equal rational persons. No longer are these notions purely transcendent and lacking explicable connections with other human conduct, for the procedural conception of the original position allows us to make these ties.[27]

If posited in the language of the third *Critique*, Rawls seeks to give sensuous form to the great Kantian notion of our freedom as moral persons who seek to regulate their behavior through an appeal to the kingdom of ends. There is a sense, then, in which Rawls insists on the imagination in helping us to represent to our empirical selves why acting justly can speak to us as human beings who seek fulfillment in our day-to-day lives. Rawls never wrote of the veil of ignorance as an aesthetic idea, but I am suggesting here that his insistence on the role of the veil of ignorance in Kantian moral theory in accord with empirical theory is exactly the kind of role Kant allows for aesthetic ideas in giving shape to the great ideas of reason that can never be conceptualized.

From the very beginning of his work Rawls is explicitly concerned with the role of the imagination as a way to shape the noumenal self so it can rest in accord with what he calls empirical theory. His first attempt to figure the restriction on information consistent with the postulation of our noumenal, or morally free, self was not, however, the veil of ignorance. To quote his early essay, "Justice as Fairness," Rawls configures another experiment in the imagination in which we would be able to envision a moral law that would guide us in the adoption of principles of justice:

> The idea is that everyone should be required to make in advance a firm commitment, which others also may reasonably be expected to make, and that no

one be given the opportunity to tailor the canons of a legitimate complaint to fit his own special conditions, and then to discard them when they no longer suit his purpose. Hence each person will propose principles of a general kind which will, to a large degree, gain their sense from the various application to be made of them, the particular circumstances of which being as yet unknown. These principles will express the conditions in accordance with which each is the least unwilling to have his interests limited in the design of practices, given the competing interests of the others, on the supposition that the interests of others will be limited likewise. The restrictions which would so arise might be thought of as those a person would keep in mind if he were designing a practice in which his enemy were to assign him his place.[28]

Rawls, then, throughout the entire body of his work is explicitly concerned with how one brings Kant's thoughts on the autonomous self to bear in empirical theory so we can actually figure why we as phenomenal beings would choose to act justly.

If we can imagine a just world based on our freedom, then we can at least potentially explain how imagination plays a crucial role in explaining how actual phenomenal beings can be motivated to justice. In the third *Critique*, Kant is concerned with the same problem that Rawls constantly returns to: how can we relate the categorical imperative to our "natural inclinations" and our everyday desires? This is precisely the question integral to aesthetic ideas, and therefore I want to suggest here that we can best understand Rawls's insistence on the mediating function of imagination through Kant's third *Critique*. From a very different standpoint, but one explicitly defending the role of imagination in political theory, Hannah Arendt argues that Kant's theory of politics can only be found in the *Critique of Judgment*.[29] The importance of aesthetic ideas is that they allow us to bring into the sensuous realm figures of the great ideas of reason that cannot be conceptualized. Therefore, Rawls is in a sense correct to note that he has made an important addition to Kant, as his work allows for this mediating function of the imagination even if the role of the imagination is never philosophically defended in Rawls. To quote Rawls:

> The missing part of the argument concerns the concept of expression. Kant did not show that acting from the moral law expresses our nature in identifiable ways that acting from contrary principles does not.
>
> This defect is made good, I believe, by the conception of the original position. The essential point is that we need an argument showing which principles, if any, free and equal rational persons would choose and these principles must be applicable in practice.[30]

Rawls in a sense, then, believes that he overcomes Kantian dualism by providing us with this hypothetical experiment in the imagination. My purpose is not to defend either of the attempts made by Rawls to figure the restraints on interest as they are consistent with the Kantian idea of the morally free person, but rather to defend the necessity for the mediating role of the imagination in something like the hypothetical experiment of putting oneself behind the veil of ignorance.

Kant's Ambivalence on the Imagination

The mediating role of the imagination is indeed a powerful and necessary way to figure the grand ideas of the noumenal self and the moral harmonizing in making the kingdom of ends, but Arendt is right that if one is to seek to give central place to the imagination in political theory then one needs to turn to the third *Critique* and not just to the *Groundwork on the Metaphysics of Morals* or the *Critique of Practical Reason*. Indeed, in the *Critique of Practical Reason*, Kant argues against the idea that we need the imagination to access the moral law. He even argues that the imagination is not even needed in order to schematize the moral law so as to apply it in particular circumstances. Whereas concepts of the understanding always require the schemata of the transcendental imagination in order to be applicable to objects of experience, an idea of practical reason, on the contrary, needs only a natural law of the understanding as the type that exhibits the moral law. This isomorphism between laws of morality and laws of nature is due to the argument made by Kant that the moral law is a fact of reason. In the *Critique of Practical Reason*, the role of the imagination is reduced to helping us grapple with whether or not we are actually following the dictates of the moral law, and its service is one of self-examination. There is great ambivalence throughout the larger body of work by Kant giving us complicated readings on the role of the imagination.

Kant, in his writing on the sublime in the third *Critique*, writes "the **inscrutability of the idea of freedom** entirely precludes any positive presentation."[31] In the case of the sublime it is precisely the failure of the imagination to the dignity of our own personhood that gives us the sense of our sublimity before the much greater forces of nature. Thus, there is certainly within Kant reason to be wary of the use of aesthetic ideas as positive representations of what the moral law demands. However, Kant is not always consistent about this, and it is precisely this inconsistency that inspires the work of Ernst Cassirer to be more precise about the role of symbolic form in Kantian critical philosophy, particularly focusing on the *Critique of Judgment*. Kant's distrust of the role of the imagination in moral theory is precisely that it tends to focus on our desires for happiness and therefore takes us away from the demands on us of the categorical imperative. But in his earlier work, *Anthropology from a Pragmatic Point of View*, Kant explicitly gives place to the imagination in that it allows us to idealize our inclinations and therefore imagine reconciliation between our "higher" tastes and the demands of morality.[32] In like manner, of course, the imagination is given a central role in presenting a moral image of the world that unites teleological ideas with natural and moral purposes. The reconciliation between virtue and nature does indeed demand the mediation of the imagination so that we can project out the historical goal, ultimately envisioning the final purpose of nature as the freedom of humanity. Thus, the teleological ideal of the world citizen specifies and gives imaginative content to the abstract ideal of an invisible kingdom of God on earth. Thus, whatever one thinks of the specific aesthetic idea of the veil of ignorance, in Rawls, there is much to be said for his implicit understanding of the role of the imagination in bringing the categorical imperative into empirical theory and thus figuring the way in which such an imperative can actually speak to our desire for self-fulfillment.

More sweepingly, the moral image of the world, to use Dieter Henrich's telling phrase, that inheres in Kant's entire critical philosophy implies the reconciliation of happiness and freedom, a reconciliation that can never be more than a regulative ideal in Kant.[33] Critical theory, for Kant, is teleological at its very core, as Paul Guyer has often reminded us.[34] The imagination plays a role here, too, for in Kant we can read the signs of the progress of history through what he calls divinatory memory. Famously, Kant argued that the spectators of the French Revolution who sympathized with the struggle of that revolution could imagine that this event, with all of its failings, could be read as a sign of progress in history. The human imagination is necessary to see the providence of such an event as a sign of progress. The ultimate teleological element of moral theory in Kant is that we must always take humanity itself as our ultimate end, and it is this which underscores the central role of the world spectator and the world citizen. Both the world spectator and the world citizen are ultimately necessary for imagining actual events as conveying the sign that humanity is progressing. For Kant, progress can never be theoretically proven, either as in Hegel through a philosophical account of the unfolding of *Geist* or as in Marx with the ultimate development of the class struggle to its fulfillment in communism. We see progress only because we can imagine that the actual events in history can be read as signs of that progress.

We do not need to go as far back as the French Revolution to see and envision such signs. Throughout the world, the day that Nelson Mandela was inaugurated as the president of South Africa after twenty-seven years of imprisonment was imagined by those of us who were spectators as a sign of everything we might achieve as human beings. It was a sign that many held on to who remained committed to progressive ideals against triumphant stories of the inevitable advance of liberal capitalism signaled to us with the fall of the Berlin Wall.[35] Kant very carefully argues that the imagination has a central, integral place in the world spectator and in the world citizen, suggesting to us that without this imagination we would not be able to read these signs as progress. We have to "divine" the meaning of history in order to project it as a regulative ideal for us in our humanity. In the second half of the *Critique of Judgment*, Kant eloquently argues that the regulative ideal of taking our humanity as our own end, which, of course, is one of the formulations of the categorical imperative, is teleological in the sense that it projects an ultimate purpose. It is a purpose that can never be known but can actually help us to imagine, and indeed even study, our place in nature. This ultimate regulative ideal, which is, of course, teleological at its heart, is the development of human culture as human freedom seeks nothing less than the kingdom of ends on earth. In the kingdom of ends we not only make humanity itself our end as an ideal but we also, as Guyer reminds us, preserve and promote human capacities to choose particular ends.

There is ultimately, then, in this telos a harmony of purpose between nature and the ideal of humanity. As Guyer has rightly argued, if we take this telos seriously as an ideal of reconciliation, then we should read Kant against himself and argue that Kant's own arguments about sexuality and suicide are not entirely consistent because these seem to suggest that our nature can somehow or another limit our ends and therefore limit our freedom. The ultimate purpose of human beings, if we are thought of as an end, can only be aesthetic in that it is an act of the imagination in which we project who and what we might become, and this would include, as I suggested in *The Imaginary Domain*, the projection of our somatic freedom.[36] Thus, I have argued that it is inconsistent with Kant's spirit, if not his own arguments, to argue that the position of any human being because of their sexual difference can be cemented by the nature of that sexual difference; that is, that women are fated to be inferior because they are born into women's bodies or that gay and lesbian sexuality is somehow against nature. To quote Guyer:

> Although Kant does use this principle, not only in some of his arguments against suicide but also in some aspects of his treatment of human sexuality, he has no justification for doing so. Any suggestion that nature itself sets certain ends for us seems incompatible with Kant's insistence upon both the unre-

stricted force and the unconditional value of human freedom, and indeed Kant himself ultimately recognizes that we cannot allow the ends of nature to override the exercise of human freedom in the choice of ends even in his treatments of suicide and sexuality.[37]

The moral image of the world imagined and projected as a teleological ideal which regulates our behavior is one in which human beings set their own ends and not only harmonize their own ends with others but, to the highest degree possible, promote the capacity and ends of every other person. To my mind, Amartya Sen has rightly claimed that his own theory of equality of well-being and capability is consistent with the moral image of the world and the broad deontological spirit of critical philosophy found in Kant.

The "as if" of the imagination is necessary if we are to project our own freedom as it can be reconciled with nature; there is a necessary "as if" quality about this form of reasoning because this moral image of the world can never be proven, but it is something that can guide our activity if we invest in it. The "as if" character of the subject of practical reason and of aesthetic judgment means that there is no theory of the subject on which we can root our hope. There is also no theory of the subject in which we can prove that the world is hopeless. As we discussed at the beginning of this chapter, it is Kant who first decenters the subject. Henrich argues that Kant's critical philosophy, including the postulation of this moral image of the world, not only allows but also mandates what he calls the second level of reflectiveness. Henrich describes this secondary level of reflection as follows:

> Reflection upon the sources of knowledge is therefore recognized as indispensable to the possibility of reliable knowledge.
>
> The emergence of critical thought that turns upon itself was fundamental to the discovery that norms can have their source in nothing other than the self-awareness of reason. Whether valid or invalid, discourses that proceed from the inward turn of reason become the basis for the insight that reason is the source of norms. Paradoxically, not only calm, rational insight, but also a peculiar *pathos* of reason, manifested as intense feelings of self-empowerment, issue from critical reflection. Even though rational discourses can in fact be the basis of error, the critical capacity of reason can be the foundation of a life free from outside control and confusion.[38]

Henrich reminds us of a pervasive third level of reflection in which reason itself is seen as nothing but an irresistible illusion, and that some other need in us or our will alone is what pushes us to survive. Survival, then, becomes the only possible goal. As a result, all world images are repudiated and any large or significant changes in world events are forsaken. This vision of the world ironically informs some of what is now called postmodern literature supposedly following a reading of Nietzsche as well as some of the work of recent political science in the form of risk management. I agree with Henrich when he argues that the second level of reflectiveness leaves us with a kind of pathos of the "as if" it might still be different. For, it is always possible that we might still live up to the ideal of the kingdom of ends.

What Kant shares with Rousseau is a deep conviction that we need a moral image of the world. Hegel and Marx much more ambitiously argue that ultimately the ideal of human freedom can be shown to actualize itself in the motor of history. It is the pathos of freedom and the intensive feeling of self-empowerment arising from it that keeps many of us going in progressive politics even when we know we cannot prove this freedom. Interestingly enough, the third level of reflection as described by Henrich gives us a kind of certainty about the subject which a Kantian-inspired critical theorist can never have, for we can never know that we cannot be better. Sen in his more recent work writes eloquently against the miniaturization of the human spirit.[39] I want to add here that this miniaturization is inevitable if we give up the pathos of a reason ultimately embedded in the imagination integral to transcendental idealism. We need this pathos and indeed, in a sense, finitude demands that we face it. That is perhaps the ultimate irony in charges that Kant gives us a theory of the subject and therefore that his theory is inevitably egocentric; it no doubt imagines a world in which nature and freedom can be reconciled, but that is what it does: it imagines it.

As Henrich eloquently argues, if we take the lessons of the *Critique of Judgment* seriously, then we will need to temper the spirit of Kantian critical theory with the knowledge of the role of the imagination in all of Kant's rational system, including as it undermines any notion of subjective self-certainty. To quote Henrich:

> We can only incorporate this conviction—that the ground of freedom differs from the self—into those comprehensive images that transcend seriously the agent's self-assertion. This means, among other things, that we must conceive of the finite subject in new ways. We can, for example, entertain the notion of a subject from whom a normative principle may be derived, even though the subject does not yet have a self-image or self-generated motivation. We need only note that such a subject need not be conceived of as an entity that explains or generates itself. Something may exhibit the form of a closed and complete system, yet be founded upon the grounds that are not accessible within the system itself. To think of ourselves in this way is to recognize that because

we are not wholly self-contained, we could not possibly generate the pathos of freedom. We can still legitimately orient conduct with respect to what we do know about the structure of the finite subject, but we must remember that pathos of freedom, which issues through us, has its origin in another source.[40]

Whether or not this tempering through the centrality of the aesthetic in Kant's thought is enough to preserve the moral image of the world that underlies Kant's critical philosophy is indeed the subject of the rest of this book. Clearly, this is a European moral image of the world. It cannot be imagined otherwise. So, as Henrich reminds us, if we were to truly promote a vision of the world that could support human rights it could not at all be based solely on the grounds of a simple image made only in the likeness of Europe. We would need to dare to imagine the ideal of humanity differently as this will come to us in other philosophical systems generated in parts of the world whose philosophy has been discredited for far too long by lingering forces of imperialism. In a complex global society we will need to rethink any moral image of the world in the context of seeking ideals capable of a worldwide reach which does not demand that everyone view the world in the same way but in which different worldviews seek to find an overlapping consensus that could support the ideal of perpetual peace and the possibility of a freed humanity worthy of our dignity. Universal validity, then, demands that we give legitimate place to clarify claims of our humanity within the context of different cultures and traditions and not simply those that arose in the West. Revision of a worldview that could give place to the ideal of freedom and the ideal of perpetual peace is of pressing concern; despite the threat of annihilation in a world eaten up by war such work opens up a limited space for self-determined life, as these ideals are animated to guide actual institutional structures of international law.

In the next chapter, I will read Heidegger and Derrida against certain received wisdoms about their truths, ultimately suggesting that the limit of what can be known is also the formation of conditional structures of the knowable itself. Ironically, when applied to our conscious life, this insight can be read against a certain strand of postmodern literature to prohibit the naturalistic reductions of consciousness that have informed the third level of reflection, to borrow the term from Henrich. Indeed, Heidegger and Derrida can help us see that even if we cannot ignore or repress our knowledge of the multifaceted limitation and dependence of conscious life upon the unknowable—either as the unconscious or some other theory of how we are constituted—it also undermines a kind of practical nihilism by rejecting the idea that the unknowable can be shown to be illusory and, in turn, be used to destroy all moral images of the world as they promise a telos of hope as a regulative ideal. We will turn first to Derrida and Heidegger and later in this book to the black philosophies of existence as this tradition has both worked through and revised the moral image of the world offered in European critical philosophy.

Notes

1. See, generally, Judith Butler, *Gender Trouble: Feminism and the Subversion of Identity* (New York: Routledge, 1999).

2. See, generally, Wendy Brown, *States of Injury: Power and Freedom in Late Modernity* (Princeton, NJ: Princeton University Press, 1995).

3. Jacqueline Rose, *States of Fantasy* (Oxford: Oxford University Press, 1998), 88.

4. Immanuel Kant, *Critique of the Power of Judgment* (Cambridge, UK: Cambridge University Press, 2001), 192 (§49, 5:314).

5. Kant, *Critique of the Power of Judgment*, 192 (§49, 5:313).

6. Jacques Derrida, "Choreographies. An Interview with Jacques Derrida and Christie McDonald," *Diacritics* 12, no. 2 (1982): 66–76.

7. Friedrich Schiller, *Essays*, ed. Walter Hinderer and Daniel Dahlstrom (New York: Continuum, 1993), 125 (13th Letter on the Aesthetic Education of Man).

8. Schiller, *Essays*, 176 (27th Letter on the Aesthetic Education of Man).

9. Kant, *Critique of the Power of Judgment*, 23 (20:220).

10. Kant, *Critique of the Power of Judgment*, 23 (20:221).

11. Kant, *Critique of the Power of Judgment*, 26–27 (20:224).

12. Immanuel Kant, *Critique of Pure Reason*, trans. and ed. Paul Guyer and Allen Wood (Cambridge, UK: Cambridge University Press, 1998), 552 (A569/B597).

13. Immanuel Kant, *Critique of Pure Reason*, 552 (A570–B598).

14. See, generally, Rudolf Makkreel, *Imagination and Interpretation in Kant: The Hermeneutical Import of the Critique of Judgment* (Chicago: University of Chicago Press, 1995).

15. Kant, *Critique of the Power of Judgment*, 121–122 (§19, 5:237).

16. Kant, *Critique of the Power of Judgment*, 173–174 (§40, 5:293–5:294).

17. Kant, *Critique of the Power of Judgment*, 124 (§22, 5:240).

18. See, generally, Kirk Pillow, *Sublime Understanding: Aesthetic Reflection in Kant and Hegel* (Cambridge, MA: The MIT Press, 2003).

19. Kant, *Critique of the Power of Judgment*, 116–117 (§17, 5:232).

20. Kant, *Critique of the Power of Judgment*, 225 (§58, 5:351).

21. See, generally, Rudolf Makkreel, *Imagination and Interpretation in Kant: The Hermeneutical Import of the Critique of Judgment* (Chicago: University of Chicago Press, 1995).

22. See, generally, Rudolf Makkreel, *Imagination and Interpretation in Kant: The Hermeneutical Import of the Critique of Judgment* (Chicago: University of Chicago Press, 1995).

23. Kant, *Critique of the Power of Judgment*, 145 (§28, 5:261–262).
24. Kant, *Critique of the Power of Judgment*, 225 (§59, 5:351).
25. Kant, *Critique of the Power of Judgment*, 192–193 (§49, 5:314).
26. John Rawls, *Political Liberalism* (New York: Columbia University Press, 1996), 24.
27. John Rawls, *A Theory of Justice* (Cambridge, MA: Harvard University Press, 1999), 226.
28. John Rawls, *Collected Papers* (Cambridge, MA: Harvard University Press, 1999), 53–54.
29. See, generally, Hannah Arendt, *Lectures on Kant's Political Philosophy*, Ronald Beiner ed. (Chicago: Chicago University Press: 1992).
30. Rawls, *A Theory of Justice*, 224.
31. Kant, *Critique of the Power of Judgment*, 156 (§29, 5:275).
32. See, generally, Immanuel Kant, *Kant: Anthropology from a Pragmatic Point of View*, Robert Louden and Manfred Kuehn, eds. (Cambridge: Cambridge University Press, 2006).
33. Dieter Henrich, *Aesthetic Judgment and the Moral Image of the World: Studies in Kant* (Stanford, CA: Stanford University Press, 1992).
34. Paul Guyer, *Kant's System of Nature and Freedom: Selected Essays* (Oxford, UK: Oxford University Press, 2005), chapter 8.
35. Francis Fukuyama, *The End of History and the Last Man* (New York: The Free Press, 1993).
36. See, generally, Drucilla Cornell, *The Imaginary Domain: Abortion, Pornography, and Sexual Harassment* (New York: Routledge, 1995).
37. Guyer, *Kant's System of Nature and Freedom*, 171–172.
38. Henrich, *Aesthetic Judgment and the Moral Image of the World*, 71.
39. See, generally, Amartya Sen, *Identity and Violence: The Illusion of Destiny* (New York: W. W. Norton, 2006).
40. Henrich, *Aesthetic Judgment and the Moral Image of the World*, 78–79.

CHAPTER TWO

Dignity in *Dasein*: Between Thrownness and Hospitality

Kant and Heidegger are often pitted against one another, particularly in some of the crasser characterizations against Heidegger as a hopeless Nazi who completely rejected the moral image of the world described in the last chapter. But, what is forgotten in this characterization is that Heidegger began his own philosophical journey through a controversial interpretation of Kant which indeed influenced his pathbreaking work *Being and Time*. In a certain sense, Heidegger developed the notion of the transcendental imagination integral to Kantian philosophy and drew out its significance for his own existential, ontological understanding of *Dasein*. Heidegger argues that Kant and his attempt to uncover a new scientific ground for metaphysics sought to resolve the seeming paradox of how a creature limited by finitude could achieve universal and necessary knowledge.[1] As Heidegger tells us, Kant does so by uncovering the truth that all of our knowledge derives from the very finitude that is also a limit and a restriction on pure reason.

Heidegger is deeply critical of traditional rationalist metaphysics and suggests to us that the essential limit of finitude is both restrictive and enabling. The enablement made possible by grasping the limit of theoretical reason is subsequently transformed in how Kant understood the central role of transcendental imagination. This central role enables us to open what Heidegger calls a horizon of objectivity, giving us a field of knowable objects that appear to us as a rule-like and lawful nature, allowing us to claim truth for knowledge of the world around us. For Heidegger, finitude and transcendence are two sides of the same coin. And, we can only understand why if we fully come to terms with the significance of the role that the transcendental imagination plays in both our receptiveness to the world around us and in our understanding of that world. Heidegger begins his analysis of how a finite creature must relate itself to the beings that make up our world by suggesting:

> A finite, knowing creature can only relate itself to a being which it is itself is not, and which it also has not created, if this being which is already at hand can be encountered from out of itself. However, in order to be able to encounter this being as the being it is, it must already be "recognized" generally and in advance as being, i.e., with respect to constitution of its Being. But this implies: ontological knowledge, which here is always pre-ontological, is the condition for the possibility that in general something like a being can itself stand in opposition to a finite creature. Finite creatures need this basic faculty of turning toward . . . which lets-[something]-stand-in-opposition. In this original turning-toward, the finite creature first allows a space for play [Spielraum] within which something can "correspond" to it. To hold oneself in advance in such a play-space, to form it originally, is none other than the transcendence which marks all finite comportment to beings. If, however, the possibility of ontological knowledge is grounded in pure synthesis and if ontological knowledge nevertheless constitutes precisely the letting-stand-against of . . . , then pure synthesis must be revealed as that which complies with and supports the unified whole of the inner, essential structure of transcendence. Through the elucidation of this structure of pure synthesis, the innermost essence of the finitude of reason is then unveiled.[2]

This elucidation of what pure synthesis entails is what Heidegger pursues in detail to show us how Kant rejected the traditional metaphysical notion of the mediational role of the imagination. Instead, Heidegger argues that the transcendental imagination is the formative core of this necessary pure synthesis. Transcendental knowledge, for Heidegger, entails transcendence in a unique sense of the word as we just read. It is only if we understand human knowledge as transcendental and necessarily entailing transcendence that we can fully grasp how and why Kant's theory of the imagination creates an earthquake in traditional Western metaphysics. For Heidegger, Kant's explanation of why synthetic a priori judgments are possible demands an inquiry into the transcendence that allows human beings to have knowledge of *Being*. Heidegger is clear about the possibility of a priori judgments, suggesting:

> In synthetic a priori judgments, however, which are now the problem before us, it is a matter of still another type of synthesis. This [other type of synthesis] should bring forth something about the being that was not derived experientially from it. This bringing-forth of the determination of the Being of the be-

ing is a preliminary self-relating to the being. This pure "relation-to . . ." (synthesis) forms first and foremost the that-upon-which [das Worauf] and the horizon within which the being in itself becomes experienceable in the empirical synthesis. It is now a question of elucidating the possibility of this a priori synthesis. Kant calls an investigation concerning the essence of this synthesis a transcendental investigation. "I entitle all knowledge transcendental that is occupied in general not so much with objects as with the kind of knowledge we have of objects, insofar as this is possible a priori." Hence, transcendental knowledge does not investigate the being itself, but rather the possibility of the preliminary understanding of Being, i.e., at one and the same time: the constitution of the Being of the being. It concerns the stepping-over (transcendence) of pure reason to the being, so that it can first and foremost be adequate to its possible object.[3]

Thus, Heidegger concludes that for Kant:

With the problem of transcendence, a "theory of knowledge" is not set in place of metaphysics, but rather the inner possibility of ontology is questioned.

If its truth belongs to the essence of knowledge, then the transcendental problem of the inner possibility of a priori synthetic knowledge is the question concerning the essence of truth of ontological transcendence. It is a matter of determining the essence of "transcendental truth, which precedes all empirical truth and makes it possible."[4]

It is only against the background of Heidegger's interpretation of how synthetic a priori judgments are possible that we can fully grasp his argument that Kant poses the problem of transcendence as the inner possibility of any ontology. Only then can we understand Heidegger's claim that Kant's theory of the imagination was not only a watershed in Western metaphysics but also led Kant to confront an abyss which, according to Heidegger, led him to make substantive revisions in the second edition of the *Critique of Pure Reason*. Heidegger echoes this idea with brevity when he tells us, "Transcendence, however, is finitude itself, so to speak."[5] We will return shortly to why Heidegger believes that Kant's theory of the transcendental imagination brought him to such an abyss, but for now let us return to Kant's own insight into what Heidegger names the finitude of subjectivity.

For Heidegger, finitude in Kant is demonstrated by how pure reason cannot reach objects of experience except through the sensible intuition of space and time. These are the finite limits laid out by the transcendental imagination and put forth by Kant in his transcendental aesthetic found in the *Critique of Pure Reason*. According to Heidegger, Kant breaks with the traditional mediational role of the imagination by presupposing the formative role of the imagination in both sensibility and understanding. The imagination, in other words, is not a derived function that comes after sensibility or after understanding; instead, Heidegger argues that in order to turn toward objects, or "take them in stride" as he writes in his own unique language, we must initially grasp how the pure understanding is rooted in pure intuition. Again, to quote Heidegger:

> In order for the horizon of the letting-stand-against as such to be able to function, however, this character of an offering needs a certain perceivability. Perceivable means: immediately capable of being taken in stride in intuition. Hence the horizon, as a distinct offering, must present itself in a preliminary way constantly as a pure look. From this it follows that the letting-stand-against of finite understanding must intuitively offer objectivity as such, i.e., that the pure understanding must be grounded in a pure intuition which guides and sustains it.[6]

There must be an image of a horizon of space and time before objects appear before us in their affinity, connectedness, and thus also in their differentiation from one another through their temporal spacing. Heidegger uses the example of substance to help us understand this complex point being made by Kant. Substance in Kant is something that persists in time. It is only by "looking" at time that we can get a preliminary view of the image of persistence which as such remains the same in the temporalization that moves it through one "now" to another. Substance, in other words, is not simply a present being. It is a being that we grasp as persistence in time, and we can only do this if we have a primordial image, a pure image, of time itself. Heidegger believes that he is expanding on Kant's own argument that "the pure image of all magnitudes (*quantorum*) for outer sense is space; for all objects of the senses in general, it is time."[7] In other words, as Heidegger reads Kant, time gives us a pure image that pre-forms the horizon of all that is experienced in empirical intuition, but since this act of pure intuition belongs to the transcendental imagination what is thus pre-formed therein must also be imagined.

But, what is this strange something that is imagined, and by definition no thing because it makes the appearance of things possible? This strange something is precisely the horizon of possibility presupposed by the empirical intuition of all actual objects.

> The imagination forms the look of the horizon of objectivity as such in advance, before the experience of the being. This look-forming [*Anblickbilden*] in

the pure image [Bilde] of time, however, is not just prior to this or that experience of the being, but rather always is in advance, prior to any possible [experience]. Hence, from the beginning, in this offering of the look, the power of imagination is never simply dependent upon the presence [Anwesenheit] of a being. It is dependent in this way to such a small degree that precisely its pre-forming [Vor-bilden] of the pure schema Substance, i.e., persistence over time, for example, first brings into view in general something like constant presence [ständige Anwesenheit]. In turn, it is first and foremost only in the horizon of such constant presence that this or any "present presence of an object" as such can show itself. Hence in the Transcendental Schematism, the essence of the power of imagination—to be able to intuit without the present presence [ohne Gegenwart]—is grasped in a way that is fundamentally more original. Finally, the Schematism also shows quite straightforwardly and in a far more original sense the "creative" essence of the power of imagination. Indeed, it is not ontically "creative" at all, but [is creative] as a free forming of images. The *Anthropology* shows that the productive power of imagination as well is still dependent upon the representations of the senses. In the Transcendental Schematism, however, the power of the imagination is originally pictorial in the pure image of time. It simply does not need an empirical intuition. Hence, the *Critique of Pure Reason* shows both the intuitive character and the spontaneity in a more original sense.[8]

Imagination in Kant, then, plays a central role in sensible intuition because of its capacity to pre-form its perceptions in light of this possible something that must be presupposed in the presentation of all objects. Even at the most primordial level of sensible perception the imagination has a certain autonomy. The peculiar way in which the imagination is placed at the root of both receptivity and understanding in its spontaneity explains why for Kant the imagination is not after the fact of our world, but it actually forms it. In Heidegger's reading, the imagination is thus both in sensibility and in understanding, a transcendental freedom in that it serves as the a priori precondition of all objectivity.

As we have seen in the case of "substance" we see an object as presence because we have a temporalized view of it as being in the horizon of the "here and now." We see an object as permanent, as a substance that persists in time, because we view it against the temporal horizon of what it means to last through the succession of "nows" yet still remain in its form. The imagination is not ontically creative, which is why Kant emphasizes that he is not an idealist in the sense of either Berkeley or Descartes. Yet, there is no object which appears to us that is not viewed in the pure image of time that gives us a horizon of both possible and actual objects. Many neo-Kantians have tried to challenge the metaphysical notion of sensibility in Kant and reduce the *Critique of Pure Reason* to being a successful deduction of the categories of understanding that need not rely on the transcendental imagination.⁹ Even if one does not accept Heidegger's reading of Kant, as it is certainly controversial, it is difficult, if not impossible, to deny that Kant's transcendental idealism turns on this metaphysical notion of sensibility and the central place that the imagination plays in our very reception of objects. But, Heidegger rightly notes that, for Kant, the imagination is not just presupposed by sensation but also by understanding. And if it were not the root of both, then it would not have created the abyss that Heidegger argues Kant was brought before. As Kant tells us, understanding owes to the imagination the capacity to shape, differentiate, and connect in general (i.e., make synthesis). This very power of synthesis points to a more primordial unity of sensation and understanding brought about by the imagination prior to the separate functioning of either faculty. As Kant writes, "This schematism of our understanding with regard to appearances and their mere form is a hidden art in the depths of the human soul, whose true operations we can divine from nature and lay unveiled before our eyes only with great difficulty."¹⁰

How does the act of synthesis precondition the understanding? The first thing to recall here is that understanding is first defined by Kant as the faculty of rules. As a result, the understanding must presuppose those unities which guide all possible modes of unification in the act of representation. But, these regulated unities, or categories as Kant usually calls them, must be included in an act even more primordial if they are to be represented and ultimately to be connected to our "making sense" of objects. In order for us to be given a law-like or rule-governed objective field that is represented as such, then the schematism must play a central role in connecting the rule-like function of the understanding with the differentiation of objects as rooted in the unity of the transcendental apperception: the "I think" which makes possible the conceptualization of the many as unified in a law-like nature.

Heidegger distinguishes Kant's difference from empiricism by summarizing the role of the schemata when he suggests, "This initial sketching-out [*Vorzeichnung*] of the rule is no list [*Verzeichnis*] in the sense of a mere enumeration of the 'features' found in a house. Rather, it is a 'distinguishing' [*Auszeichnen*] of the whole of what is meant by [a term] like 'house.'"¹¹ Heidegger argues that the "I think," or the transcendental ego, does not exist alone or in its own right but is itself rooted in the productive imagination which projects the unification of all possible and actual objects. The "I think" in other words projects itself against the pure image of time and can only grasp itself in its permanence as it remains the same through the temporalizing of its own being. Kant underscores this point when he argues in the third section of the transcendental deduction that "only the **productive synthesis of the imagination** can take place *a priori*."¹² What this denotes is that the deduction of the categories of the understanding originates in the synthetic act of the imagination in which, and against which, the transcendental "I" must project itself as the basis of what in turn represents the world of objects beyond it. Heidegger underscores the significance of the dependence of the deduction of the categories on this particular reading of how they must be integrally tied to the transcendental "I" of apperception as follows:

> The representing of unity, as pure thinking, necessarily has the character of the "I think." The pure concept, as consciousness of unity in general, is necessarily pure self-consciousness. This pure consciousness of unity is not just occasionally and tacitly carried out, but rather it must always be possible. It is essentially an "I am able." "This pure, original, unchangeable consciousness I will now name *Transcendental Apperception*." The representing of unity which lets something stand against it is grounded in this apperception "*as a power*." Only as the constant, free "I can" does the "I think" have the power to allow the Being-in-opposition of the unity to stand against itself, if in fact linking remains possible only with reference to an essentially free comporting. The pure understanding, in its original holding of unity before itself, acts as Transcendental Apperception.¹³

As Heidegger reads Kant, he is the first Western thinker to think of the unthought aspect of human existence as the root of all knowledge. This unthought cannot be objectified because it lies behind us and shapes both who we are as finite creatures and how we know such finitude amid the possibility of its beyond. The imagination is, in this sense, the secret behind our vision of a law-like universe in which we can sketch out what an object is through the central role of the schematism. The imagination, in other words, resists the objectifying tendency Heidegger has already so militantly refused in *Being and Time*. Heidegger is much more on the side of Kant than he admits in his famous 1929 Davos debate with Ernst Cassirer, a debate to which we will return in the next chapter.

Of course, it is undoubtedly the case, for those who wish to emphasize the central role Kant played in grounding scientific law, that Kant did indeed tell us how our determinate judgments of nature can claim to be true. But Kant only did so, as Heidegger reminds us, in a way that challenges some of the most basic assumptions of Western metaphysics, such as in the antithesis of reason and sensibility or the opposition of the permanent soul and the temporal self. The "I" of transcendental apperception is only abiding as it presupposes a horizon of identity and permanence in a primordial image of time.

How things are, and how they are knowable after Kant, including objects in their so-called immediacy, can no longer be thought of, then, without addressing the subject in time whose understanding of the world can only proceed through a horizon of possibility rooted in what Heidegger describes as the a priori freedom that underlies both understanding and sensibility. Again, to quote Heidegger:

> "Experience," understood as experiencing in distinction from what is experienced, is intuiting which takes things in stride and which must let the being give itself. "That an object is given" means that it "is presented immediately in intuition." But what does this mean? Kant answers: "to relate the representation {of the object} to experience (be it actual or still possible)." This relating, however, wants to suggest: in order for an object to be able to give itself, there must in advance already be a turning-toward such an occurrence, which is capable of being "summoned." This preliminary turning-one's-attention-toward . . . [*Sichzuwenden zu*] occurs, as the Transcendental Deduction shows and as the Transcendental Schematism explains, in the ontological synthesis. This turning-one's-attention-toward . . . is the condition for the possibility of experiencing.
>
> And yet, the possibility of finite knowledge requires a second condition. Only true knowledge is knowledge. Truth, however, means "accordance with the Object [*Objekt*]." In advance, then, there must be something like a with-what [*ein Womit*] of the possible accordance which can be encountered, i.e., something which regulates by giving a standard. It must open up in advance the horizon of the standing-against, and as such it must be distinct. This horizon is the condition for the possibility of the object [*Gegenstand*] with respect to its being-able-to-stand-against [*Gegenstehenkönnens*].[14]

Ultimately, Heidegger openly acknowledges his debt to Kant in *Being and Time*; indeed, as thinkers like Richard Kearney have suggested, *Dasein* can be read as a recasting of Kantian insight into the finitude of subjectivity imposed by both the reproductive and productive role of the transcendental imagination. As Kearney succinctly poses in reflection upon what is often seen as dense Heideggerian analysis, there is "no *Sein* without *Dasein*, no *Dasein* without time, and no time without imagination."[15]

Shepherding Being against Our Thrownness

Undoubtedly, Heidegger goes beyond Kant in privileging *facultas praevidendi* over and against the other two aspects of the imagination, *facultas formandi* and *facultas imaginandi*, which respectively give us images of the past and the future. However, this privileging of the projection of a future horizon can, and to my mind should, be thought as Heidegger foregrounding the significance of the a priori freedom he associates with Kant's transcendental imagination. His project does indeed seem, then, to be a reinterpretation of Kant rather than a break with his thinking, as Cassirer constantly reminds him during the debate at Davos. And, the heart of this recasting and foregrounding of the a priori freedom of the imagination remains wedded to the pride of place of our freedom as finite beings. Indeed, in a thought-provoking reinterpretation of the relationship between theoretical reason and practical reason in *Kant and the Problem of Metaphysics*, we see Heidegger deepening something like the moral image of the world envisioned in the last chapter. Heidegger notes that the feeling for respect found in the *Critique of Practical Reason* is nothing less than respect for the moral law itself. It is best understood by connecting the self-imposition of the law that defines us as persons with the receptive and intuitive function of the imagination.

The moral self manifests itself in action and duty; the person is not some natural being that is just there, the person who is submitting to the law is also projecting himself or herself as a person who acts morally. This projecting, for Heidegger, involves the basic possibility of authentic acting. We do not know ourselves to be moral apart from our enactment of the law and the imagined projection of our personhood. As we saw in the last chapter, Kant himself was suspicious of the role of the imagination in practical reason. Yet, we should be able to use Heidegger's rephrasing how we receive the moral law as a fact of reason. In the reworking of respect as susceptibility or having a feeling for the law, Heidegger is arguing that the imagination should not just play a role in practical philosophy as hypothetical experiments in the imagination such as the one developed by John Rawls. Ultimately, Heidegger's reading of the imagination explains how we can receive the law and, indeed, form ourselves as persons even as we manifest ourselves in accordance with the moral law:

> Respect as such is respect for the moral law. It does not serve [as basis] for the judgment of actions, and it does not first appear after the ethical fact to be something like the manner in which we take a position with respect to the consummated act. On the contrary, respect for the law first constitutes the possibility for action. The respect for . . . is the way in which the law first becomes accessible to us. At the same time we find therein: this feeling of respect for the law does not also serve, as Kant puts it, for the "grounding" of the law. The law is not what it is because we have respect for it, but the reverse: this respecting having-a-feeling for the law, and with it this determinate manner of

making the law manifest, is the way in which the law, as such a respecting having-a-feeling for in general, can be encountered by us.[16]

In Heidegger's reading of Kant, it is due to our susceptibility, or having a feeling for the law, that we can also feel ourselves called to manifest our person as it is necessarily in relation to other persons. Thus, this moral person, then, is not rooted in an empirical faculty of the soul as in previous metaphysical explanations of why human beings can feel it right to be moral.

Heidegger argues that Kant should best be read consistently with the larger body of his own argument, especially in the *Critique of Practical Reason*, as suggesting respect is a moral feeling providing us with the transcendental structure of receptivity of both the subject of theoretical reason and the moral self of practical reason. As such, he challenges the dualism of theoretical and practical reason, at least as it relates to Kant's argument that the transcendental imagination should have no place in practical reason because the moral law is not a schematizable object. To quote Heidegger:

> The self-submitting, immediate, surrender-to . . . is pure receptivity; the free, self-affecting of the law, however, is pure spontaneity. In themselves, both are originally one. And again, only this origin of practical reason in the transcendental power of the imagination allows us to understand the extent to which, in respect, the law as much as the acting self is not to be apprehended objectively. Rather, both are manifest precisely in a more original, unobjective, and unthematic way as duty and action, and they form the unreflected, acting Being of the self [*Selbst-stein*].[17]

In a profound sense, Heidegger's reading of Kant's *Critique of Practical Reason* is such that the moral self is also understood to rest on the transcendental imagination, does not undermine the moral image of the world inherent in Kant's critical philosophy and the other great works of German Idealism, but instead helps us to understand how we can have the possibility of a view of the world that includes our freedom as basic to our finitude since this moral image can itself be understood to inhere in the faculty of receptivity. In this manner, I would argue that Heidegger should be read to deepen our understanding of being human as a nonobjectifiable project of freedom rooted in the finitude of our being pointed toward death. Yet, in distinguishing his own position from the existentialism of Sartre which foregrounds "man's" freedom even if in a way different than Heidegger and his reading of Kant, Heidegger no doubt backs away from these extraordinarily provocative pages on the role of the transcendental imagination in practical philosophy. To understand why he does so we have to trace a fundamental shift in his assessment of

Kantian critical philosophy and the place Heidegger gives it in emphasizing the a priori freedom of the transcendental imagination. We have to return again to Heidegger's reassessment of what he took to be Kant's finest accomplishment: the demonstration of the possibility of an object with the Kantian notion of truth as *Gegenstehenkönnens*.

Heidegger frankly acknowledges his debt to Kant in *Being and Time*. As we have seen, Kant's notion of the imagination, as well as the relationship of time to the imagination, serves as a point of philosophical departure for Heidegger in his conceptualization of *Dasein* as being "thrown into the world" in the past and yet projected toward a future of possibility. For Heidegger, it is Kant who first shows us the necessary connection between the questions What is a thing? and Who is man?:

> What Kant hit upon and what he constantly tried to grasp anew as the fundamental happening is that we human beings have the power of knowing what is, which we ourselves are not, even though we did not ourselves make this what is. To be what is in the midst of an open vis-à-vis what is, that is constantly strange. In Kant's formulation this means to have objects standing against us as they themselves, even though the letting encounter (*das Begegnenlassen*) happens through us. How is such possible? Only in such a way that the conditions of the possibility of experiencing (space and time as pure intuitions and the categories as pure concepts of the understanding) are at the same time the conditions of the standing-against of the objects of experience.[18]

As we have seen, Heidegger accomplishes another Copernican revolution by profoundly rethinking the significance of the subject. Heidegger notes the change in the meaning of that word: subject. The subject undergoes a change in the course of philosophical development from being what underlies, as for example the modern subject of a sentence and the matter of the thing, to its modern meaning as the person in the subjective. But, in Kant there is another fundamental shift in that now the "thing that underlies" is our own thinking through of the highest principle of synthesis in the transcendental "I" of apperception.

For Kant, as we have seen, the unity of all things, and of space and time, indeed of all necessary connections, is possible only through the unity of the "I think." The necessary representation of the oneness of our thinking is what underlies, to use Heidegger's phrase. For example, when we count units we take them along with this "I" and unite them as we go on thinking. We must represent the subject that counts two as the same subject that counted one. If we drink a glass of wine, to give another example, the subject that sees yellow must also be the subject that tastes the wine, otherwise the taster and the viewer would not be the same and there would be no experience of drinking such wine. The subject in this sense, then, "bears" persistence in the thought unity of the experiencer. This highest synthesis, for Kant, entails what Heidegger calls transcendence in our relationship to objects. We only encounter objects in Heidegger as this relation between the human experiencer and thinker as this relation, in turn, is only possible if we postulate and represent an "I" that endures in time. Without this necessary between, as Heidegger tells us, there would be no field of objectivity, no object defined as *Gegenstand*, in Kant's unique sense of the word, and therefore no metaphysically sound explanation of the objectivity of our judgment.

Heidegger explains the relationship between his own notion of transcendence and Kant's transcendental idealism as follows:

> The transcendental is what concerns transcendence. Viewed transcendentally, thought is considered in its passing over to the object. Transcendental reflection is not directed upon objects themselves nor upon thought as the mere representation of the subject-predicate relationship, but upon the passing over (*Überstieg*) and the relation to the object *as this relation*. (Transcendence: 1. Over to [the other side]—as such [*Hinüber zu—als solches*] 2. Passing up, passing beyond [*Über weg*.]) (For Kant's definition of "transcendental," compare *Critique of Pure Reason*, A 12, B 25. In a note (Academie edition, *op. cit.*, xv, No. 373), it reads as follows: "A determination of a thing with regard to its essence as a thing is transcendental.")[19]

This necessary transcendence opens up Heidegger's exploration of what this "necessary passing over" means for *Dasein* as a "dimension" which "reaches out beyond things and back behind man."[20] Heidegger underscores, in the most profound sense, that things are not the same after Kant, and neither are we. The thinking of this "between" changes how things are revealed to us, and how we in turn are related to ourselves as other to them. We know things, then, as we transcend them. But, this transcendence is only possible in that we must be with things in the first place as they are actually other to us. Since we are not God, we are not ontically creative. We are not in this sense transcendent. We meet instead with our world through a transcendence that is unique to a finite rational creature whose thought partially shapes the world around us. This transcendence in Heidegger's terms is thought of in Kant as the essence of how we can know things and yet are other to them. This otherness becomes crucial for Heidegger in the thinking of *Dasein* and freedom as transcendence in *Being and Time*.

In Kant, as we say, this "I think" can never be an object, although there is a "me" that is an object in the phenomenal world as all phenomenal objects must be in time. The "I think" then is instead the unity we must represent in the process of knowing sensory objects. For Heidegger, this "I" resists objectification because, as the basis for our grasp of the world, it must be represented as necessarily behind us, but as "necessarily behind" it is ungraspable. Again, as we discussed earlier, this ungraspability of the "I" is what makes the root of knowledge itself unknowable. In this sense, the "I" is a limit to what can be objectified and turns itself into a graspable "what." This "I," as such, at least as Heidegger reads Kant, points to Heidegger's fundamental insight into how human beings are always before and after themselves. The ultimate unity of the "I think," as being discussed, explains why, in Kant, rational logic is no longer valid, independent of the receptivity of intuition. Sensation, then, is no longer separated from thought, nor is it reduced to confused thought that must be clarified through derivable axioms. Rather, the sensory given and rational thought in their connection are two different, and yet necessary, conditions of any experience.

Thought can only be true if we think its necessary foundation in our own finite thinking. As human and finite, then, our axiomatic thinking is limited to its role in the makeup of sensory experience. And, this experience is only made-up through the transcendental imagination. What a priori means in the most basic sense is this valid but limited role of our thinking and judging which has already occurred whenever we experience an object as *Gegenstand*. We do not add on our thought after we experience something. Underscoring this point, Heidegger suggests, at length:

> That which shows itself (*Sichzeigendes*) must have in advance the possibility of coming to a stand and constancy, so that what encounters, what shows itself, i.e., what appears, can come before us at all as standing before us (*Gegenstehendes*). However, what stands in itself (*Insichstehendes*) and does not fall apart (*Nichtauseinanderfahrendes*) is what is collected in itself (*Insichgesammeltes*), i.e., something brought into a unity, and is thus present and constant in this unity. This constancy is what uniformly in itself and out of itself exists as presented toward. (*Die Ständigkeit ist das einheitliche in sich von sich aus An-wesen.*) This presence to it is made possible *with* the participation of the pure understanding. Its activity is thought. Thought, however, is an "I think"; I represent something to myself in general in its unity and in its belonging together. The presence (*Präsenz*) of the object shows itself in the representing, in which it becomes present *to me* (*auf mich zu Präsentwerden*) through the thinking, i.e., connecting representing. But to whom this presence of the object is presented, whether to me as a contingent "I" with its moods, desires, and opinions, or to me as an "I" that puts behind itself everything "subjective," allowing the object itself to be what it is, this depends on the "I," namely, upon the comprehensiveness and

the reach of the unity and the rules under which the connecting of the representations is brought, i.e., fundamentally upon the range and kind of freedom by virtue of which I myself am a self.[21]

Heidegger and Kant agree that we know our world only through an approach to nature. The role of philosophy in Kant is to think the fundamental principles of such an approach. Kant was deeply convinced that the Newtonian approach to nature was truly basic to all human experience; clearly, Heidegger argues to the contrary, insisting that approaches are historically variable, if not variable through our will or agency. But that disagreement, in all of its significance, still does not keep Heidegger from attributing to Kant his status as the thinker that demonstrates to us how we ground our scientific principles in a deeper metaphysical grasp of the essence of our being. Kant's specific way of thinking "the between" and his delineation of a knowable object as *Gegenstand* approaches nature through the domination of what Heidegger calls the mathematical.

The central problem of critical idealism lies precisely in how we grasp objects and thus come to know ourselves as a particular kind of maker of our world. It is the integral connection between the grasp of the object as *Gegenstand*, the domination of the mathematical, and Kant's own humanism in his ethical philosophy that Heidegger understands as inseparable aspects of Kant's great critical system. Heidegger's turn from his provocative insight into the role of the transcendental imagination in Kant's moral theory, and indeed from the project of critical philosophy, turns on Heidegger's understanding that our freedom in Kant is inseparable from a particular kind of thinking of "the between" linking human beings to the world around them. Indeed, Heidegger turns from his own development of transcendence as the heart of human freedom in *Being and Time* because this work still remains tied to human beings as a particular kind of maker under the domination of the mathematical. To understand this movement we need to review how Heidegger understands the shift that takes place in the creation of modern science.

Heidegger argues that the basic character of modern science is missed if one says that it only differs from earlier science by being experimental. Modern science is experimental but only in a specific sense. The modern notion of the experimental is the result of nature now coming to us in an axiomatic form. An experiment in modern science always first sets up a hypothetical framework in which the results of an experiment are to be judged. Heidegger argues that objects, in, say, science, found in ancient Greece are both understood and indeed made in a way similar to the way we make and develop knowledge of tools, which is ultimately dependant on practice. Heidegger gives us the example of how we come to use a weapon, suggesting that the weapon builder must have advanced knowledge of how the weapon is to be built and this knowledge determines the structure the builder will give to such an object when he makes it according to the plan inherent in such weaponry. This form of foreknowledge is what Heidegger identifies as the mathematical, as it was broadly construed in Greek philosophy. The mathematical, however, shifts its meaning from the foreknowledge we have of tools that demand we lay out a plan in advance for their creation or production. Heidegger demonstrates this shift in the mathematical in the broader meaning by giving us the example of Isaac Newton and his first law.

Famously, Newton argued that every body left to itself moves uniformly in a straight line. The phrase "every body" is already a key to the significant difference. For, we are no longer analyzing how we make specific objects like tools. We skip over the specificity of the thing as we abstract what is common to all bodies. In a related manner the idea of motion also changes its meaning. In Aristotle the capability for motion lies in the nature of the body itself. The kind of motion of the body and its relation to place depends on the nature of that body. Thus, for example, the velocity of natural motion increases the nearer the body comes to its proper place. Even velocity is expressed in this way as dependent on the fundamental nature of that body. Earthly bodies move downward in Aristotle because earthly things have their proper place under the fiery realm. To summarize, each body has its place according to its kind, and it moves toward that place with more or less velocity according to its nature. But this account of motion is fundamentally rejected by Newton. Motion is now understood axiomatically as an assertion about the law of motion for every body indifferent now to its nature. This law reduces motion to a change of relative position as measurable distance between places. With this law as an example, Heidegger argues that the very idea of nature has itself changed:

> Therefore, the concept of nature in general changes. Nature is no longer the *inner* principle out of which the motion of the body follows; rather, nature is the mode of the variety of the changing relative positions of bodies, the manner in which they are present in space and time, which themselves are domains of possible positional orders and determinations of order and have no special traits anywhere.[22]

Nor do we get these kinds of scientific laws from observing experience and then generalizing from it. As Heidegger tells us, scientific laws abstract from actual bodies. We come to know what is true of all of them but only if truth is conceived in a particular way such as in the mathematical. As Heidegger explains in reference to Newton's law:

> How about this law? It speaks of a body, *corpus quod a viribus impressis non cogitur*, a body which is left to itself. Where do we find it? There is no such body. There is also no experiment which could ever bring such a body to direct perception. But modern science, in contrast to the mere dialectical poetic conception of medieval Scholasticism and science, is supposed to be based upon experience. Instead, it has such a law at its apex. This law speaks of a thing that does not exist. It demands a fundamental representation of things which contradict the ordinary.
>
> The mathematical is based on such a claim, i.e., the application of a determination of the thing, which is not experientially created out of the thing and yet lies at the base of every determination of the things, making them possible and making room for them.[23]

To summarize, for axiomatic science all things are only as we mathematically make them. Nature works for us within the terms we present. This insight is the basis of Kant's famous claim that we only know in nature what we have put into nature. That the experimental is another aspect of its axiomatic character is what makes modern science unique.

If Heidegger "turns" from Kant's critical philosophy, and indeed on the interpretation offered here it is a "turning" in his earlier writing which attempts to radicalize it, he does not do so because Kant is wrong. Kant, indeed, has it right in his metaphysical grounding of the mathematical. In later work by Heidegger he emphasizes that Kant's humanism, which springs from the delimitation of theoretical knowledge and what can be known axiomatically, is still tied to a system of transcendental idealism and thus ultimately the subject finds itself framed by the mathematical. Thus, for Heidegger the way in which questions of the subject of moral freedom and agency are raised in Kant ultimately ensnares us in the forgetfulness of who we truly are as the guardian of Being. In all of his work, Heidegger has reminded us that beings inevitably reveal themselves to us by our approach to those beings. But, Being is not identical with the beings that we approach. Being is a possible interaction, "the between" to use a phrase from Heidegger. This "between" is a "third" which is in a sense "first" because it is something behind us which lets us be.

Being as beings is only partial disclosure, and this partiality is, in turn, different in our historical approaches to Being. Our partiality is the necessary result of our finitude. It is this otherness of Being that forms all beings as what gives all things to come to be and perish. Heidegger attributes this thinking of Being to the pre-Socratics and as "what lies behind all that is," or what reveals itself in presence but is as such never present. For Heidegger, since Plato Being is taken instead as what is already defined and constituted. Being is what is actually formed, present, and what works. Heidegger in his thinking turns on the structure of technology which frames us as *Gestell*. Not only might human beings blow up the world with their fancy technological machinations, but technology itself has, for Heidegger, gone too far in making human beings its own appendage: making humanity into a thing whose "nature" can only articulate itself within this limited frame of technological projecting. It is in such a world that all things, including ourselves, come to be graspable only as formed, calculable objects. Things, then, are reduced to standing in reserve for their possible use by modern technology. As Heidegger writes:

> What kind of unconcealment is it, then, that is peculiar to that which results from this setting-upon that challenges? Everywhere everything is ordered to stand by, to be immediately on hand, indeed to stand there just so that it may be on call for a further ordering. Whatever is ordered about in this way has its own standing. We call it the standing-reserve [*Bestand*]. The word expresses here something more, and something more essential, than mere "stock." The word "standing-reserve" assumes the rank of an inclusive rubric. It designates nothing less than the way in which everything presences that is wrought upon by the revealing that challenges. Whatever stands by in the sense of standing-reserve no longer stands over against us as object.[24]

For Heidegger, this particular kind of enframing deepens the danger of turning nature into an object for us, which is a particular form of objectification. The calculable complex is what we draw on, but we who draw on these standing reserves become their servant.

For Heidegger, this ensnarement is a particular kind of destiny as to how Being presents itself, or perhaps more precisely, withdraws itself, in that we have been banished, indeed rendered homeless, by the very hubris of modern technology. This is a primary danger for Heidegger because it fundamentally and violently blocks the gift of Being to us and therefore undermines what Heidegger will try to salvage as a non-metaphysical salvation of the dignity of *Dasein*. We are for Heidegger lost in the illusion that we are the lords of the earth, for we ourselves are now captured and incapable of even knowing and thinking our own capture. We challenge nature, we force nature to yield to us and in the course of so doing destine ourselves to being consumed by what we purportedly create. Heidegger continues this line of thinking and suggests:

> Yet when destining reigns in the mode of enframing, it is the supreme danger. This danger attests itself to us in two ways. As soon as what is unconcealed no longer concerns man even as object, but exclusively as standing-reserve, and man in the midst of objectlessness is nothing but the orderer of the standing-reserve, then he comes to the very brink of a precipitous fall; that is, he comes to the point where he himself will have to be taken as standing-reserve. Meanwhile, man, precisely as the one so threatened, exalts himself and postures as lord of the earth. In this way the illusion comes to prevail that everything man encounters exists only insofar as it is his construct.[25]

Dasein, for Heidegger, is thrown into the truth of Being and it is only, in a certain sense, through us that the gift of Being can be received. But, in the "Letter on Humanism," Heidegger tries to reevaluate his own writing in *Being and Time* to suggest not that Being is dependant on us, but that it is our destiny to be the shepherd of Being so that Being can illuminate itself as well as hold itself in its otherness. Since Being is the gift of all that is in the world, it is in a certain sense simultaneously in-and-beyond-beings as what yields to their becoming and yet is not identical with any being in particular.

Thinking attests to the unfolding of Being as the ultimate destiny of *Dasein*. Heidegger's rethinking of what it means for *Dasein* to *ek-sist* is that we will think from within our own destiny, which is to hold ourselves open to the nearness of Being even if as we hold ourselves open, Being only reveals itself as the most profound absence. More precisely, we experience the absence of Being because Being has withdrawn its gift as we try to hold sway over beings. As Heidegger tells us in his rethinking of what our thrown projection into our historical being now means, that it is not *Dasein* but Being itself which sends human beings into their essence and therefore calls them home. For Heidegger, Marx and Hegel—as two great thinkers—reflect on this homelessness in the fundamental estrangement of human beings from themselves. Indeed, Heidegger speaks favorably of historical materialism à la Marx precisely because it is for him all about the history of this estrangement:

> What Marx recognized in an essential and significant sense, though derived from Hegel, as the estrangement of man has its roots in the homelessness of modern man. This homelessness is specifically evoked from the destiny of Being in the form of metaphysics, and through metaphysics is simultaneously entrenched and covered up as such. Because Marx by experiencing estrangement

attains an essential dimension of history, the Marxist view of history is superior to that of other historical accounts.[26]

Again, as Heidegger always tells us, the great thinkers are not wrong per se, but they are, whether or not they know it themselves, speaking the truth of Being as it is revealed to them. This is why we do not refute any of the great thinkers, for rather then refute them we instead think how Being comes to be revealed in their works.

Revelation in a history is nothing less than the history of Being as it can only find itself in such great philosophers. Heidegger suggested:

> The happening of history occurs essentially as the destiny of the truth of Being and from it. Being comes to destiny in that It, Being, gives itself. But thought in terms of such destiny this says: it gives itself and refuses itself simultaneously. Nonetheless, Hegel's definition of history as the development of "Spirit" is not untrue. Neither is it partly correct and partly false. It is as true as metaphysics, which through Hegel first brings to language its essence— thought in terms of the absolute—in the system. Absolute metaphysics, with its Marxian and Nietzschean inversions, belongs to the history of the truth of Being. Whatever stems from it cannot be countered or even cast aside by refutations. It can only be taken up in such a way that its truth is more primordially sheltered in Being itself and removed from the domain of mere human opinion. All refutation in the field of essential thinking is foolish. Strife among thinkers is the "lover's quarrel" concerning the matter itself. It assists them mutually toward a simple belonging to the Same, from which they find what is fitting for them in the destiny of Being.[27]

Does Heidegger reject the dignity of man by writing that "man is not the lord of beings. Man is the shepherd of Being"?[28] Certainly, Heidegger would not agree and would instead suggest such a glossary reading of his intention overlooks his more profound insight. Indeed, Heidegger tries to tell us that it is a metaphysical notion of human beings as rational animals that degrades *Dasein* and violates the dignity of *Dasein*. For, we are not, in Heidegger, simply an animal that thinks. We are in a profound sense different from animals in that our body is a project that turns on the meaning we give to it in our struggle to turn the thrownness of our past into an authentic future in which we turn toward our own finite destiny of death. The human being, then, is not fundamentally reducible to an organic thing; whatever the most serious animal-rights activists might think, Heidegger is arguing that we are not one among others and that it degrades human beings to abandon them to the essential realm of animal existence. We are "other" to ourselves in

Heidegger precisely because we are "in time" as was said in the beginning of this chapter. Of course, Heidegger in a sense is challenging one notion of dualism in which human beings live as subjects amid objects, but this does not mean that he in any way wants to reduce human beings to another kind of thing, even organic.

Our otherness, however, as Heidegger interprets moral agency in Kant, lives but in our thrownness (*Geworfenheit*) into our true essence in which we come to care for the dignity of ourselves as the site in which Being can disclose itself and be acknowledged as the gift, indeed the ultimate gift. As Heidegger explains, there is an integral connection between care for our dignity and our care for Being as shepherds:

> But "substance," thought in terms of the history of Being, is already a blanket translation of *ousia*, a word that designates the presence of what is present and at the same time, with puzzling ambiguity, usually means what is present itself. If we think the metaphysical term "substance" in the sense already suggested in accordance with the "phenomenological destructing" carried out in *Being and Time*, then the statement "The 'substance of man is ek-sistence'" says nothing else but that the way that man in his proper essence becomes present to Being is ecstatic inherence in the truth of Being. Through this determination of the essence of man the humanistic interpretations of man as *animal rationale*, as "person," as spiritual-ensouled-bodily being, are not declared false and thrust aside. Rather, the sole implication is that the highest determination of the essence of man in humanism still do not realize the proper dignity of man. To that extent the thinking in *Being and Time* is against humanism. But this opposition does not mean that such thinking aligns itself against the humane and advocates the inhuman, that it promotes the inhumane and deprecates the dignity of man. Humanism is opposed because it does not set the *humanitas* of man high enough. Of course the essential worth of man does not consist in his being the substance of beings, as the "Subject" among them, so that as the tyrant of Being he may deign to release the beingness of beings into an all too loudly bruited "objectivity."
>
> Man is rather "thrown" from Being itself into the truth of Being, so that ek-sisting in this fashion he might guard the truth of Being, in order that beings might appear in the light of Being as the beings they are. Man does not decide whether and how beings appear, whether and how God and the gods or history and nature come forward into the clearing of Being, come to presence and depart. The advent of beings lies in the destiny of Being. But for man it is ever a question of finding what is fitting in his essence that corresponds to such a destiny; for in accord with this destiny man as ek-sisting has to guard the truth of Being. Man is the shepherd of Being. It is in this direction alone that *Being and Time* is thinking when ecstatic existence is experienced as "care."[29]

Metaphysics in Heidegger, then, is reductive in that it reduces Being to actual beings and seeks to study them in such a way. Thus, we lose the experience of *Dasein* as the site in which Being reveals itself and instead identify ourselves anthropologically as the maker of values. Indeed, for Heidegger understanding ourselves as the maker of all values and therefore grasping ourselves as having the highest value because it is humanity that gives value to the world is still a dangerous form of subjectivism.

Valuation is subjectivism because it says that Being is only as we give it a particular form of validity in that we say that it is something valuable. But this act of valuing still turns Being into objects of value for us as well as making ourselves lord of all things, therefore, falling prey to the very danger to which we are destining ourselves in the era of technology. Again, to quote Heidegger:

> But what is a thing is in its Being is not exhausted by its being an object, particularly when objectivity takes the form of value. Every valuing, even where it values positively, is a subjectivising. It does not let beings: be. Rather, valuing lets beings: be valid—solely as the objects of its doing. The bizarre effort to prove the objectivity of values does not know what it is doing. When one proclaims "God" the altogether "highest value," this is a degradation of God's essence. Here as elsewhere thinking in values is the greatest blasphemy imaginable against Being. To think against values therefore does not mean to beat the drum for the valuelessness and nullity of beings. It means rather to bring the clearing of the truth of Being before thinking, as against subjectivising beings into mere objects.[30]

For Heidegger, the word *ethics* comes from "ethos"; we ponder the ethos of *Dasein* when we think about our true dwelling in this world. To think about our true dwelling in this world is inseparable for Heidegger from thinking about the truth of our *Dasein* as the one who exists to be the shepherd of Being. This thinking is ontological in one sense, and indeed Heidegger called this kind of thinking the fundamental ontology, but in his later work he even critiques this notion of fundamental ontology in that it still remains caught in something like the radicalization or ontologization of Kant's transcendental idealism. Even the word ontology, then, if it seeks to ground Being in some primal element of humanity—even paradoxically an element that is not an element in that *Dasein* is only a future projection—still ties us into trying to think the gift of Being by thinking ourselves first or before it. We are instead only ourselves through Being as it gives itself to be in us.

So, what is to be done? In the deepest sense of the word nothing if doing is to remain in the metaphysical tradition. Heidegger tells us that from

Plato through Aristotle, thinking itself becomes a form of *techne*; thinking becomes a process of reflection in service to doing and making. For Heidegger, then, we must turn from a thinking that renders itself practical so that we can truly think. Does thinking accomplish anything? Yes, but only in Heidegger's own unique sense of the word accomplish. For Heidegger, indeed, thinking is a kind of action if we mean by action the accomplishment of some effect. What we do in thinking is accomplish the relation of Being to the essence of *Dasein*. Thinking does not make or cause such a relationship and at some level Heidegger is rejecting Kant and the notion that the world we live in is the one we think. Thinking, instead, now tries to hold true to the offering of Being as it takes us over in language. We do not express Being but if we do, if we can accept the gift of Being, then we can reveal it in *poesis*, for as *Dasein* reveals Being we come to dwell in its truth as the gift of our own being as well as the gift of all other beings. If we can accept this gift called thinking, then we might once again—if we ever did—be able to dwell in the truth of who we are.

Being is ultimately the home in which all things are rooted. As Heidegger tells us, this home is protected by the great thinkers who are the guardians of Being. When we think of ourselves as the guardians and render ourselves patient before this gift, we can accomplish our true essence by allowing it to unfold. To lead anything into its fullness is to accomplish it. This is why Heidegger tells us that only "what is" can be thought, and thus accomplished. But, this "what is" in Heidegger is not present beings, but it is the "isness" of all those beings which gives them to be at all. Thus, if there is a "solution" to the ultimate danger, if there is to be a freedom for humanity worthy of its name, it must be the freedom of Being to reveal itself. Thought in this way is connected to the freedom of Being in that human beings can think the realm of the destiny of Being and therefore we are never fated to take up our dignity, even if paradoxically it is our highest destiny. In Heidegger, our freedom entails that we think this destiny against the fate of the so-called technological revolution that tells us even we only have meaning through our efficiency and utility. As such, Heidegger redefines freedom:

> Freedom governs the free space in the sense of the cleared, that is to say, the revealed. To the occurrence of revealing, i.e., of truth, freedom stands in the closet and most intimate kinship. All revealing belongs within a harboring and a concealing. But that which frees—the mystery—is concealed and always concealing itself. All revealing comes out of the free, goes into the free, and brings into the free. The freedom of the free consists neither in unfettered arbitrariness nor in the constraint of mere laws. Freedom is that which

conceals in a way that opens to light, in whose clearing shimmers the veil that hides the essential occurrence of all truth and lets the veil appear as what veils. Freedom is the realm of the destining that at any given time starts a revealing on its way.[31]

Too many commentators misunderstand Heidegger's pitting of destiny against fate and therefore interpret him as denying freedom altogether. Whatever one makes of this definition of freedom, the dignity of humanity is still in accord with what Heidegger calls freedom. By doing nothing in the sense of reducing our thought to the service of things, we can open ourselves to questioning. Thus, our thinking that claims our destiny as the guardian of beings can itself become a saving power in that it preserves the higher essence of *Dasein* as what can open *Dasein* to its guardianship.

We are endangered as well, of course, and Heidegger certainly recognizes such. We are endangered with obliteration. But, given that humanity is never reducible to its bare life or its bodily existence, it is not even obliteration that is the worst danger: it is ourselves enframed and imprisoned so that we cannot enter into the more original revealing and return ourselves to this world as our true home. When we challenge nature we refuse it as a gift. Thus, the thinking that questions fate but poetically holds on to the destiny of the dignity of *Dasein* as the shepherd of Being might, just might, create an opening to a poetic dwelling that might enhance the saving power inherent in the grace of Being. Again, Heidegger writes:

> Thus, questioning, we bear witness to the crisis that in our sheer preoccupation with technology we do not yet experience the essential unfolding of technology, that in our sheer aesthetic-mindlessness we no longer guard and preserve the essential unfolding of art. Yet the more questioningly we ponder the essence of technology, the more mysterious the essence of art becomes.
>
> The closer we come to the danger, the more brightly do the ways into the saving power begin to shine and the more questioning we become. For questioning is the piety of thought.[32]

Does Heidegger produce nihilism or promote it as some sort of necessary destruction so that out of the ashes some new world might arise? Not at all; Heidegger's entire point is that human achievement alone may never banish this danger and, indeed, we can never directly encounter it because it does not directly come from us.

Nihilism is not the thinking of the namelessness for Being, if by *namelessness* we mean uncapturable by any of the names of beings. Practical nihilism, as defined here, is enframement by technology. So, far from seeking to produce nihilism in the sense just given, Heidegger is actually trying to think a way through this enframement so as to illuminate how it ensnares us. In this other way we might hold on to the saving power of *Dasein*. So, it is a serious error to call Heidegger's thinking nihilistic. Nor, as we have seen, does he reject a special place for human beings in the universe which has always been at the heart of all humanism. What he rejects is that this special place is reducible to our dignity as the makers of all value. Emmanuel Levinas agrees with this fundamental perspective, suggesting it is in and through the moral ethical action of human beings that holiness is brought into the world. Holiness, in Kant, is the human orientation toward freedom through the great regulative ideal of the kingdom of ends. It is this orientation and the ideal, one that is never present but always an aspiration for struggle, that yields a moral image of the world in which we can be not only different but also better in the sense of living more justly together. For Heidegger, on the other hand, holiness comes to irradiate the world around us only when Being has been illuminated and experienced in its truth. We do not bring holiness into the world for at best we can only prepare for it. I sincerely hope that I have presented Heidegger in the profundity of his thought so he can be rescued from false accusations of destructive thinking. For, Heidegger sought to "do no other" but to save *Dasein* from a seeming fate in which we are nothing other than commodities and utilities without purpose other than to serve the great god of money and the ultimate technological structure which we now call the Military Industrial Complex, whose sole purpose is to produce capital for a handful of human beings on this planet.

Yet, at the end of the day there is a fundamental difference between those that still hold we certainly need to rethink this moral image of the world that Kant first illuminates and those who, like Heidegger, argue that what is to be done now is that we must heal ourselves by questioning technology with the slight hope that Being might ascend into grace. Evil in Heidegger does not consist of the baseness of human nature, but instead in "malice of rage."[33] Such rage can only come from the concealment of Being since if we were to grace ourselves with our true dignity we would be able to receive Being. Our rage, to use this word deliberately, is an impotent resistance to the technological enframing that has taken us over. I do not want to deny the elitism in Heidegger, for it is certainly present, and indeed I want to emphasize here that it is Kant who first fundamentally breaks with elitism in that each and every one of us can heed the categorical imperative and struggle to live our lives in the freedom it provides and demands of us. But, at the same time we need to confront Heideggerian pessimism in Heidegger's own meaning. Even in his most despairing moments suggesting that only God can save us now, to paraphrase, Heidegger is hoping that we can be saved so that we can be returned to our proper place as the shepherds of Being.

So, can we preserve the moral image of the world defended, even reimagined as all aesthetic ideals must be continually reimagined, against Heidegger's pessimism about all subjectifying attempts to change the world? Heidegger, in a sense, takes his place and claims to take his place as one of the great thinkers of Being who thus can show us, or at least question, the truth of Being as it has been revealed. We can know the history of Being as it is thought in the great thinkers; thus, we can know how we are enframed and why we can do nothing about it or why we cannot humanize our world in a Marxist dream of socialism because this too will fall prey to the errancy of technology. While Heidegger is clear about the gift of *Dasein*, he stands paradoxically contrary to his own deontological premises in *Being and Time*, which offers us a knowledge of human finitude yet without fate to find itself comported away from or disclosed toward the trueness of our guardianship as shepherds of Being. Yet, if we cannot know Being in its entirety by its definition, then how can we know how we have been fated "to be" by the unconcealment of Being from us? How can we know that there is only one destiny that remains open for us if we seek to preserve the dignity of man? How do we know that this moral image of the world might not take us into a different relationship, not only with each other but, perhaps by so doing, with technology and with other beings with whom we share this planet? *Dasein*, laying claim to its dignity, may find momentary unconcealment in heeding the call by any other for hospitality.

Heeding the Call of Hospitality

In *The Philosophy of the Limit*, I argued that the force of Jacques Derrida's deconstruction of Heidegger's own definition of truth as errancy—the errancy inherent in that Being is a gift that we cannot claim—turns against any notion that we can know our fate, distinguish it from our destiny, and decisively reject the great ideals of the European enlightenment—freedom, equality, and fraternity—as if these were to be inevitably tied to a resubjectification of our world that would once again ensnare us in the error of technology and the ultimate danger to the dignity of *Dasein*.[34] But, how does Derrida's deconstruction engage Heideggerian pessimism? Here I do not intend to review the extensive body of work Derrida left behind after his death. There is so much that could be said about Derrida's lifelong engagement with Heidegger and the spirit of Heidegger's writing. But, I do want to bring to the fore a certain sense of Derrida because there have been such grievous misunderstandings about deconstruction in some academic circles in the United States. So, I will emphasize how a "certain" Derrida, to use one of his famous phrases, deconstructs Heideggerian pessimism in the name of an ethical responsibility that is inseparable from Derrida's highly original engagement with the meaning of hospitality.

Famously, as we have seen, Heidegger writes that the oblivion of Being has allowed the distinction between Being and beings to be eclipsed so that we are in danger of disrespecting our own dignity as the unique being whose destiny it is to care for the gift of "how all that is has come to be." Derrida engages the Heideggerian text in his essay on *différance* by turning Heidegger's own conclusions against themselves. If, as Heidegger writes, Being both reveals and conceals itself, indeed if truth is necessarily involved in what Heidegger terms errancy, then we cannot know what the truth of Being is. Even if we were to take seriously Heidegger's call for us to witness to the danger of *techne* we must remember that if Being hides itself, then we are not in the position to assert what has been hidden, for things might always be otherwise.

Indeed, if Heidegger is to think such danger, then this thinking itself entails thinking the trace of what, even if concealed, has left its mark on the oblivion of the distinction between Being and beings. To quote Derrida:

> Since the trace is not a presence but the simulacrum of a presence that dislocates itself, displaces itself, refers itself, it properly has not site—erasure belongs to its structure. And not only the erasure which must always be able to overtake it (without which it would not be a trace but an indestructible and monumental substance), but also the erasure which constitutes it from the outset as a trace, which situates it as the change of site, and makes it disappear in its appearance, makes it emerge from itself in its production. The erasure of the early trace (*die frühre Spur*) of difference is therefore the "same" as its tracing in the text of metaphysics. This latter must have maintained the mark of what it has lost, reserved, put aside. The paradox of such a structure, in the language of metaphysics, is an inversion of metaphysical concepts, which produces the following effect: the present becomes the sign of the sign, the trace of the trace. It is no longer what every reference refers to in the last analysis. It becomes a function in a structure of generalized reference. It is a trace, and a trace of the erasure of the trace.[35]

It is impossible, as Derrida tells us, to think *différance* except from within metaphysical inscriptions because in a certain sense it is the movement of all things into time and space that allows things to even be at all. It is not the gift of some static Being known only as the trace of what has been withdrawn, but the movement of spatialization and temporalization that must be there if things can appear to us. Here, Derrida seems to be echoing Kant in that he is writing of the necessary temporalization and spatialization of all experience for human beings of the things around them. But, in his attempt to be true to Heidegger, Derrida is also arguing that this trace of the force of movement is not simply a transcendental horizon for us, but must indeed be actually thought if we are to be able to engage with the world around us as it presents us with things marked in their singularity.

This "marking off" of things is something like an interval which allows things to be present only by pointing to the force of "presencing" that is both beyond them and at the same time present in their temporalization and spatialization. Again, to quote Derrida:

> Let us go on. It is because of *différance* that the movement of signification is possible only if each so-called "present" element, each element appearing on the scene of presence, is related to something other than itself, thereby keeping within itself the mark of the past element, and already letting itself be vitiated by the mark of its relation to the future element, this trace being related no less to what is called the future than to what is called the past, and constituting what is called the present by means of this very relation to what it is not: what it absolutely is not, not even a past or a future as a modified present. An interval must separate the present from what it is not in order for the present to be itself, but this interval that constitutes it as a present must, by the same token, divide the present in and of itself, thereby also dividing, along with the present, everything that is thought on the basis of the present, that is, in our metaphysical language, every being, and singularly substance of the subject. In constituting itself, in dividing itself dynamically, this interval is what might be called spacing, the becoming-space of time or the becoming-time of space (*temporalization*). And it is this constitution of the present, as an "originary" and irreducibly nonsimple (and therefore *stricto sensu* nonoriginary) synthesis of marks, or traces of retentions and protentions (to reproduce analogically and provisionally a phenomenological and transcendental language that soon will reveal itself to be inadequate), that I propose to call archi-writing, archi-trace, or *différance*. Which (is) (simultaneously) spacing (and) temporalization.[36]

As a force that points beyond itself, and as Derrida tells us force is only one of the many approaches one can make to *différance*, it both allows things to be presented and at the same time disrupts the idea of any notion of absolute presence. But, it also disrupts the notion of the division between the ontic and the ontological difference, such that it is seemingly frozen into an epoch that we can historically apprehend as the unfolding of the truth of Being. This disruption, for Derrida, which is paradoxically a force that allows things to come into being and yet is never actually present per se, is the basis of what Derrida dares as Heideggerian hope:

> There will be no unique name, even if it were the name of Being. And we must think without *nostalgia*, that is, outside of the myth of a purely maternal or paternal language, a lost native country of thought. On the contrary, we must *affirm* this, in the sense in which Nietzsche puts affirmation into play, in a certain laughter and a certain step of the dance.
>
> From the vantage of this laughter and this dance, from the vantage of this affirmation foreign to all dialectics, the other side of nostalgia, what I will call Heideggerian *hope*, comes into question. I am not unaware how shocking this word might seem here. Nevertheless I am venturing it, without excluding any of its implications, and I relate it to what still seems to me to be the metaphysical part of "The Anaximander Fragment": the quest for the proper word and the unique name. Speaking of the first word of Being (*das frühe Wort des Seins: to khreon*), Heidegger writes: "The relation to what is present that rules in the essence of presencing itself is a unique one (*ist enine einzige*), altogether incomparable to any other relation. It belongs to the uniqueness of Being itself (*Sie gehört zur Einzigkeit des Seins selbst*). Therefore, in order to name the essential nature of Being (*das wesende Seins*), language would have to find a single word, the unique word (*ein einziges, das einzige Wort*). From this we can gather how daring every thoughtful word (*denkende Wort*) addressed to Being is (*das dem Sein zugesprochen wird*). Nevertheless such daring is not impossible, since Being is always and everywhere throughout language."[37]

In a certain sense Derrida writes that *différance* is not even adequately thought of as force if it is to be thought as something present or at hand in things themselves. It is the beyond that is indicated, and yet only indicated, by things that are in space and time and in a profound sense forced "to be" if there are to be singular beings. What I want to emphasize here is not whether or not Derrida is successful in displacing Kantian critical idealism as he suggests must be done if we are to deepen our understanding of how Being gives things to be only in time and space as that this is a gift from something other than ourselves and is irreducible to the conditions of possible knowledge for us. I obviously do not think Derrida is entirely successful in this displacement, or perhaps more strongly put, that we can think the truth of Being beyond our experience of it as finite creatures. But, this being said, Derrida from the beginning of his writing holds out that deconstruction is an experience that points beyond the presence of things and our knowledge of them to what is other to them, and that even if we cannot know this other—indeed by definition as an experience of the impossible we cannot know it—it must not be forsaken if we are to attend to the gift of Being; for, this gift (*es gibt*) is never reducible to what is given, as Heidegger eloquently writes.

However, is this holding on to the trace illuminating the trace of what is beyond some sort of negative theology as Jürgen Habermas argues? Not at all. For what Habermas misses in Derrida is that Heideggerian hope is inseparable from the ethical demand of hospitality on us. If all things in a play of forces are irreducible to a static Being that withdraws and conceals itself from the beings who are to illuminate its gift, then we cannot with certainty differentiate between Being and beings, for what is "other" is only indicated in beings themselves. Of course, to write on hospitality is to echo the great ideal which Kant writes about in "Toward Perpetual Peace." Hospitality, in Kant, is explicitly anti-imperial and extraordinarily radical. This right to visit, for Kant, this right to be treated well when one is a foreigner, carries with it the inverse responsibility that those who visit do not violate the hospitality that is offered. It is precisely in hospitality that Kant condemns what we would now call imperialist actions. He is almost prophetic when he writes:

> If one compares with this the *inhospitable* behavior of civilized, especially commercial, states in our part of the world, the injustice they show in *visiting* foreign lands and peoples (which with them is tantamount to *conquering* them) goes to horrifying lengths. When America, the negro countries, the Spice Islands, the Cape, and so forth were discovered, they were, to them, countries belonging to no one, since they counted the inhabitants as nothing. In the East Indies (Hindustan), they brought in foreign soldiers under the pretext of merely proposing to set up trading posts, but with them oppression of the inhabitants, incitement of the various Indian states to widespread wars, famine, rebellions, treachery, and the whole litany of troubles that oppress the human race.[38]

Derrida is, of course, in accord with Kant's anti-imperialist spirit. And, indeed, many of his specific political proposals—such as the "city of refugees," which would allow refugees a space of freedom from persecution for their so-called illegal status in big cities throughout Europe—is certainly consistent with this spirit. Many of these refugees have fled their home countries because of the inhospitable behavior of the state. For Derrida, then, hospitality is tested in our openness to the stranger who seeks shelter among us.

In Derrida we can never know that the other to Being may not present itself to us in an actual human being. Perhaps there could be no other way for this other to present himself to us, so we must attend to this other as if this other may well be the messiah for whom we have waited. Levinas, and we will return to his ideas in the next chapter, always insists that the other man is my neighbor—and he uses the word *man*, as Luce Irigaray reminds us—because he is my universal brother in my humanity. But, for Derrida, there is no promise that the figuration of the other will appear to us in human form; truly, the other might actually be other than human and we would not be able to know in advance that this is indeed the other who will redeem us. Derrida makes the distinction between those whom we invite and those who visit us, as the larger notions of visitation and invitation are used to distinguish the seemingly incompatible sides of hospitality. Derrida knows that the demand for hospitality in our world is exceedingly real, which is why he advocates and defends the institutionalization of the "city of refuge." Thus, we are called to prepare ourselves by developing something close to a radicalized culture of hospitality. Indeed, Derrida goes so far as to argue that hospitality is culture itself, and here again he echoes Kant's mocking of the so-called European states of high culture who fall into the state of nature when they land on foreign soil. So, we must prepare in both politics and ethics to shelter refugees and those who seek shelter within us.

For Derrida, again echoing Heidegger, since we cannot know who is to arrive we must also be open to the incompleteness and inadequacies of any of our preparations. Derrida explains to us:

> But, *on the other hand*, the opposite is also nevertheless true, simultaneously and irrepressibly true: to be hospitable is to let oneself be overtaken [*surprendre*], to *be ready to not be ready*, if such is possible, to let oneself be overtaken, to not even *let* oneself be overtaken, to be surprised, in a fashion almost violent, violated and raped [*violée*], stolen [*vole*] (the whole question of violence and violation/rape and of expropriation and de-propriation is waiting for us), precisely where one is not ready to receive—and not only *not yet ready* but *not ready, unprepared* in a mode that is not even that of the "not yet."[39]

Indeed, Derrida refers to deconstruction as the experience of the apprehension of this impossible hospitality. It is impossible because we cannot prepare for who is to arrive and what it might mean for us. It might, to paraphrase Derrida, even take us by surprise with a truly frightening visitation in the form of an animal or a specter. This being might only appear as monstrous because we view this other as shut out from the reach of humanity, but for Derrida it is simply not enough to grit our teeth and extend our vision so that we can see as human what we have formally denied as seeming like ourselves. For, if we are truly to welcome the other as other, if we are truly to accept and dare to open ourselves to the gift of what might be truly different from what is now, then we must be willing to yield even our idea of what is human as the basis of any act of welcoming.

We are ultimately responsible to extend ourselves to the breaking point of all that is familiar to us and must refuse to make it familiar by saying, "After all, this other is truly like ourselves." Derrida elaborates on this point, suggesting:

> If every concept shelters or lets itself be haunted by another concept, by an other than itself that is no longer even its other, then no concept remains in place any longer. This is about the concept of concept, and this is why I suggested earlier that hospitality, the experience, the apprehension, the exercise of impossible hospitality, of hospitality as the possibility of impossibility (to receive another guest whom I am incapable of welcoming, to become capable of that which I am incapable of)—this is the exemplary experience of deconstruction itself, when it is or does what it has to do or be, that is, the experience of the impossible. Hospitality—this is a name of an example of deconstruction. Of the deconstruction of the concept, of the concept of concept, as well of its construction, its home, its "at-home" [son chez-soi]. Hospitality is the deconstruction of the at-home; deconstruction is hospitality to the other, to the other than oneself, the other than "its other," to an other who is beyond any "its other."[40]

Heidegger tells us that as beings thrown into the world, we are in a certain sense "guilty" and called to an attention that we cannot adequately give. This is an unusual use of the word *guilt* because it is associated with our finitude and the danger of a lack of attention which inheres in such finitude, particularly when it refuses the stark confrontation of death. But, Derrida deepens the Heideggerian understanding of guilt by suggesting that those of us who have survived what he often refers to as the infinite horror of our world have placed upon us a demand for our forgiveness by the other that has gone before.

Derrida constantly reminds us that the unforgivable occurred not only in Auschwitz but also in apartheid, Rwanda, and Palestine. To take on this a priori acceptance that we must be forgiven by the other who has gone before us is integral to the compassion that Derrida insists can only arise if we open ourselves to suffer what the other has gone through even while knowing we can never do so.

> Besides, regarding everything for which Auschwitz remains both the proper name and the metonymy, we would have to speak of this painful but essential

experience which consists in reproaching oneself as well, in front of the dead, as it were, with having survived, with being a survivor. There would be, there is sometimes is, a feeling of guilt, muted or acute, for living, for surviving, and therefore an injunction to ask for forgiveness, to ask the dead or one knows not who, for the simple fact of being there [être là], alive, that is to say, for surviving, for being here, still here, always here, here where the other is no longer—and therefore to ask for forgiveness for one's being-there [être là], a being there originarily guilty. Being-there: this would be asking for forgiveness; this would be to be inscribed in a scene of forgiveness, and of impossible forgiveness.[41]

We are always, in a profound sense, guilty of giving too little and arriving too late. Derrida is serious when he writes that none of us is in a position to have a good conscience. But, this forgiveness, which is inseparable from attending to the gift of how we are left to be, is integrally connected to the passivity and the patience demanded by what he writes of as an impossible hospitality. It is impossible because we must be willing to take in what is beyond our experience and therefore might shatter the very idea we have of it. And, again to return to Habermas and his insistence that this is negative theology, we have to see that since we cannot know who is in advance this other that comes to us we must always be willing to invite her in and shelter her. Thus, this is not some kind of negative gesture on Derrida's part in which we pray to the trace of the other and hope that they might arrive. Truly, these others are arriving among us all the time. And, we must create institutional structures from a "city of refugees" to immigration laws so as to actively reach out to this other.

Some of these thoughts on hospitality may seem abstract and perhaps deserve a more illuminating example. I am a part of a peace group, Take Back the Future, which was asked in 2002 by the Muslim Circle of North America to participate in a demonstration outside the former immigration services office. Muslim men from many different countries were being asked to reregister their legal status because they were citizens of countries being dominated by governments supposedly affiliated with Islamic fundamentalism. This is a mundane example of how the other arrives with a demand that we live up to our hospitality. Our group aimed to accomplish just that, and we did indeed demonstrate in support of these groups; although, sadly, we were one of the only groups of white U.S. citizens who participated. It is this kind of arrival that Derrida tells us we must take infinitely seriously, for we can never know that we might find ourselves redeemed by giving shelter to this other. Redemption, in Derrida, is hospitality; it is not some future forgiveness that may be bestowed on us. It is how we ask for forgiveness by taking on what is other to ourselves that makes us responsible, and it is in this responsibility that we find an opening to the future of how we can shape the world around us into a radically different place.

Truthfully, there is a certain sense in which Derrida argues this is a messianism without the messiah because this emancipatory promise is not only always available to us but something that is always asked of us. Again, to quote Derrida:

> Well, what remains irreducible to any deconstruction, what remains undeconstructable as the possibility itself of deconstruction is, perhaps, a certain experience of the emancipatory promise; it is perhaps even the formality of a structural Messianism, a Messianism without religion, even a messianic without Messianism, an idea of justice—which we distinguish from law or right and even from human rights—and an idea of democracy—which we distinguish from its current concept and from its determined predicates today [permit me to refer here to the "Force of Law" and the *Other Heading*]. But this is perhaps what must now be thought and thought otherwise in order to ask oneself where Marxism is going, which is also to say, where Marxism is leading and where is it to be led [*où conduire le Marxisme*]: where to lead it by interpreting it, which cannot happen without transformation, and not where can it lead us such as it is or such as it will have been.[42]

So, we cannot simply affirm that things will always be different, and suggest this is meeting our responsibility. We must always offer hospitality. To offer hospitality we must take positions and negotiate so that there are actual institutions that seek to realize this ideal. Of course, hospitality is not an ideal as Kant described ideals and it is also not reducible to ideals precisely, because if we are truly hospitable to the other we may have to revise what we mean by something like the word *ideal* itself.

Derrida has written that the affirmation of the gift of Being should be affirmative in that we attend to the forces of *différance* that allow things to always be otherwise. For Heidegger, our hands are already dirty as finite creatures. We cannot simply affirm things as they are or as they might be otherwise, for we are always already in a concrete situation that puts demands on us to live up to hospitality. Thus, we are called to negotiate:

> Let us begin by distinguishing affirmation and position. I am very invested in this distinction. For me it is of the utmost importance. One must not be content with affirmation. One needs position. That is, one must create institutions. Therefore, one needs position. One needs a stance. Thus, negotiation, at this particular moment, does not simply take place between affirmation and negation, position and negation: it takes place between affirmation and position, because the position threatens the affirmation. That is to say that

in itself institutionalization in its very success threatens the movement of unconditional affirmation. And yet this needs to happen, for if the affirmation were content to—how shall I say it—to wash its hands of the institution in order to remain at a distance, in order to say, "I affirm, and then the rest is of no interest to me, the institution does not interest me . . . let the others take care of that," then this affirmation would deny itself, it would not be an affirmation. Any affirmation, any promise in its very structure requires its fulfillment. There is no promise that does not require its fulfillment. Affirmation requires a position. It requires that one move to action and that one do something, even if it is imperfect.[43]

In Derrida, we cannot wait, we are called to act now, and indeed to pay attention to those forces that are marginalized or excluded that lie at the very heart of our responsibility to the future. Ultimately, as I argued many years ago in The Philosophy of the Limit, deconstruction is fundamentally ethical in that it serves as the protector of what is still yet to come.[44] The limit of theoretical knowledge stands against Heideggerian pessimism in that it is impossible to know definitively what is possible or impossible in terms of political change. Thus, we cannot know that our activities to reform the world will necessarily enhance the oblivion of Being by reinforcing the subjectification of everything. We must not only think, but we must also act if we are to be hospitable. Deconstruction is inseparable from this call to action; we do not wait for God or moan about the absence of God. But, can the moral image of the world, even if it need be radically rethought after deconstruction, survive deconstruction?

Derrida tells us again and again that the great ideals of humanity, freedom, and equality are never obsolete, and this is not just because they are ideals and never reducible to historical reality. In a deep sense, how do we negotiate, how do we engage with legal and political institutions without these great ideals? If we are called to negotiate then we are called to negotiate with ideals themselves. Thus, as I argued in The Philosophy of the Limit, we are responsible to the context into which we are thrown and this historical context includes no less than these ideals, damaged as they are by the horrific reality of the twentieth and twenty-first centuries.[45] Because it calls us to take positions, deconstruction as it seeks fidelity with hospitality is aligned with nothing less than practical philosophy.

Notes

1. Martin Heidegger, *Kant and the Problem of Metaphysics*, 5th ed., trans. Richard Taft (Bloomington: Indiana University Press, 1997).

2. Heidegger, *Kant and the Problem of Metaphysics*, 50.
3. Heidegger, *Kant and the Problem of Metaphysics*, 10.
4. Heidegger, *Kant and the Problem of Metaphysics*, 11.
5. Heidegger, *Kant and the Problem of Metaphysics*, 64.
6. Heidegger, *Kant and the Problem of Metaphysics*, 63.
7. Immanuel Kant, *Critique of Pure Reason*, trans. and ed. Paul Guyer and Allen Wood (Cambridge: Cambridge University Press, 1998), 274 (A142/B182).
8. Heidegger, *Kant and the Problem of Metaphysics*, 92–93.
9. See, for instance, the works the Marburg School, such as Hermann Cohen, *Kants Theorie der Erfahrung*, 2nd ed. (Berlin: Dimmler, 1885).
10. Kant, *Critique of Pure Reason*, 273 (A141/B180).
11. Heidegger, *Kant and the Problem of Metaphysics*, 67.
12. Kant, *Critique of Pure Reason*, 238 (A118).
13. Heidegger, *Kant and the Problem of Metaphysics*, 55–56.
14. Heidegger, *Kant and the Problem of Metaphysics*, 83.
15. Richard Kearney, *Poetics of Imagining: Modern and Postmodern* (New York: Fordham University Press, 1998), 54.
16. Heidegger, *Kant and the Problem of Metaphysics*, 110–111.
17. Heidegger, *Kant and the Problem of Metaphysics*, 112.
18. Martin Heidegger, *What Is a Thing?* trans. W. B. Barton and Vera Deutsch (South Bend, IN: Gateway Editions, 1967), 242.
19. Heidegger, *What Is a Thing?* 176.
20. Heidegger, *What Is a Thing?* 244.
21. Heidegger, *What Is a Thing?* 188–189.
22. Heidegger, *What Is a Thing?* 88.
23. Heidegger, *What Is a Thing?* 89.
24. Martin Heidegger, "The Question Concerning Technology," in *Martin Heidegger: Basic Writings*, ed. David Krell (San Francisco: Harper Collins, 1993), 322.
25. Heidegger, "The Question Concerning Technology," 332.
26. Martin Heidegger, "Letter on Humanism," in *Martin Heidegger: Basic Writings*, ed. David Krell (San Francisco: Harper Collins, 1993), 243.
27. Heidegger, "Letter on Humanism," 239.
28. Heidegger, "Letter on Humanism," 245.
29. Heidegger, "Letter on Humanism," 233–234.
30. Heidegger, "Letter on Humanism," 251.
31. Heidegger, "The Question Concerning Technology," 330.
32. Heidegger, "The Question Concerning Technology," 340–341.
33. Heidegger, "Letter on Humanism," 260.
34. See, generally, Drucilla Cornell, *The Philosophy of the Limit* (New York: Routledge, 1992).
35. Jacques Derrida, "Différance," in *Margins of Philosophy*, trans. Alan Bass (Chicago: University of Chicago Press, 1982), 24.
36. Jacques Derrida, "Différance," 13.

37. Jacques Derrida, "Différance," 27.

38. Immanuel Kant, "Toward Perpetual Peace," in *Practical Philosophy*, trans. Mary Gregor (Cambridge: Cambridge University Press, 1996), 329 (8:359).

39. Jacques Derrida, *Acts of Religion*, ed. Gil Anidjar (New York: Routledge, 2002), 361.

40. Jacques Derrida, *Acts of Religion*, 364.

41. Jacques Derrida, *Acts of Religion*, 382–383.

42. Jacques Derrida, *Specters of Marx: The State of the Debt, the Work of Mourning, and the New International*, trans. Peggy Kamuf (New York: Routledge, 1994), 59.

43. Jacques Derrida, *Negotiations: Interventions and Interviews, 1971–2001*, trans. and ed. Elizabeth Rottenberg (Stanford, CA: Stanford University Press, 2002), 25–26.

44. See, generally, Drucilla Cornell, *The Philosophy of the Limit* (New York: Routledge, 1992).

45. See, generally, Drucilla Cornell, *The Philosophy of the Limit* (New York: Routledge, 1992).

CHAPTER THREE

Symbolic Form as Other: Ethical Humanism and the Vivifying Power of Language

Today, the domination of the world by Europe and the United States is being challenged politically, ethically, and philosophically. Throughout this challenge, will the moral image of the world associated with Kant's critical philosophy survive? Should it, indeed, survive this challenge? Can we reconcile the grand vision of universality evoked by the ideal of humanity that makes its own history even if under conditions our humanity does not make or choose? The great Kantian ideal of humanity still allows for and, indeed, demands the struggle for a more just world worthy of that ideal. Did this idea, beginning with Kant yet informing so many important philosophical and political struggles such as Marxism, die with the fall of the Berlin Wall? Are we left with nothing but local struggles on the ground? Philosophically are we fated to a relativism that argues there can be no universal standards by which we judge the different efforts of human beings to survive in the world culturally, politically, and ethically?

Heidegger's ominous witnessing to the danger of technology, even if it encounters critical philosophy, remains tied to both a grand vision of the place of *Dasein* in the world and of the true dignity of *Dasein*. Thus, Heidegger critiques critical philosophy because it remains spellbound by a subjectivity that blinds us to our destiny as the being that must ultimately care for beings. Yet, Heidegger is certainly not with the relativists or those who would reduce human beings to mere statistical analysis and objects for instrumental study, prediction, and control. Heidegger, ironically, remains tied to the moral image of the world that insists on the grandeur of humanity precisely because he insists on a more cosmological sense of the state of things and the special place of *Dasein* in the universe. Of course, Heideggerian pessimism has now been challenged as just one more form of Eurocentrism. If European culture and society are in demise, so the story goes, the world and our humanity finds itself in a similar position of demise. As we have seen in his "Letter on Humanism," Heidegger still not only retains but seeks to protect the dignity of *Dasein*, even as he also argues that Kant's critical philosophy undermines the dignity he seeks to make the hallmark of a moral image of the world.

Throughout the rest of this book we will return to the ethical and political significance of challenges to Eurocentrism for critical theory and critical philosophy. We need to begin to confront this challenge so as to start considering the philosophical and ethical terms framing the debate. We will do so by acknowledging the debate is not between relativism and universalism, but between a universality that respects the plurality of cultural forms and symbols as integral to the moral demand put on us by the ideal of humanity itself. In this chapter, we will focus on the work of Ernst Cassirer, who reinterpreted the critical philosophy of Immanuel Kant and, indeed, the central place of the *Critique of Judgment* in critical philosophy as the basis for a philosophy of symbolic forms that shows us the inevitable plurality of such forms and yet does so as part of the ethical commitment to the moral vision of the world in which human beings can take responsibility for the world into which we are thrown.

Cassirer's contribution, as we will review it for the purposes of this book, is fourfold. First, Cassirer defends a sophisticated understanding of symbolic form that can undo the pessimism Heidegger holds about *Dasein*'s efforts to reform the world and a social order dominated by technocratic reason. Second, Cassirer overcomes the famous dualism ascribed to Kant by interpreting our freedom as a force that makes us in our personhood and which we in turn reshape through symbolic formation, allowing us to grapple with the world in the first place. Cassirer's understanding of symbolic forms is not reducible to the naive humanism to which it has so often been reduced. Rather, Cassirer does indeed defend the possibility of transformation and our responsibility for the state of the world in which we live.

Third, Cassirer is one of the first thinkers to recognize the inevitable plurality and infinite variability of symbolic forms giving rise to the worlds inherent within such forms. Cassirer rejects the idea that any one symbolic form can simply exist in a privileged space above other symbolic forms. As such, there is no one justified position to suggest "scientific man" renders all other symbolizations of reality obsolete. All simple neo-Hegelian versions of history culminating in the victory of "European Man" are rejected. If there is progress in Cassirer, and there is, it is through the increasing complexity of symbolic forms and their intertwinement with one another. I will not deny that there is a lingering Eurocentrism in Cassirer, but I will argue that it is not at the heart of his philosophy and indeed runs against his profound understanding of the inevitable plurality of symbolic forms.

Fourth, if Cassirer critically reworks the insights of Kant into the central distinction of human thought as the ability to distinguish between reality and possibility, he does so in such a way as to place human beings in a continuum with animals. Cassirer is one of the first thinkers to give animals their rightful place as creatures that can think, plan, or indeed have a future. The difference between animals and humans along this continuum ultimately presents itself in the fact that animals have a less rich vocabulary and do not have the capacity to distinguish between the possible and the actual. We are no longer to understand "man" as "the" rational animal. Part and parcel of this rethinking of what makes human beings significant as symbolic creatures stands aligned with the insight by Kant regarding the finitude of human thought as now reconciled with a historical dimension, since forms of thought even as basic as time and space are represented and expressed differently in different symbolic forms.

In Cassirer we cannot and should not choose between historicism and the fundamental insight offered by Kant that human beings always experience a world that has already been represented in the transcendental imagination. Our thought is limited by the forms of time and space and the "I" of the transcendental apperception; however, these very limitations simultaneously enable us to know our world in the specific form of knowledge available to a creature whose sensible experience of the world can indeed produce images of both possibility and actuality. It is impossible to even begin the project of fully elaborating the rich philosophical work of Cassirer, but we can at least begin to show its place in rethinking neo-Kantianism so as to make it more salient; indeed, this is a necessary beginning if we are to meet the challenge of what has been mundanely dubbed multiculturalism, on the one hand, and postmodernism, on the other hand.

Human Beings as Symbolic Creatures

Cassirer begins *The Philosophy of Symbolic Forms* by arguing that the conception of the human being as the rational animal is completely inadequate to its own aspirations, which is to distinguish what is unique in our humanity and why we have a special place in the chain of being. Cassirer reveals the symbolic quality of reason, and the realization of such truth, as integral to the development of civilization:

> Reason is a very inadequate term with which to comprehend the forms of man's cultural life in all their richness and variety. But all these forms are symbolic forms. Hence, instead of defining man as an *animal rationale*, we should define him as *animal symbolicum*. By so doing we can designate his specific difference, and we can understand the new way open to man—the way to civilization.[1]

Cassirer, as we have already suggested, was one of the first thinkers to take animals seriously as having complex intellectual processes through which they relate to the world. Cassirer makes the crucial distinction between animals and humans as one between signals and symbols. Cassirer was a careful reader of research on animals conducted during his lifetime and strongly defends the notion that animals are capable of grasping signs and expressing signals to one another. Through these signs animals both emotionally articulate feeling and communicate at even a rudimentary level with one another. Animals can manipulate tools and learn from their experience while teaching this experience to other animals, and they can self-correct if a tool being used does not achieve the desired result. In one sense, then, animals do live in some sort of temporal sequence and can distinguish between past and future as learning demands at least a primitive sense of time.

Animals also have some sense of identity, of existing as a being separate from other things and other similarly appearing animals, suggesting perhaps also a rudimentary sense of spatiality. Cassirer describes the difference between human intelligence and animal intelligence as follows:

> If by intelligence we understand either adjustment to the immediate environment or adaptive modification of environment, we must certainly ascribe to animals a comparatively highly developed intelligence. It must also be conceded that not all animal actions are governed by the presence of an immediate stimulus. The animal is capable of all sorts of detours in its reactions. It may learn not only to use implements but even to invent tools for its purposes. Hence some psychobiologists do not hesitate to speak of a creative or constructive imagination in animals. But neither this intelligence nor this imagination is of the specifically human type. In short, we may say that the animal possesses a practical imagination and intelligence whereas man alone developed a new form: a symbolic imagination and intelligence.[2]

Animals are also capable of responding to simple commands and are thus capable of language in the limited sense of reacting to signs and signals as well as expressing emotions. For Cassirer, then, animals clearly have intelligence and some sense of being individuals with emotions and learning capacities. However, the faculties of human intelligence are capable of constituting a different level of symbolic formation.

Throughout his work, Cassirer uses three dimensions distinguishing symbolic forms and explaining their coherent formation: representation, expression, and significance.[3] While animals can express emotion and have practical representations of their world, they do not have the experience of significance in a way entirely similar to human beings. Significance, as Cassirer defines it, is the possession of an established set of symbols. Symbols must be established through conventional meaning so that these symbols can come to have universal applicability for those fluent in a particular language. It is this universal applicability that allows human beings to designate an object that can be recognized as an object repeatedly, even if the actual object is not present in our immediate experience. The images that animals have are triggered by receiving information from the concrete world around them. They cannot, in other words, proceed directly from the abstract to the concrete. Again to quote Cassirer:

> Diverse as the animal cries and calls may be—cries of fear or pleasure, mating calls, and calls of warning—they do not go beyond the sphere of mere sounds expressing sensation. They are not "significant" in the sense of being correlated as signs with definite things and happenings in the outside world. According to the observations of W. Koehler, even the language of the most highly developed anthropoid apes, rich as it is in direct expressions for the most diverse subjective states and desires, remains confined to this sphere: it never produces a sign or designation for an object.[4]

To draw out the significance for a human being of a designated world of universal names, Cassirer movingly tells the story of Helen Keller being mesmerized by the world of objects that appears to her once she finally grasps the profundity of naming. For Cassirer, a human world arose for Helen Keller only when she was able to master this function of universal applicability. Said differently, we are able to learn what water means through all of the experiences we have with water, ranging from putting our hands under a faucet to running across the falling tides coming in from the sea. Water can operate in many different ways in the experiences of human beings and we are still able to give significance to water as a universalizable object. Yet while animals can also have different experiences of wetness, they are not capable of representing water outside their practical experiences of wetness because they do not have a symbolic system that can designate it beyond a particular moment of temporality and spatiality.

For Cassirer, the capacity for objects to have a name of potential universal applicability within a symbolic form is only one of the prerogatives of human language. Cassirer steadfastly rejects empiricist notions of language, and instead reminds us that there is no thing existing outside the designation of language. Such designation not only gives us the world in symbol but also provides our very experiential relationship to the world in actuality. This means that different languages naming with the force of different symbolic formations are indeed representing different things in the world. What is important in Cassirer is not the designated world per se or that that words actually function as names; rather, Cassirer aims to explain that human beings who speak different languages do indeed live in different and divergent worlds of things. Yet, despite this particular difference in naming our linguistic experience, human beings share important commonalities. The key, for Cassirer, is the general function of the architectonic form of human language. While Eskimos may indeed have more than thirty different names for snow, making our sensible understanding of snow seem simple and indeed lackluster in comparison, Cassirer would remind us that the architectonic function of language vivifies so as to allow language to make the signs speak the whole of the world to those wielding a given language.

Applicability, Versatility, and Vivification

It is this vivifying power of language that allows human beings to share knowledge of sameness across forms of language, even if they live in seemingly different worlds of symbolic forms. Thus, the architectonic function of language also allows for the possibility of translation as it emerges through a constantly negotiated struggle to come to terms with the designation of words vivified in other languages. Thus, the inherent flexibility given in the infinite malleability of symbolic forms operates as a bridge between the worlds of different languages, demanding those who wish to pass over such a linguistic bridge open themselves to how material signs vivify the world differently in diverse languages. Through such thinking, Cassirer contributes to the continuing debate of commensurability and incommensurability and suggests that by grasping architectonic forms of language we can understand not only how human language designates but also the fact that different languages designate differently. By struggling with our experience of forms of designation, we can potentially open ourselves to the worlds of others as they have signified the worlds they are living in.

If universal applicability is one key component to the form of human language as symbolic form, another is versatility; again, it is the versatility of human symbolization as well as the architectonic function of a name that allows for the possibility of translation. Designation and versatility, in turn, allow human beings to abstract relationships between objects so that it is only the relationship that can become the focus of symbolization. Symbols can be brought into a relational system that is further abstracted from sensory experience. It is the versatility of symbolization that Cassirer often refers to as the free ideality of language, allowing human beings not only to abstract from actual relations between symbols but also to reflect on those relationships. Reflection is broadly described by Cassirer as the power to isolate certain elements and focus only on those while excluding others. We are both enabled by our human process of symbolization and also in a profound sense ensnared within such a system. Truly, there is no human experience outside our symbolic systems. To quote Cassirer:

> Man cannot escape from his own achievement. He cannot but adopt the conditions of his own life. No longer in a merely physical universe, man lives in a symbolic universe. Language, myth, art, and religion are parts of this universe. They are the varied threads which weave the symbolic net, the tangled web of human experience. All human progress in thought and experience refines upon and strengthens this net. No longer can man confront reality immediately; he cannot see it, as it were, face to face. Physical reality seems to recede in proportion as man's symbolic activity advances. Instead of dealing with the things themselves man is in a sense constantly conversing with himself. He has so enveloped himself in linguistic forms, in artistic images, in mythical symbols or religious rites that he cannot see or know anything except by the interposition of this artificial medium. His situation is the same in the theoretical as in the practical sphere. Even here man does not live in a world of hard facts, or according to his immediate needs and desires. He lives rather in the midst of imaginary emotions, in hopes and fears, in illusions and disillusions, in his fantasies and dreams. "What disturbs and alarms man," said Epictetus, "are not the things, but his opinions and fancies about things."[5]

While Cassirer anticipated what has now been called the linguistic turn in philosophy, speech as we live in it and language as we write with it are only two of the symbolic systems Cassirer studies.

For Cassirer, work and economic action are symbolic systems. Capital, as Karl Marx told us long ago, is a symbolic form even as it turns itself through the fetishism of commodities into the fantasy of reality. Cassirer, then, is not making a distinction between symbol and material since what is material for us always already comes to us in a symbolized form. Giving his own interpretation of Kant, Cassirer suggests that it is not that human beings know the world around them in language and that it is the only world we can know as important, but rather that as finite creatures we must always come to the world represented to us through the distinction of actuality and possibility. Cassirer rightly notes it is only in the *Critique of Judgment* that Kant finally articulates the distinction between possibility and actuality as what is truly unique to human knowledge. Specifically, Kant contrasts our human distinction between possibility and actuality to divine knowledge. In the realm of divine knowledge, *actus purus*, everything conceived is ontically created by God. Kant was not defending the actuality of a God with this kind of ontic power, but instead was deploying divine knowledge so as to contrast it with human knowledge and the limits of finite human understanding. Heidegger also emphasizes the significance of finitude for *Dasein* as not ontically creative. Ultimately, the distinction between the actual and possible is a crucial difference between humans and animals whose practical intelligence remains within the sensory world.

Kant famously wrote in the *Critique of Pure Reason* that "thoughts without content are empty, intuitions without concepts are blind."[6] It is only, however, according to Cassirer, in the *Critique of Judgment* that Kant fully understands that it is the heterogeneous elements of our discursive understanding that also undergird the faculty of our reason to make distinctions between actuality and possibility. For Cassirer, and this is a crucial aspect of his original contribution to critical philosophy, we need to also realize that human intelligence is not only in need of images but human knowledge is crucially in need of symbols. Cassirer achieves this remarkable addition to the large body of critical philosophy through his original recasting of the schema in Kant.

Cassirerian Critique of the Kantian Schema

For Cassirer, the significance of the *Critique of Judgment* is in part due to the advance that Kant made from the abstract schematism appearing in the *Critique of Pure Reason* to the more concrete forms that Kant studies in both nature and art in the *Critique of Judgment*. For Kant, the schema is the solution to the dilemma as to how an abstracting, transcendental logic can be applied to sensuous content. Kant is not concerned with how this actually happens, as the very word *happens* suggests that the matter could be otherwise when indeed Kant argues that there is no experience without the melding of concepts and intuitions. So, we need then to think *via media* between conceptual intuition and the actual construction of specific knowledge by the human understanding. The schema, in Kant, is the underlying representation, or the synthetic medium, in which forms of the understanding and sensuous intuitions are assimilated so they can constitute experience. While the schema compresses the categories of the understanding it also at the same time contains more than the categories can supply. In this respect, we can say that the schema is something beyond the simplicity of a mere "category," for it is what makes possible an experience that neither logical form nor sensuous content could yield by themselves. Thus, the schema holds something of both sensuous and intellectual form. But, the schema is not merely the medium through which the sensual and intellectual are brought into unity.

We are not to forget that whatever is a matter of sensuous apprehension always appears in the universal form of time. The schema, then, must be a relation of the concepts of the understanding with temporal appearances. Thus, for example, cause and effect is a concept relevant to the succession of events in the world and makes definite the necessary connection of things that occur in time. The schemata of pure concepts are both schemata of sensibility and the first realization of the categories as they give us a knowable world. In this fashion, the schema is more complete than either the category or the form of time or sensuous content, for a schema is all of these together in their synthesis. No wonder, to paraphrase Kant, he marveled at the schema as a mysterious power of the soul. As such, the schema is not merely logical but it is real in the sense of a phenomenon of being, a concrete constituent of appearances. It is striking that the schema itself should be called a phenomenon insofar as it is consistent with the form of understanding, for this means that the schema is no longer a hidden transcendental factor only conceivable in and of analysis, but it is a real presence because there is no phenomenon in its absence.

Cassirer's *Philosophy of Symbolic Forms* is in many ways a development of Kant's notion of the schema. Indeed, Cassirer saw many of the key developments of German Idealism as rooted in creative reworkings of the schema. For Cassirer, the *Critique of Judgment* brings forward the best articulation by Kant of the way in which human experience is inevitably formed through schematization. It is the unity of concept and intuition that remains central to Cassirer's understanding of symbolic forms, as these forms also bring together concept and intuition as the experience of the sensuous. For Cassirer, the Kantian notion of the schema pushed Kant himself beyond his own conceptualizations of how human beings only know their world through an already represented set of forms starting with time and space. Cassirer in a sense began where Kant left off: in comprehending symbolic form as a union between intuition and structural form in a manner similar to the schema. For Cassirer, language itself can be understood to possess this schema as an architectonic form whose function is precisely to vivify a world through sensuous signs which come to be understood as a system of representation, expression, and significance.

However, Cassirer does not mean to suggest that Kant was mistaken about the absolute necessity of images for human knowledge, as images remain an integral, core component of symbolic function. However, the productive and reproductive imagination now recast is the difference between the passive images necessary for the representation of our world in time and space and the symbols that are created by the intellect itself. Said differently, the images of the reproductive imagination are delimited differently than the symbols used to communicate with the productive imagination. While symbols are in part created, they, of course, are not shaped out of nothing, but instead out of the established resources of symbolic forms such as language, myth, and science that have been inherited throughout human history and kept alive in conventional usage. And, although human beings cannot be ontically creative, there is still a profound sense in which symbols are made with something like a power of creation. We can use the example of language to help clarify this relationship. Words are themselves sensuous images in all of the capacities in which they are experienced. Anyone who has ever listened to a rap song knows that the art of rap involves bringing language to its full potential for sensuous representation where the whole world can live in a single word. But, words are used with meaning and so they are also employed so as to abstract from the reality which they seek to represent. As Cassirer writes at the end of the first volume of *Philosophy of Symbolic Forms*:

> The characteristic meaning of language is not contained in the opposition between the two extremes of the sensuous and the intellectual, because in all its achievements and in every particular phase of progress, language shows itself to be *at once* a sensuous and an intellectual form of expression.[7]

For Cassirer, life and *Geist*—the sensuous and the spiritual—are always mediated by one another in symbolic form. Language, as one symbolic form, is part of the sensuous world and makes the intellectual world of abstract ideas possible at the same time. This way of thinking about language affirms the unity of the sensual and spiritual which Cassirer argues is crucial for recasting the Kantian notion of the schema.

What is involved when an image is used to serve as a symbol is a complex relationship of expression, significance, and representation. The special function of symbolization must now be elaborated, and this is exactly the project Cassirer undertakes in his four-volume work. There have, of course, been many meanings of symbolization prior to Cassirer's neo-Kantian interpretation. In regards to language, for instance, it had been supposed in the eighteenth century that the mind notes similar properties of things and then pins a label upon each one of these images. This word-label then serves to recall any one of those designated objects. But, in this understanding of symbolization in language, language serves only to recapitulate what has been given and does not have the power to reveal or develop a new meaning. This notion of a word-for-thing symbolization is precisely what Cassirer challenges. Remember here that Cassirer is always working with what he sees to be the unique distinction of our human finitude: our distinguishing between actuality and possibility. Language is inseparable from this fundamental distinction in the service it provides us. Language actually serves humans better than the thing-for-word notion of symbolization. Language is also a means to new knowledge and indeed allows us to disclose new worlds. The reason language is able to do so is that much more is involved in the function of symbolization than was defended and articulated in the eighteenth-century model of a symbol.

For Cassirer, nothing is truly a symbol if it is only a mark of something already given and enables us merely to talk about it again. The "it" we denote with a word is only perceived in the first instance in light of our whole previous experience of the world already revealed to us in language. It is identified as what it is, even as an object necessarily in space and time by the relations of whatever is given by other known contexts of experience. There is such a whole, always present, in the moment of remaking any particular given, since that given only takes on meaning in relationship with other known contexts of experience. There is also such a whole, always present, in the moment of remaking any particular given as any symbol derives its own significance from that whole experience represented in language. For readers more familiar with Wittgenstein, Cassirer is emphasizing the point that meaning only arises in a form of life that also then represents the very meaning of its symbolic system. For Cassirer, language as symbolic form only exemplifies what is universally the case of how human beings come to know their world. Cassirer, as we have seen, retains the Kantian conception of consciousness as a holding of the many contents of experience together in unity, but he reframes this notion of synthetic unity by redefining it through a symbolic function which expresses the meaning of experience in and through the same content which is represented against the whole. Particular symbols, in other words, are full of meaning conferred upon them by the totality of experience already represented. But, the symbolic does not hold solely to the image or content taken as representative or expressive of meaning, for it pertains no less to the forms in which meaning is intelligible so that they are in a deep sense capable of their symbolizing function only as part of a system of established and conventional meaning and forms.

Cassirer, in his comprehensive meditations on language, returns to what he takes as the basic insight of Kant's conception of the schema. As we have seen, every schema of the understanding is a phenomenon of the imagination which is at once intellectual and sensuous. Because of the latter aspect there is sensible meaning through reference to objects, and because of the former there is agreement with the categories or forms through which anything whatsoever has meaning to the human mind. Thus, we symbolize our images in order to know anything at all, and these symbols are intermeshed with the phenomena themselves. There is no thing outside of the word, and the word becomes a sensuous reality when it vivifies things. This basic symbolic function has various directions and symbolic forms are precisely those directions in which meaning is realized and revealed in human consciousness as this consciousness, in turn, always unfolds in and through systems of representation that give to us a seemingly unified world.

Inevitable Plurality of Symbolic Forms

From his understanding of the constitutive function of symbolization in all experience, Cassirer concludes that science, as one of the "artificial" symbolizations of human beings along with myth, language, religion, and art, is but one of the directions of the symbolizing process of human consciousness. While there are basic forms such as space and time and the categories of the understanding, there are also special constructions for each one of the symbolic forms. Indeed, each one of the sciences has a different theoretical constitution in terms of the divergent symbolic forms of its language. The meaning of concept in any scientific discourse depends upon the whole structure or system in which it is used and will vary within the general theory in which it is conceived. As Cassirer succinctly writes, "The facts of science always imply a theoretical, which means a symbolic, element."[8] Thus, for example, even the symbols of mathematics will be deployed differently and indeed have a different meaning within the context of a different science because such different science will inevitably be based on different theoretical assumptions. When we move any mathematical system from one context to another we will have to be sensitive to the way in which the symbols themselves and the principles in which they are given meaning will also shift in signification. For example, algebra can be used in social science, but it will only be effectively used if it is consciously deployed within the recognition that what this science studies implies a different objective reality than that of natural objects and therefore a different set of theoretical assumptions. We will return to a longer discussion of Cassirer and objectivity shortly, but the point here is that even mathematics as a symbolic system only derives its ultimate meaning within the context of the theories in which it is used. As those theories differ, the type of the mathematics employed will also have to differ.

Every symbolic form, including science, is a condition either of the knowledge of meaning or the human expression or representation of meaning. Within the symbolic realm of art the image or content has its significance in virtue of the formal structure according to which the work of art is made. There is a form of music and poetry, and myriad other symbolic forms in more general and particular terms. Besides the general form of art there is the individual form or style of the particular artist. Always some universal form of discourse is involved in anything that has significance. Mythical thinking, for example, has its own symbolic form of constructing a world. Myth as a formal mode of symbolization both expresses the world of things we live in and also, according to Cassirer, has a poeticizing function. The manner of art is not identical to it since it is a separable form. Cassirer suggests that "myth embraces the first attempt at a knowledge of the world, since it perhaps also represents the earliest and most universal product of the *aesthetic fantasy*."[9] One crucial aspect of mythical consciousness is its concrete richness, which is related to its own form of producing an inner world that seeks to limit the abstract factors of understanding things—including the limit imposed upon the richness of a concrete universe by reflection—and thus distance from the sign itself. Cassirer understood myth as a form of separation of human beings from their reality in which they were vulnerable; however, this separation in which human beings seek to reintegrate themselves into a reality that includes them creates a magical world where we can both know our human place and find some sense of design in the things themselves as they create a reality as cognitively palatable to our ability to orient ourselves in existence.[10]

The creative aspect of myth in Cassirer inheres in the generative aspect of language, and they both have their roots in metaphor. Myth is primarily expressive and representative. The significance of meaning itself is caught in the rich concreteness of the images of myth and their representations as the basis of a magical world. This does indeed create a medium of thought, but it does so in such a way so as to constrain abstract reflection on the meaning of the images. But as in any symbolic form, expression, representation, and significance interact; thus, for Cassirer, there is absolutely nothing irrational about myth, even if as a symbolic form it limits attention to the conceptual which also inheres in the condensation of meaning in language. It is beyond the scope of this book to explore what Cassirer has right and wrong about the form of mythical consciousness; however, he was one of the first thinkers not only to recognize myth as an important form of knowledge but also to forcefully argue that mythical thinking—and indeed, for Cassirer, it is thinking—can never be eclipsed by another symbolic form such as science because it is integral to metaphor and metaphor inheres in the expressive capacity of language. It is no wonder that Cassirer remains a deep friend of so many anthropologists.

Imaginative Projective and Symbolic Form

Language is symbolic in the same way as myth, art, and science. So-called realist theories of language are wrongheaded for Cassirer, as indeed are nominalist theories of language because they fail to understand the world disclosing power of language as a symbolic form. World disclosure is not simply discovery but also an act of recollective imagination which creates new possibilities in all forms of our shared human endeavors. The properties and other aspects of objects are only defined by the symbolizations and experience which lies behind the intent to use words to designate things. An already symbolized world then is drawn upon in every word which is used in the process of naming. Words and mathematical symbols are always given meaning in a system of thought that proceeds them, allows them to be understood, and also allows the bigger picture to leave open the possibility of reshaping or redefining any word or symbol, which in turn, of course, will ultimately have an impact on the system of thought in which it is encased. As Cassirer remarks, the diversity of language—since it is always caught up in what Wittgenstein called a form of life such as our day-to-day speech or a conceptual system such as algebra—is always connected to a particular approach to the world and an outlook on the world connected to that approach. In a sense, language should be considered the basic artifice by which all cultural forms are related.

Mathematical language is the most extreme example of the conceptualizing, abstracting power inherent in everyday language which then can be effectively translated into an organization of relational systems. Each symbolic form has its own autonomy even as it is ultimately connected back to some relationship to language and the autonomy of its own image world. For Cassirer, science, too, has an image of the world, an image, of course, that must be symbolized in mathematics, but mathematics for Cassirer is never freed from the image of the world of a law-like nature in which it is embedded. We never confront a reality just given to us for there is no content whatsoever that is not construed in some form and no form that is not embedded in an image of the world. Whatever human consciousness appropriates for any purpose whatsoever is already possessed of a form. It is not just the mode of knowledge that is different; it is not what we usually think of as an epistemological question only. Cassirer argues that the bases of phenomena are actually different in different forms of knowledge. There are also different ways to understand knowledge and things as they are represented and given significance in their different forms.

There is no kind of knowledge that is better or more accurately expressive of the world than the rest. Science, in other words, does not bring us closer to reality than art, but it simply gives us a different reality. Cassirer remarks:

> Categories such as "empiricism" or "rationalism" relate to the question of the "origin" of knowledge, not in the genetic sense, but in the sense of their "dignity." Must we look for the "origin" of knowledge and the criterion of its truth in "reason" or strictly in "experience"? Is "sense" or the "understanding" the foundation of certainty and of validity, and to which does truth originally belong? The different schools of thought in the theory of knowledge part company according to how they answer this question.[11]

Cassirer has shown us how any symbolization always gives us a world of both actual and possible objects. For Cassirer, even scientific hypotheses precede through an as-if of conjectural reasoning. The scientist often proceeds through the seeming paradox of projecting what cannot exist in order to grasp what does exist as a law of nature. Nature, as we have seen in Kant, is not the assemblage of material things; nature, as Kant famously writes, "is the existence of things insofar as it is determined according to universal laws."[12] Galileo and other great scientists project this order onto nature, a rule-like order which projects a system of unified rules as a regulative ideal. This regulative ideal is, in a sense, a second order of possibility that inheres in human knowledge. The system is not real but is projected as a possible unity. Cassirer is now emphasizing that science often conjectures about this image of nature often by imagining objects that do not and will probably never actually exist. There never will be a knowable actual object that is still in space, unmoved by any external force. And yet, it is precisely this imagined object that Galileo projects in order to grasp one of the laws of modern physics.

As Kant famously tells us, the scientist comes as a judge and actually puts a demand on nature that it be graspable according to the principles that science endeavors to use to understand it, not as it is but as it is ordered by the human mind. Galileo could not have measured the magnitude of acceleration in the freefall without the conception of acceleration itself as well as having a measuring apparatus adequate to this task. But, he begins his experiments with an imagined object that will never exist.[13] Cassirer, then, emphasizes how science depends on the human ability to distinguish between actual and possible objects, both in that symbolic forms often proceed by projecting imaginative objects and because it proceeds by projecting a system of nature that is not actual but only a possible unity. This possible unity is not only a regulative ideal but also an absolutely necessary one for the great ambitions of modern science. To put this idea in its most radical and succinct form: even in science we must imagine otherwise to know the truth of what is. Of course, in political philosophy this distinction between actuality and possibility also has a long history. Cassirer's analysis of Rousseau's famous state of nature defends this state of nature as an imagined object used by Rousseau to vivify what is wrong with the France of the Third Estate. Imagining otherwise becomes the envisioned standpoint for a critical assessment of current social reality. Of course, then, imagining otherwise is also the basis for all of the great aesthetic ideas we discussed in chapter 1, including Rawls's famous experiment in which we imagine ourselves as behind a veil of ignorance. If we could not distinguish real from actual objects we would not be able to imagine the veil of ignorance, let alone symbolize the significance of this representation of the otherwise for the meaning of equality in a theory of justice.

Imagining otherwise, of course, as an act in and of itself does not necessarily bring about a new and more just world. No one has ever been foolish enough to think such; only political struggle and ethical commitment can accomplish such a task. What we learn from Cassirer—and we will return to this point in the next chapter when we discuss Frantz Fanon and the challenge by black philosophers of existence—is that these political and ethical struggles also inevitably have a symbolic projection, including the projection of a better and more just future. But, we cannot emphasize this point enough since it runs against the grain of the empiricist and even the materialist versions of Marxism that drove so many of the Communist parties. All material reality is always grasped by human beings as always already symbolized. Capital, as a symbolic form of human life, can only be replaced by another symbolic form of life. This is the significance of Cassirer's insight that there is no material and ideal dualism for human beings; our material forms of life are always also symbolic. The versatility of symbolization not only makes, to coin a word often used in current debates, the iterability of language possible, but it in a certain sense makes it inevitable. The transformative power of language in Cassirer is not reducible to iterability, for language always has within it a pull toward stabilization and toward transformation of the possible worlds embedded in any symbolic form. Various symbolic forms differently organize this tension between transformation and stabilization but the pull and tension is present in Cassirer for each one. Language has a free ideality, to use Cassirer's expression, as the other side of the universal applicability inherent in the power to name. Language, then, pushes us to generalization precisely through this power to name. But it is not simply this push to generalization and abstraction that explains the full force of the free ideality of language, for naming is not the true key to language.

Following Wilhelm von Humboldt, who plays such an important role in Cassirer, language is also a productive force because the very power to name ultimately relies on an appeal to a world image and some form of accepted significance. In this context, any linguistic proposition appears not as a mere copy of meaning which is already fixed and given in the consciousness of the speaker, but as a vehicle for the conferring of meaning and the disclosure of possible new worlds. Cassirer uses his own interpretation of Humboldt to articulate a new meaning for Kant's fundamental distinction between possibility and actuality as the hallmark of human thinking. Language is, therefore, no longer merely instrumental as constituted by human beings who are always a necessary link in the process of symbolization. Our creativity, then, is always part of how symbols come to mean something in our lived experiences. For Cassirer, the inner subjective domain of language is both *energia* and *ergion*, creative rule and creative potential. This is why he refuses to oppose *Geist*, or spirit, to life as he argues against Bergson.[14]

The "I" Standpoint

Language vivifies our world and our experience in it because although we are marked and delimited by language, we are also enabled by it to express, represent, and give significance to our lives. Different symbolic forms may mark out the "I" that is the necessary link in the chain of being represented, even if this "I" standpoint as a judgmental possibility is expressed differently; there is, however, an "I" standpoint in all symbolic forms, including myth, and therefore the "I" who judges for Cassirer is not some unique development for modernity. To quote Cassirer:

> Every kind of symbolic formation works in its own way and with its own aim toward such a pure sense of the I, which is specifically distinguished from a mere ego-meaning. This sense of the I appears in language most characteristically where it is able to achieve the kind of expression most adequate to it,

where it sharply and clearly distinguishes the "is" of the copular—which expresses the validity and stability of a pure relation—from assertions of mere existence, assertions about spatial and temporal *Dasein*.[15]

This "I" standpoint is true in science as a judgmental possibility, as it is true in art and as it is true in religion. To put this in the language of the current debates: symbolic forms that do indeed delimit us, also produce an "I" standpoint that endows us with some kind of creative productivity because the space for judgment in one form or another is allowed. Cassirer, then, enters into the modern debate about the social construction of the self in an important way. Yes, we are produced by language, socially constructed, or more precisely symbolically constructed. But, in those constructions there is also an "I" that is constituted through judgmental possibility. Again, to emphasize this point, the subject is constituted through an ascertainability whose other side is transformability. Outside of symbolic form there is no subject and there is no world. Cassirer, then, consistently gives a new meaning to Kant's privileging of judgment over the conceptual as a practice of freedom that inheres in the human distinction between the actual and the possible, as this is now, in turn, understood to be integral to all symbolic forms. To use Heidegger's language, *Dasein*'s being in the world is integrally tied to the projection of possibility.

How Is Objectivity Possible?

However, is there objectivity for our judgments in the different symbolic forms for Cassirer? The answer is yes. In each symbolic form, given the limits of our humanity, there is something like an inner necessity. This is, for example, what Kant demonstrated in respect to scientific representation of phenomena. All phenomena in Kant are necessarily represented in time and space and this inner necessity allows us to represent a law-like nature. But, as Cassirer tells us, even Kant in his *Critique of Judgment* concluded that his defense of scientific objectivity was too narrow to include the many forms in which the human mind displays its world. In both Kant and Cassirer, what delivers the necessary form, and thus objective character of any phenomenon, is always exactly the element of form that is inseparable from the image world in which it is embedded. It is the conforming of the factual with the theoretical that enables the former to have its inner necessity not only in science but also in art and myth. Yet, we would and should not ever collapse the specific objectivity of any symbolic domain into that of something specific like scientific cognition. The key for Cassirer is to grasp the form of the various human projects by which we come to know and live in our world. This means that for Cassirer there is no ontic, let alone ontological, distinction between the symbolic form and its contents. We can only struggle to know the form as it is represented and expressed with full respect given to its own autonomy. There is no privileged place for science as there is also no privileged place for philosophy if we identify philosophy as producing an overarching standard by which to judge other symbolic forms. Nor, for Cassirer, can we root any of these forms in some ultimate ontology of man or *Dasein* separate from the actuality of these forms. As we will see this is the heart of Cassirer's disagreement with Heidegger.

Cassirer forcefully argued that no philosophy can aspire to such rationalization of itself, as Hegel famously attempted, because all formations of *Geist*, including that of philosophy, rest on image worlds. We are creatures marked by an "ideality" from which we are inseparable. Ideality is not quite the right word here because it echoes the dualism Cassirer rejected. But, there is another sense in which the retention of the human need to think, live, and work through images of a specific kind rooted in the finite imagination remains the basis of Cassirer's thought. Our ideality, as we discussed in the last chapter, is also definitively reworked by Heidegger as the other side of our finitude. But in Cassirer, it is the space of judgment inseparable from the form of symbolization that allows us to claim our freedom and to assume our responsibility. Cassirer always insists that our ethical world is always in the making and there is no one but ourselves who makes it. It is in a sense, then, in the character of a human being to judge, which is inseparable from our finitude and makes us responsible. We can at least struggle to live up to our own ideals of justice even if we accept and respect these as symbolic formations. There is, for Cassirer, a moral image of the world implied in all forms of human endeavor. It is as this being capable of moral judgment and action, the very being who judges and poses questions before physical nature, in which Cassirer finds the grandeur of the ideal of humanity. Judgment in all forms testifies to a "subject" not lost among the phenomena of any objective world, even if it is ultimately, of course, part of a world of symbolization. In judgment we find the "I" that remains even if that "I" following Kant can never be theorized as an outside place where we can safeguard our judgments of what "I" means.

Cassirer and Progress

Cassirer read the history of human beings as a *Bildung*, as a ground of self-discovery, or at least he did so in his more optimistic moments and he famously ends his *Essay on Man* with the ethical task he argued informs his philosophy as a whole:

> Human culture taken as a whole may be described as the process of man's progressive self-liberation. Language, art, religion, science, are various phases in this process. In all of them man discovers and proves a new power—the power to build up a world of his own, an "ideal" world. Philosophy cannot give up its search for a fundamental unity in this ideal world. But it does not confound this unity with simplicity. It does not overlook the tensions and frictions, the strong contrasts and deep conflicts between various powers of man. These cannot be reduced to a common denominator. They tend in different directions and obey different principles. But this multiplicity and disparateness does not denote discord or disharmony. All these functions complete and complement one another. Each one opens a new horizon and shows us a new aspect of humanity. The dissonant is in harmony with itself; the contraries are not mutually exclusive, but interdependent: "harmony in contrariety, as in the case of the bow and the lyre."[16]

Cassirer did believe that reflection on the plurality of symbolic forms could enlarge our understanding of our own creativity, which ultimately allows us to appreciate all the richness of these forms and at the same time seek to understand their own unique inner necessity and ultimate interdependence. But, as the modest man Cassirer was, he knew that he had just begun and that this project lay in the future. It is certainly the case that the spirit of his work is to fight against what Amartya Sen has defined as the miniaturization of the human spirit.[17]

Ultimately, if there is development or progress of human knowledge in Cassirer, it is through the appreciation of complexity that would allow us to see our way more clearly through the shadows that might ensnare human beings in fears driven by their vulnerability. Although Cassirer sometimes spoke as if the modern European world gave us an appreciation of complexity that was not present in myth, he did so provisionally and in the name of that complexity. Cassirer emphasized again and again that we can only know the truth of symbolic forms in and through them, and that this insistence has led to the charge against him that he is a relativist. Before we turn to two of his great critics, Levinas and Heidegger, I want to emphasize again that Cassirer is not a relativist in the sense often used: a refusal of any universal truth about *Dasein*. Cassirer does offer us a universal insight as we have seen throughout this chapter through his original reinterpretation of the uniqueness of human knowledge given in symbolic form: the distinction between possibility and actuality. In this sense, he offers us an insight into the formal aspect of our humanity as symbol-making creatures. Cassirer is mistakenly called a relativist even by his great critics because, given his central insight into what is universal about what constitutes the uniqueness of our being human, we can never know the content separately from the form and each symbolic form will have its own objectivity. I want to emphasize here that Cassirer leaves us, however, with an ethical call that is often confused with relativism: his ethical call is a demand for the respect of the plurality of symbolic forms as integral to the Kantian ideal of humanity.

The Davos Debate

In 1929 the young Heidegger met Cassirer in Davos to debate their differences. Cassirer's *Philosophy of Symbolic Forms* was already in print and had been for a number of years. Cassirer had become a controversial figure within the circle of neo-Kantians because of his radical interpretation of the transcendental imagination into a new form of symbolization. The debate with Cassirer was over his continuing emphasis on the imagination and his insistence on the central place of the *Critique of Judgment* in Kant's philosophy. Many of the neo-Kantians in Germany at that time, including those who identified with the Marburg School, had defended the position that the transcendental imagination was both an inconsistent and unnecessary idea for Kant's logical derivation of the categories of the understanding. The focus of the Marburg school was almost entirely on the *Critique of Pure Reason* with some attention to the *Critique of Practical Reason*. Cassirer enters the debate with Heidegger as if they were allies when it came to the fundamentals of the reading of Kant. Heidegger refused this alliance. Unfortunately, I cannot spend as much time on the debate as it deserves, but the setting was undoubtedly dramatic.

Germany was in a state of serious crisis. The Nazi Party was gaining popularity. The young Emmanuel Levinas was present at Davos and like so many of the other graduate students he was enamored with Heidegger. A group of graduate students put on a skit mocking the old-fashioned, scholarly Cassirer. Levinas played Cassirer and later in life deeply regretted that decision, and it is the essay that he wrote on Cassirer's work that will be the focus of my own discussion. The drama of the setting as it has come to be understood in the horrific events that followed has undoubtedly marked the scholarly reception of the debate. Perhaps we should not separate the debate from the violent aftermath of history within which it was situated. In the ten years that followed Davos, Cassirer would be fired from his professorship and exiled from Germany because he was Jewish and Heidegger was to become the rector of the

University of Freiburg for a brief period of time. Levinas was to spend the war years in a concentration camp. What has sadly been forgotten as a result of the taboo against taking Heidegger seriously in some circles due to his Nazism is precisely that the young Heidegger was in part inspired by Kant.

There are two main points that should be highlighted in this rich debate so that we can grasp the significance of the larger exchange at Davos. Cassirer emphasizes what the two share in their reading of Kant as follows:

> On one point we agree, in that for me as well the productive power of imagination appears in fact to have a central meaning for Kant. From there I was led through my work on the symbolic. One cannot unravel this [the symbolic] without referring it to the faculty of the productive power of the imagination. The power of the imagination is the connection of all thought to the intuition. Kant calls the power of imagination *Synthesis Speciosa*. Synthesis is the basic power [*Grundkraft*] of pure thinking. For Kant, however, it [pure thinking] does not depend simply on synthesis, but depends instead primarily upon the synthesis which serves the species. But the problem of the species leads into the core of the concept of image, the concept of symbol.[18]

As we saw in the last chapter, Heidegger's response accepts that he does indeed begin with a reworking of Kant's notion of the transcendental imagination. But this reworking will demand a completely different kind of ontology of finitude that, according to Heidegger, Kant did not undertake but only anticipated. Both thinkers agree that truth is indeed relative to *Dasein* and that they are following Kant in saying as much. To quote Heidegger's summation of what was at stake in their difference:

> In this question of the going-beyond of finitude, we find a wholly central problem. I have said that it is a separate question to ask about the possibility of finitude in general, for one can formally argue simply: As soon as I make assertions about the finite and as soon as I want to determine the finite as finite, I must already have an idea of infinitude. For the moment this does not say much—and yet it says enough for a central problem to exist here. From the fact that now this character of infinitude comes to light precisely in what we have emphasized as the constituent of finitude, I want to make it clear that I would say: Kant describes the power of the imagination of the Schematism as *exhibito originaria*. But this originality is an *exhibito*, an *exhibito* of the presentation of the free self-giving in which lies a dependency upon a taking-in-stride. So in a certain sense this originality is indeed there as creative faculty. As a finite creature, the human being has a certain infinitude in the ontological. But the human being is never infinite and absolute in the creating of the being itself; rather, it is infinite in the sense of the understanding of Being. But as Kant

says, provided that the ontological understanding of Being is only possible within the inner experience of beings, this infinitude of the ontological is bound essentially to ontic experience so that we must say the reverse: this infinitude which breaks out in the power of imagination is precisely the strongest argument for finitude, for ontology is an index of finitude. God does not have it. And the fact that the human being has the *exhibito* is the strongest argument for its finitude, for ontology requires only a finite creature.[19]

Both philosophers also put pride of place on the centrality of freedom for *Dasein*. And, indeed, the two men argue that they are providing a radical reading of Kant that insists that it is only the theoretical ungraspability of freedom that allows *Dasein*'s freedom as a possibility.

However, for Heidegger this possibility must be revealed as the truth of *Dasein* through a new ontology of *Dasein*'s existence as a creature who is marked by being toward death. Heidegger defines the difference between his understanding of freedom and Cassirer's as follows. In Cassirer, we have seen that freedom is our power to reshape things even as we are shaped by them because symbolic forms always leave open a space for judgment. Heidegger responds as follows:

> Cassirer's point is to emphasize the various forms of the shaping in order, with a view to these shapings, subsequently to point out a certain dimension of the shaping powers themselves. Now, one could say: this dimension, then, is fundamentally the same as that which I call *Dasein*. But that would be erroneous. The difference is clearest in the concept of Freedom. I spoke of a freeing in the sense that the freeing of the inner transcendence of *Dasein* is the fundamental character of philosophizing itself. In so doing, the authentic sense of this freeing is not to be found in becoming free to a certain extent for the forming images of consciousness and for the realm of form. Rather, it is to be found in becoming free for the finitude of *Dasein*. Just to come into the throwness of *Dasein* is to come into the conflict that lies within the essence of freedom. I did not give freedom to myself, although it is through Being-free that I can first be I myself. But now, not I myself in the sense of an indifferent ground for explanation, but rather: *Dasein* is the authentic basic occurrence in which the existing of man, and with it every problematic of existence itself, becomes essential.[20]

The task of the philosopher as it is articulated in this debate is to unveil the truth of *Dasein*'s freedom as transcendence. We are, as we saw in chapter 2, always ahead of ourselves, thrown into the world, one out of which we yet project a future partially marked by our own making but that ultimately takes us toward the nothing of our own death. We are, in other words, the being who knows at the deepest level that we ourselves are only who we are by confronting nothingness. In this confrontation, however, with what is not and can never be known we find our authentic humanity and we transcend the conditions of sociality that bog down most human beings in the chatter and distractions of the "they." Transcendence inheres in our throwness into a world of objects in which we are also other. In our experience and confrontation with the nothingness that marks our finitude we find what Heidegger calls the eccentric character of man.[21]

Freedom comes to us as transcendence, a future project by which we make ourselves into an authentic being whose freedom is unveiled in the confrontation with nothingness, and this means for Heidegger that the traditional metaphysical notion of "man" as a thinking subject is completely inadequate to the true dignity of humanity. As we have already seen, it was Kant, not Heidegger, who first undermined the possibility of a theory of the subject. Heidegger does not seek such a theory, but he does aspire to a new existential analytic of the fundaments of our being in time. And, it is through understanding *Dasein* that we would also understand the particularities of any form of *Dasein*'s objectification, such as mythical thinking. Hence, Heidegger accuses Cassirer of relativism and uses his discussion of the form of myth as pointing to a fundamental problem in Cassirer's philosophy:

> Yet if this interpretation of myth is to be judged not only with regard to what it achieves as a guide in the positive sciences but also with regard to its *own philosophical* content, then the following questions arise: is the predetermination of myth as a functional form of creative consciousness adequately grounded on its own terms? Where are the foundations for such an admittedly unavoidable grounding to be found? Are the foundations themselves sufficiently secured and elaborated? Cassirer's *grounding* of his guiding predetermination of myth as a creative force [*bildender Kraft*] of spirit ("symbolic form") is essentially an *appeal* to Kant's "Copernican revolution," according to which all "actuality" is to be considered as a formation of productive consciousness.[22]

Cassirer's response to Heidegger is that, indeed, he will not ground his philosophy of symbolic forms in any philosophy of *Dasein* which turns on some overarching, philosophical notion of "man's" existence, including "man's" existence as transcendence which gives him an eccentric character.

Thus, for Cassirer it is ironically Heidegger who is retreating from the radicalism of the transcendental imagination. If we are to be faithful to Kant we must remain true to his fundamental lesson that we cannot have any theory of man, even a non-"metaphysical" one. As Cassirer explains his own understanding of Kant's central insight of the finitude of reason:

What is new in this [Copernican] turn appears to me to lie in the fact that now there is no longer one single such structure of Being, but that instead we have completely different ones. Every new structure of Being has its new a priori presuppositions. Kant shows that he was bound to the conditions for the possibility of experience. Kant shows how every kind of new form now also refers to a new world of the objective, how the aesthetic object is not bound to the empirical object, how it has its own a priori categories, how art also builds up a world, but also how these laws are different from the laws of the physical. For this reason, a completely new multiplicity enters into the problem of the object in general. And for this reason, the new Kantian metaphysics comes into being precisely from out of ancient, dogmatic metaphysics. Being in ancient metaphysics was substance, what forms a ground. Being in the new metaphysics is, in my language, no longer the Being of a substance, but rather the Being which starts from a variety of functional determinations and meanings. And the essential point which distinguishes my position from Heidegger's appears to me to lie here.[23]

I agree with Cassirer that he has eloquently summarized his difference from Heidegger. The key difference between the two philosophers for the purpose of this book is that Heidegger's philosophy cannot yield the respect for the plurality of symbolic forms that is at the very heart of Cassirer's philosophy. Behind all of the objectifications of *Dasein*, in Heidegger is a new existential analytic of the fundaments of our finitude. There cannot and should not be such an existential analytic in Cassirer because we only know *Dasein* in *Dasein*'s multiplicity. There is no *Dasein* other than in and through that multiplicity. Thus, even an analytic of the fundaments of our finitude is not possible. It is this call to respect for plurality that makes Cassirer a necessary beginning to defend the continuing ethical importance offered by the moral image of the world. Of course, Heidegger as we saw came to disagree with his own earlier work in *Being and Time* and correspondingly the position he took with Cassirer in the Davos debate. As we saw, Heidegger critiques himself for holding on to a notion of man as the subject of transcendence that further distances us from the truth of Being and more desperately leads to the complete domination of technocratic reason. The Cassirerian answer to the later Heidegger is that such sweeping pessimism runs afoul of Kant's insight into our finitude.

As we saw in Cassirer's responses to Heidegger, it is multiplicity that is the other side of our inevitable ensnarement in symbolic forms. More specifically, myth cannot be eclipsed as long as there is language because myth is integrally tied to the metaphoric power of language. Thus, mythical thinking cannot and will not completely die out as long as human beings vivify themselves in language. There are, of course, many reasons for us to be pessimistic about our future but that is what they are: reasons. These reasons will always come to us in symbolic forms embedded in the image of the world in which they are represented. We are not God, but for Cassirer, it is up to us to create a more just world for humanity. Indeed, it is our responsibility to do so. For, a practical ethics can be read into the content of our experiences and the possibility of a future world met in the vivifying power of language. Certainly, a little help from God would be nice, or at least this writer would welcome it, but for Cassirer it is up to us to transform our world, not only with the great ideals of Europe but also with the recognition that they are but one of the symbolic manifestations of humanity.

Levinas's Engagement with Cassirer

However, for Levinas the problem with Cassirer's philosophy was not only that it seemed relativist but that it rooted transformation in a cultural subject even if that subject is to be conceived as a transsubjectivity. In his moving answer to Cassirer, in which he echoes his repentance for his participation in the skit at Davos, Levinas defends the idea of how meaning arises, which is itself critical to understanding his entire work. For Levinas, symbols cannot contain the moral imperatives that ultimately drive them. For example, Levinas argues that the primordial ethical demand "thou shalt not kill" comes before its enunciation in words. This command originates as we confront our encounters with the face of the Other. The face of the Other for Levinas comes beyond any given system of meaning. To quote Levinas:

> In other words, before it is a celebration of being, expression is a relation with the one to whom I express the expression and whose presence is already required so that my cultural gesture of expression can be produced. The Other who faces me is not included in the totality of being that is expressed. He arises behind all collection of being, as the one to whom I express what I express. I find myself facing the Other. He is neither a cultural signification nor a simple given. He is, primordially, *sense* because he lends it to expression itself, because only through him can a phenomenon such as signification introduce itself, of itself, into being.[24]

Levinas's worry is that Cassirer's philosophy of symbolic forms reduces the Other, in Levinas's own terminology, to an order of the same through the argument that through symbolization we can reach out to others, draw them toward us, and make them present to ourselves. Again, to quote Levinas:

The face is abstract. This abstraction certainly does not correspond to the raw sensible given of the empiricists. Nor is it an instantaneous cut in time, where time would "cross" eternity. The instant pertains to the world; it is a cut that does not bleed. Whereas the abstraction of the face is visitation and advent that disturbs immanence without being set in the horizons of the World. Its abstraction is not obtained from a logical process going from the substance of beings, from the particular to the general. On the contrary, it goes toward beings but is not engaged with them, retires from them, is ab-solved. Its wonder lies in this *elsewhere* whence it comes and where it already retires. But this coming from *elsewhere* is not a *symbolic reference* to this *elsewhere* as to a term. The face presents itself in its nakedness; it is not a concealing—but thereby indicating—form, a base; it is not a hiding—but thereby betraying—phenomenon, a thing in itself. Otherwise the face would be confounded with a lack that precisely presupposes it. If signifying were equivalent to indicating, the face would be insignificant.[25]

For Levinas, the expression of the Other can only be represented as unreachable—in that sense before culture—that blows apart any self-certainty of the subject and calls her to an ethical response.

The difference between what Levinas names the Saying and the Said is crucial here. The Saying is the actual discourse, to use Cassirer's terms, in which we come to symbolize ourselves. The Said is more original than any human Saying. Thus, for Levinas, the spirit, or indeed the Said, of the primordial command "thou shalt not kill" originates not only in the face of the Other but it is paradoxically there before it is proclaimed in the written Torah. The written Torah in that sense only Says what has already been Said in the spirit of the revelation of the face. For Levinas, the ethical relation as the trace can never be contained by any symbolic form. Indeed, the ethical relation breaks up all symbolic forms and points beyond them. It would be impossible to provide anything like a full answer from a Cassirerian point of view without discussing his own writings on religion and ruminations on Judaism as these informed his philosophy. But, Levinas is correct that for Cassirer the finite creatures we are can only know the Other as the other comes to us in symbolic forms. We can already reach out to each other with preestablished forms of meaning even if in that very reaching we seek to break out of the symbolic forms that seek to contain and enable us to understand one another.

In *The Philosophy of the Limit* I argued that Derrida rightfully points out that the asymmetry of the Other turns on a phenomenological symmetry if we consider that Other as a human face.[26] As we have seen, in the discussion of the difference between Heidegger and Cassirer, Cassirer tells us that the sameness of our humanity is rooted in symbolic multiplicity. This sameness cannot even be evoked as the eccentric character of *Dasein*. We are the same as symbolizing creatures and as the same we are also different, other to one another, because we are never outside the symbolic forms that give us our divergent worlds. It is at the heart of Cassirer's work that the respect for plurality demands the respect for otherness, and the uniqueness of other cultures, other peoples, and the other worlds they live in. What Cassirer and Levinas share in their disagreement with Heidegger, to use Levinas's words, is "to find a sense to the human without measuring it by ontology."[27] For Cassirer, the true Copernican revolution begun in Kant leads to respect for the plurality of symbolic forms, and what is more necessary now than such respect in the so-called postcolonial world?

Notes

1. Ernst Cassirer, *An Essay on Man* (New Haven, CT: Yale University Press, 1972), 26.
2. Cassirer, *An Essay on Man*, 33.
3. Ernst Cassirer, *The Philosophy of Symbolic Forms: Volume 4: The Metaphysics of Symbolic Forms* (New Haven, CT: Yale University Press, 1996), 4–8.
4. Ernst Cassirer, *The Philosophy of Symbolic Forms: Volume 3: The Phenomenology of Knowledge* (New Haven, CT: Yale University Press, 1957), 109.
5. Cassirer, *An Essay on Man*, 25.
6. Immanuel Kant, *Critique of Pure Reason*, trans. and ed. Paul Guyer and Allen Wood (Cambridge: Cambridge University Press, 1998), 193–194 (A51/B75).
7. Ernst Cassirer, *The Philosophy of Symbolic Forms: Volume 1: Language* (New Haven, CT: Yale University Press, 1955), 319.
8. Cassirer, *An Essay on Man*, 59.
9. Ernst Cassirer, *The Philosophy of Symbolic Forms: Volume 2: Mythical Thought* (New Haven, CT: Yale University Press, 1955), 23.
10. Cassirer, *The Philosophy of Symbolic Forms: Volume 2*, 24.
11. Cassirer, *The Philosophy of Symbolic Forms: Volume 4*, 167.
12. Immanuel Kant, *Prolegomena to Any Future Metaphysics That Will Be Able to Come Forward as Science*, trans. and ed. Gary Hatfield (Cambridge: Cambridge University Press, 1997), section 14.
13. Cassirer, *An Essay on Man*, 16 (and generally chapter 1).
14. Cassirer, *The Philosophy of Symbolic Forms: Volume 4*, chapter 1.
15. Cassirer, *The Philosophy of Symbolic Forms: Volume 4*, 99.
16. Cassirer, *An Essay on Man*, 228.
17. See, generally, Amartya Sen, *Identity and Violence: The Illusion of Destiny* (New York: W. W. Norton, 2006).
18. Martin Heidegger, *Kant and the Problem of Metaphysics*, 5th ed., trans. Richard Taft (Bloomington: Indiana University Press, 1997), 194.

19. Heidegger, *Kant and the Problem of Metaphysics*, 197.
20. Heidegger, *Kant and the Problem of Metaphysics*, 202–203.
21. Heidegger, *Kant and the Problem of Metaphysics*, 204.
22. Heidegger, *Kant and the Problem of Metaphysics*, 186.
23. Heidegger, *Kant and the Problem of Metaphysics*, 206.
24. Emmanuel Levinas, *Humanism of the Other* (Chicago: University of Chicago Press, 1972), 30.
25. Levinas, *Humanism of the Other*, 39.
26. See, for example, *The Philosophy of the Limit* (New York: Routledge, 1992), 54–55, where I argued that "Derrida argues that the relegation of the Other to pure externality is itself a form of self-containment. To be self-enclosed, to deny the 'trace' of the Other in oneself, is to be impenetrable, safe from the contamination of the 'outside.' '*Différance* is difference under erasure,' not the glorification of phenomenological asymmetry."
27. Levinas, *Humanism of the Other*, 57.

CHAPTER FOUR

Decolonizing Critical Theory: The Challenge of Black Existentialism

An Afrikaans friend of mine once told me a terrible joke from his childhood. While the joke itself has many versions, the punch line always remains the same. Some Afrikaners had gone to the Transkei and wondered, rather curiously, why there were no people there. W. E. B. Du Bois famously wrote that the process of negrification allows blacks only to appear as a problem, and not as human beings carrying on in the course of their day-to-day life. Here we also have an example of a distorted vision held by whites who cannot see their fellow Africans as human beings. In the work of black philosophers of existence and their reinterpretation of phenomenology we will continuously return to what Du Bois called the double consciousness imposed upon blacks in that they cannot only see themselves being looked at but also develop a second sight where they, too, can envision how the whites are seeing them as less than human.

W. E. B. Du Bois, Frantz Fanon, and a number of younger thinkers have not only opened up a new branch of phenomenology and the black thinking of existence but they also poignantly demonstrate the full force of the collapse of the ethical due to the subconscious and also institutionalized belief that black people are somehow below the register of what can be envisioned as human. Cassirer's brilliant insistence that human beings are not rational creatures but symbolizing beings—and that there is no one symbolic practice that becomes the pinnacle from which all other practices are to be judged—explicitly challenges what Fanon called the principle of exclusivity. The principle of exclusivity in Fanon suggests that all black cultural formations will be systematically degraded as below reason in a way that such formations stand below any truly significant lasting and symbolic contribution to what we think of as the culture of humanity. It is not surprising that many thinkers associated with black philosophies of existence and Africana phenomenology have returned to Cassirer as a thinker very much on the side of the close study of the diverse forms of human symbolization, as these forms must be studied within their own histories of development and the standards by which they judge themselves. But, neither Cassirer nor Levinas directly faced what Du Bois and Fanon tell us we must confront if there is to be a human world and indeed a new and critical thinking of humanism.

We must face—and the "we" here refers to whites both in the academy and outside it who care about building a world worthy of the ideal of humanity—nothing less than the collapse of the ethical brought on by colonialism in which the black man, and, of course, the black woman, are captured by a strange kind of invisibility, one in which they are present as the absence of an interior of a subjectivity that fights for freedom and brings value into the world. As I hope to show in this chapter, Fanon is indeed a critical humanist and such humanism drives all of his work. But, such humanism is an empty dream if it does not directly face both the full political and ethical demands of decolonization and the elevation of blacks to their full human significance in any struggle to change the world. As Lewis Gordon reminds us, "Black power demands, among its values, first and foremost the recognition and valuing of black people as sources of value."[1]

I am making the distinction between black existential philosophy and black philosophies of existence following the lines of Lewis Gordon and Paget Henry who, among others, suggest that while Fanon is certainly a thinker who worked with the tools of European existential philosophy, he and the others who have followed him have also used different philosophical tools. The key here is that black philosophies of existence begin with the actual struggles of black people to liberate themselves from racism and colonialism. Indeed, what makes Africana phenomenology unique is that the occasion for transcendental reflection is the confrontation with the searing force of racism and what Du Bois called negrification rather than in Husserl, often considered the founder of European phenomenology, the crisis of European reason. In this sense, black philosophies of existence attempt to respond to the ontological imposition that W. E. B. Du Bois often remarked was the central question for a black human being: What am I other than a problem in white society? Questions of identity, of course, are always placed in the social, political, and symbolic context in which identity has to struggle to find an answer to the question of "What am I?" when that "what" has been demoted beneath the realm of humanity. If I can dare to assert that there is a shared answer as to how one answers the question of ontology implicit in black philosophies of existence, it is that such questions are inseparable from the question of liberation which is always foregrounded in the work of the thinkers discussed hereafter.

Gordon succinctly defines the difference between the ontological question of identity and the liberation question as follows:

> In the libratory question, we head, too, through a series of philosophical turns. Although the two meet on the question of *who* is to be liberated, the liberating animus charts a course of value that at times transcends being although not always essence. Liberation is a concern about purpose, a concern about *ought* and *why*: Whatever we may be, the point is to focus energy on what we *ought* to become.[2]

The black philosophers of existence do indeed provide us with powerful moral images of freedom, but they offer us something much greater and more difficult in demanding that freedom is inseparable from the actual struggles of black human beings to be free and to bring themselves out from beneath the despairing weight of racism and colonization. It was Albert Camus who wrote that suicide is the only true philosophical question in the twentieth century, but thinkers from Frederick Douglass to W. E. B. Du Bois have rightfully reminded us that the question of why blacks continue to live has always had a peculiar and terrifying twist. What does it mean to go on in the face of overwhelming oppression that affects every aspect of your life? What does it mean to struggle to be a human being in the onslaught of the very denial of your humanity? What does it mean to confront a white world that is Manichean in its demand that you be cleansed through the projected purity of whiteness? The only answer is that freedom will have to be fought for and the very opening of the ethical will have to be reasserted against its fundamental violation by colonial conditions and obviously implicit racism. In a certain sense blacks must be Other in the full existential sense of being a human being that limits the totalizing impulses of colonization before the ethical can once again begin.

Of course, we have arrived at the fundamental ethical challenge to all of us who are white by black philosophies of existence. Again, to quote Gordon:

> Here we see why the demands of classical liberalism and Kantian humanism fail: they depend on symmetry. White-black relations are such that blacks struggle to achieve Otherness; it is a struggle to be in a position *for the ethical to emerge*. Thus, the circumstance is peculiarly wrought with realization of the *political*. Fanon's book ends, then, politically and existentially. Politically, like the author's romanticized African American, the call is to fight, to struggle

against the system of his oppression. But in that struggle, Fanon calls for a pedagogy to build ("*édifer*," "to edify," "to build") a questioning humanity. This building takes the form of a prayer. From anger, to laughter, to tears, he concludes with prayers—prayers to, of all realities, his *body*. Fanon beseeches his body to make of him a man who questions, a being that is open and, consequently, a being who is a *human* being. By 1960, in *The Wretched of the Earth*, he concludes with the same thesis, that material and conceptual struggles that open possibilities are needed to set afoot a new humanity.[3]

The moral image of freedom offered by black philosophies of existence is inseparable, then, from how blacks are envisioned in their struggle to change the world and how as whites we must come to terms with what it means to be positioned as white. In our case, too, the mark of skin color gets intertwined with the denial of our humanity. We are returned here to the fundamental phenomenological questions of how we embodied beings see and live in our world. Paget Henry has succinctly defined phenomenology: "By phenomenology, I mean the discursive practice through which self-reflective descriptions of the constituting activities of consciousness are produced after the 'natural attitude' of everyday life has been bracketed by some ego-displacing technique."[4] As all of the great phenomenologists remind us, as embodied consciousness we have at least three different perspectives on the world: the dimension of seeing, the dimension of being seen, and the dimension of being conscious of being seen by others. What does it mean to be a human being in the Transkei who was not being seen? What does it mean to be a human being who could not only not see other people but not know that those people were looking back? What does it mean to be a white person surrounded by other human beings and not see them as such? Both Du Bois and Fanon tell us that all of us have lost our humanity when we are put in such a position and allow ourselves to slip into a certain myopic ignorance. For Du Bois, there were two possible ways for black Africans to find a way beyond the double consciousness imposed upon blacks in which the "we" of shared cultural traditions has been shattered by negrification. The first is that one can overcome the tragedy of second sight in which blacks see themselves as a dehumanized other by projecting and producing ways of being a "we" that goes beyond the stereotypes of black face. Paget Henry has eloquently written the Rastafarians are an excellent example of this first way of at least challenging the dominance of second sight. The other is what Du Bois called the withdrawal into a tower in which one seeks to cultivate not a "we" but an "I" of first sight in which the black person can at least see himself or herself as a thinking subject. Although Fanon would certainly agree with Du

Bois that there must be cultural reassertion on the part of black Africans, he wrote at a time of revolutionary possibility in which revolution was the only true answer to the achievement of a nonracial world and the recovery of our humanity. But, let us turn now to Fanon and his own unique call to all of us to join in the struggle to form a world in which we can truly claim our humanity.

Black Skin, White Masks

Fanon begins his classic study *Black Skin, White Masks* by exploring how the black man undergoes the denial of his humanity on a day-to-day basis. For Fanon, all human beings seek to assert themselves and to exercise their own subjectivity so they feel themselves to be a presence in the world. In this very act of self-assertion we cannot help but confront others. The great existential philosopher Jean-Paul Sartre had much to say about the dynamics of self-assertion as such dynamics immediately run up against others trying to do the same. Our very attempt to be present in the world is always an attempt to be present with others. We do not assert ourselves so as to enter into an empty void but to enter into relations with other people to declare, "Here I am." But this very assertion—"Here I am"—carries within it a language in which the "I" lives, asserts itself, and makes itself present as a unique being with a name.

As Cassirer tells us, language is one of our most primordial symbolic systems and with every language we get an entire world and not just an arbitrary naming system. If we do not allow ourselves to listen carefully to the language of others as we enter into their symbolic world, then we will be unable to meaningfully translate our being in communion with one another. We can use Cassirer's insight of how fundamental language is to all human beings as a symbolic system to deepen our understanding of the first chapter in *Black Skin, White Masks*. Of course, this is not meant in any way to suggest that Fanon is dependent on Cassirer. Dutifully, my intentions here are to heed the warning against symbolically freezing black philosophies of existence into continued legacies of European thought. Instead, the point here is to emphasize Cassirer's attempt to dramatize the horrifying wrong in denying public standing to the language of others so that there literally becomes a profound existential dilemma for blacks in the colonial situation where they are compelled to make a seeming choice but one that ultimately ends with identical outcomes. As Fanon reminds us:

> No, speaking pidgin-nigger closes off the black man; it perpetuates a state of conflict in which the white man injects the black with extremely dangerous

foreign bodies. Nothing is more astonishing than to hear a black man express himself properly, for then in truth he is putting on the white world.[5]

Either the colonized can speak their "own" language and stand belittled because it remains unacknowledged on the horizon of human symbolization, or they may take on the language of the colonizer and find themselves again belittled because such a language system remains integrally connected to the violence of the colonial oppression.

When black men and women give in and take on the language of the oppressor, they do not find themselves sheltered symbolically in equality to the oppressor. By internalizing such a symbolic system, one must also inherit the imago that goes with it such that one seeks to become and see oneself as French, for it is only a French person who speaks French. Fanon recounts a familiar scene where a family is waiting for a young black man returning from studies in the thick of the colonized university system, deliberating whether or not to get off the ship speaking his own dialect or the language of the colonizer. As Fanon explains:

> To speak a language is to take on a world, a culture. The Antilles Negro who wants to be white will be the whiter as he gains mastery of the cultural tool that language is. Rather more than a year ago in Lyon, I remember, in a lecture I had drawn a parallel between Negro and European poetry, and a French acquaintance told me enthusiastically, "At bottom you are a white man." The fact that I had been able to investigate so interesting a problem through the white man's language gave me honorary citizenship.[6]

The problem, of course, is that no black man or woman is ever truly seen as white nor heard as white but is instead glimpsed as something that can only approximate a good puppet, a puppet that just might "seem" white if you do not look too closely or listen too carefully. This almost "seeming" white but never being able to achieve whiteness is what creates a crack in the black men and women attempting to symbolize themselves. In either situation, these black men and women accept their demotion from the world in which only the language and symbolic systems of the colonizer can be valued. There is no way to put together a coherent imago bolstered by a symbolically protected place in the world capable of giving it meaning.

There is a sense, then, that the very power of language undermines black men and women in their struggle to assert themselves as individual beings. They cannot find themselves in a publicly reinforced symbolization of who they are that allows them to invest in their own equality along with other human beings. It becomes difficult, therefore, to project a coherent imago that allows one to see oneself as a human subject among other human subjects; it also becomes difficult, if not impossible, to actually enter the public world. For, in colonization there is only the public world of the colonizer whose language not only is not your own but is itself the language of oppression.

At the beginning of *Black Skin, White Masks*, Fanon discusses at length individual self-assertion in conditions of colonization. Such self-assertion ultimately fails because it imprisons the black man and woman on the horns of a dilemma: either reduce yourself by trying to mimic the whiteness of the colonizer or hold on to your own language, which in the colonized situation is always already disparaged as not really language at all. Fanon is speaking of what happens when an individual thinks they can solve the problem of racism by themselves. Famously, language and rebellions around language have often inspired collective action. In 1976, thousands of young South African black students rose up against being taught in the language of the oppressors—Afrikaans—insisting that their own languages be given the respect they deserved. The Soweto Uprising was a powerful revolutionary insistence by young blacks to receive the public space for their own languages which would be respected and not marked as a sign of inferiority. It is important to underscore the difference between a collective struggle around language from the dilemma of an individual attempting to resolve the problem alone. In a deep sense, Fanon is arguing that there are no individual solutions to end racism and colonialism—not for blacks and not for whites. Yet, Fanon tells us that the individual does not easily find his or her way through the direness of what the overthrow of colonialism will demand.

However, if a black man or woman cannot assert themselves in one of our most primordial forms, such as language, and find themselves, then can they still find themselves in other residues of society where race does not dominate everything? Fanon analyzes relationships between black men and white women and black women and white men within this context for the struggle of self-assertion and achieving some form of subjectivity away from the racist world. Fanon is not presenting an argument giving us a general commentary on the legitimacy or illegitimacy of interracial relationships. Instead, he is writing about a desperate situation of people who, having internalized the public self-hatred of their blackness, try to seek a private configuration in which either they might be human or possibly elevated beyond the stamp of blackness by being loved through someone who is worshipped as the holder of humanity: the white man or woman.

Fanon, of course, tells us that this is tragic and terrible dead end. For, no black woman ever truly becomes white by being loved by a white man. In the case of the black woman, the deep desire to be beautiful in the eyes of the lover becomes the desire to be seen as almost white, almost white because there is no beauty that is not white. At every step in the story Fanon relates how Mayotte Capécia takes herself further and further away from her own self-affirmation. We see a woman who tries to take solace in the fact that her grandmother was white, giving her a terrible hope that somehow the bit of white blood coursing through her veins will imbue her with enough whiteness to mask her blackness. Capécia fantasizes that she might even give birth to a white boy since there is that bit of white blood somewhere in her body. The fantasy, of course, is that Capécia might able to free her lineage from the curse of which she is seeking to escape. But, of course, to see yourself as a curse from which you must escape is to live with an imago that is fractured into a state of perpetual trauma which easily collapses into delusional fantasy.

Similarly, in the case of the black man pursuing white women we are returned to a basic dilemma of self-worth. The black man wants to be loved not only for himself but ultimately loved by someone who can make him other than his own black self. After all, if a white woman loves you, then you are not truly black. Such a relationship represents a psychological trophy indicating that the worth of blackness should be awarded a higher standing in the hierarchy of humanness. It may take several generations, but if your children are mixed and continue to mix only with whiteness then perhaps the dreaded coloration could find itself someday cleansed. However, like all lovers the demand for love of your unique being turns against itself as this form of self-assertion masquerading as a fantasy of escape ultimately demands one be loved as other than what one sees one's self to be: a black man.[7] Again, Fanon is in no way making a political or ethical judgment on interracial relations but is instead telling us tragic stories of those who seek to escape the denial of their public symbolization as human beings with equal dignity by finding a private place in which they can be other to this racist system. Such an attempt at escape, just like the individual who pretends to be French, cannot survive on an individual level and must, as Fanon reminds us, take place instead through a more powerful symbolic restructuring of the world:

> The sexual myth quest—the quest for white flesh—perpetuated by alienated psyches, must no longer be allowed to impede active understanding.
>
> In no way should my color be regarded as a flaw. From the moment the Negro accepts the separation imposed by the European he has no further respite, and "is it not understandable that thenceforward he will try to elevate himself to

the white man's level? To elevate himself in the range of colors to which he attributes a kind of hierarchy?"

We shall see that another solution is possible. It implies a restructuring of the world.[8]

Thus, for Fanon, there are two ways for the imago to defend itself against the horrors of colonialism and the struggle for self-symbolization: a self-defeating retreat into the individual fantasy of conflated personhood or the collective action of liberation to remake, literally, the symbolization of the world giving equal standing to all people.

The Paradox of Black Invisibility/Anonymity

To truly grasp a sense of the starkness imbued in these equally debilitating individual solutions, we need to examine two key concepts for Fanon: overdetermination and invisibility. The black man, of course, is only too visible to himself and to others, but he has presence only as the absence of his being human. Thus, he is visible as a fixed absence of humanity. This overdetermination of an absence of humanity, which appears as pure black skin, explains why for Fanon there can be no coherent black imago under colonialism. For, if one asserts one's presence as black, then one has also, at the same time, asserted oneself as not human, making the very desire for self-affirmation turn against itself:

> I move slowly in the world, accustomed now to seek no longer for upheaval. I progress by crawling. And already I am being dissected under white eyes, the only real eyes. I am *fixed*. Having adjusted their microtomes, they objectively cut away slices of my reality. I am laid bare. I feel, I see in those white faces that it is not a new man who has come in, but a new kind of man, a new genus. Why, it's a Negro!
>
> I slip into a corner, and my long antennae pick up the catch-phrases strewn over the surface of things—nigger underwear smells of nigger—nigger teeth are white—nigger feet are big—the nigger's barrel chest—I slip into corners, I remain silent, I strive for anonymity, for invisibility. Look, I will accept the lot, as long as no one notices me![9]

There is, in a deep sense, no way out of such a situation. This experience of having no way out is one in which blackness comes to pervade identity only as demoted by its very designation, and this means that blackness also takes on an estranging anonymity.

Within such a system of anonymity every black person can stand in for every other black person. This is why so often we are told that the problem of racial exclusion in employment has been solved by counting the number of black people brought into an organization, for example, academicians boasting about having three "blacks" in the faculty. Within such a discourse we are not required to utter anything beyond the mere statistical figure, and certainly would never dare to call attention to the institutional racism cemented into the many fissures of the university experience, because black people do not count as individual scholars but merely within the ephemeral category of blacks. Fanon's point is that this way of measurement implies that those who are already present in significant numbers represent normalcy, while those being counted are the unfortunate anomaly. In all of my years as an academic I have never heard anyone count how many whites are on the faculty. Indeed, Fanon is right that this way of counting would sound strange. Our deepest imagined conception of the university sees it blanketed in whiteness.

Indeed, it is a peculiar form of anonymity in which one black person is symbolically able to stand in for another black person. Both Fanon and Gordon suggest such exchangeability is at its core an antihuman form of anonymity. Gordon defines anonymity as follows:

> Alfred Schutz speaks of anonymity as the mundane ability to stand for another in the realm of understanding. Anonymity both wipes away and preserves the very notion of a private language and epistemological privilege. In this regard, anonymity is restricted to a form of universality of human presence, where the rules *qua* rules are expected to apply to all human beings. Implicit in anonymity, then, is its own limitation. There is a dialectic of private life in virtue of a public life that is so mundane that it ceases to function as a general concern of any one else. When concern emerges, it is in terms of recognizing an individual's uniqueness, that although one can stand in another's place as a human being, one cannot stand in the place of another's life.[10]

Indeed, for Gordon both oppression and liberation are uniquely tied to this notion of anonymity. Oppression for Gordon, as he defines it, "is the imposition of extraordinary conditions of the ordinary upon individuals in the course of their efforts to live 'ordinary' lives."[11] It is important to note that Alfred Schutz describes anonymity, as interpreted by Gordon, as what allows us to get through our daily lives without endlessly being stalled by the need to intelligibly unravel the nuanced experiential details of simple acts such as getting on a bus or buying a cup coffee.[12]

One need only remember Rosa Parks, a domestic worker who simply wanted to ride on the bus to get home from work, who was made to sit in the back of the bus because she was black. Every time Rosa Parks got on a bus she had to confront herself as a woman who was oppressed. By challenging an ordinary act any white person does without encountering the reflective truth of a deeply lived oppression, Rosa Parks turned a mundane performance of anonymity into a heroic act by refusing to move, and she stands rightly as a hero of the civil rights movement. But, it is that endless blockage to self-assertion that lingers, wrongly, as the fact of blackness. Such obstruction is both Manichean and phobogentic, meaning closed in on itself.

Part of the overdetermination of the black man and woman as absence is that they are blocked in the most normal forms of anonymous behavior and forced to collapse into a version of the self that supposedly does not exist in the first place. To the degree that blacks are not given meaning as persons within a white symbolic world, such black people are made into the projection of abjected impulses in the white imaginary, as this imaginary turns blacks into terrifying beings embodying the negative value of their world. Of course, we are all familiar with the fantasy positioning the black person as threatening. But, as we will also see, such a projection can give meaning to the black as a kind of savior of the white man and woman as figures who cannot own up to their full humanity. Using the phenomenological language of Schutz, so importantly reworked by Gordon, anonymity gives us a shared life-world in which we can take many things for granted but this shared world is also what allows us to engage in empathy. For, we are one among others living in overlapping symbolic languages that allow us to fashion together meanings of experience, which allow us to empathize with their undertakings as free human subjects in a shared, common world. Oppression is ethically devastating because it forecloses this kind of empathy. There are two popular cultural examples that can help to draw out how a peculiar form of anonymity imposed on black men and women undermines the capacity for empathy and at the same time denies them their freedom as unique human beings.

In the movie *Finding Forrester* we are told of a young black male struggling to be a writer and who seeks to find standing in the stereotypical anonymity of young black men. He is an average student who enjoys basketball, but much to the surprise of everyone at school he scores very high on standardized tests and is given a scholarship to a downtown, independent school in New York City. The young man has, on a dare, run into a white male author who secluded himself from the world after the trauma of his brother's death and the insignificance of continuing as a writer in the aftermath of such loss. The young black man sneaks into his apartment to show his friends that he will be true to his dare and leaves behind his bag. The white writer finds his notebooks and takes the time to comment on them to the young black man.

The promise between the two is that their friendship can continue only if the young black man never speaks of it.

Although the young black man is given a scholarship on academic merit, he is expected to play basketball even though it is not the great love of his life. He excels in school and more specifically in his creative writing class, prompting his teacher to designate him as a fraud. After all, there is no way a young black man can masterfully weave together the words of a white society. Later, the severity of such plagiarism is intensified when the young man falters at a crucial moment in an important basketball game making his value to the school questionable; after all, why else would a black man be allowed to go to school except to play basketball? As a result of these confusing circumstances, the young black man is denied the chance to participate in a creative writing competition. Ultimately, the isolated white writer saves the day by coming out of his seclusion. The white writer takes a letter written to him by his young friend and because of his fame is allowed to read it during the competition despite not being on the program or involved with the school. While everyone naturally assumes that the letter being read contains the words of the white author, it is finally revealed that the work being delivered aloud is, indeed, the talent of the young black man, Jamal Wallace. Despite the misplaced shock of the audience, Wallace is allowed to continue to study at the school.

This movie has been widely interpreted as a touching portrayal of white-black intergenerational friendship. What follows is not meant to undermine or devalue that aspect of the movie, but instead attempts to exemplify the problem of anonymity for a young man who does not want to leave his peers and does not want to stand out in public despite his aspirations to be a writer. Here we see the dilemma of overdetermination articulated by Fanon writ large as Gordon has brought out its implications for anonymity. When the young black man does try to articulate himself as a writer, he is accused of plagiarism, yet it is only when he fails in sports that he is considered a failed student. Ultimately, the only way to announce the truth of talent innate to this young black man is through the defense given by a white man reading his words in public, allowing Wallace to be a writer in the shadow of the famous white author. The young black man is seen because the white man vouches for his talent. This is exactly what Gordon is drawing out as the worst kind of oppression. A young person wants to have friends, wants to be excellent in sports, and wants to strive for a life as a writer. The white students are doing this as a matter of course in their fancy school. All of Jamal Wallace's activities should have been understood as mundane, ordinary efforts of a young man to assert himself in the world and to strive for excellence as an artist. But, these become undertakings of enormity because he is black, and there would be no happy ending to the story without the white man giving the pronouncement that the black man is a person. When Fanon speaks of the Manichean aspect of colonial racism in which blackness either has to be weeded out altogether or projected onto the white man or woman's repressed aspect of the self, he does not mean that there are not positive stereotypes but that such stereotypes are only readable through such a confined dualistic purpose.

Similarly, though providing a different viewpoint, in the movie *Bringing Down the House* a straight, white, male lawyer mistakenly sets up a date with an ex-convict black woman mistaken for a lawyer and played by Queen Latifah. The straight white male lawyer is exactly such a stereotype. He has lost his wife because of his boring superficiality and Walter Mitty life, and lives next door to a racist neighbor who happens to be the sister of one of the senior partners in his law firm. The so-called comedy results from the fact that the ex-convict demands the boring lawyer take her case, one in which she has been fraudulently arrested, or she will embarrass him before the next-door neighbor by making her presence all too visible and getting him in trouble for the crime of all crimes: associating with black people! It should be noted, this film was not made in the 1950s but in 2003. The lawyer agrees to represent the ex-convict and takes her in under the guise of his children's nanny. Of course, there are many "out of this world" advantages to having a black nanny: she saves his daughter from a misguided date, teaches the boring lawyer how to dance, and even gives uncanny advice on how to have wild sex with his wife. The happy ending emerges when the life of the boring lawyer is enriched by the ex-convict, who helps him erase his stereotypical white, suburban repression, allowing him ultimately to rekindle his marriage, quit his tiresome job, and finally kiss his wife with passionate gusto. This scenario depicts the flip side of the dark, scary black man. We have the sexy black female figuration able to raise this white man into a more complete manhood; however, for Fanon, this merely gives us two stereotypes that are the flip sides of each other and ultimately belie their Manichean origins.

Bad Faith in Bad Times

Blackness becomes a white projection that can only be yielded any space to have meaning as long as it remains the tame return of the repressed. Again, to quote Gordon:

> Antiblack racism calls for causal explanations and typifications that come to their conclusions, figuratively and literally, in the lynch mob trailing behind bloodhounds in pursuit of a black body. The pursuit, if Manichean in purpose,

is an effort to weed out the pollution of blackness from the purity of whiteness. It is also, in its essence, theodicean. For in such a world, blackness functions as an aberration that has to be explained without blaming the system in which it emerges. The system of antiblack racism is lived as a self-justified god in its institutions and its inhabitant's flesh. Emersed in itself, it can only see its faults as "contaminations" of the system. As a consequence, the bloodhound pursuit of a black body takes on a logic premised upon an identity relation between fact and value. The system is fact; it is "what is." It is absolute. Whatever "is" is what ought to be and hence ought to have been. The inferior Other becomes a fundamental project for the establishment of the Superior Self, whose superiority is a function of what *is*.[13]

Gordon's analysis of bad faith may also help us in beginning to think of what kind of struggle we must take on if we are to actually change forms of oppression that are so pervasive that they almost become unnoticeable and, due to their pervasiveness, demand radical transformation of all of us in our day-to-day activities and the depth of our being. The phobogentic quality of racism suggests that such racism closes itself in so that black pathology becomes itself a fact of blackness, which is yet another aspect of overdetermination. It is not just that the black man is viewed as a criminal; it is that blackness and criminality become combined as an empirical concept. This combination, in which a value judgment elides into a factual statement, is how Gordon analyzes the spirit of seriousness in which the judgments that make assertions fall below the realm of reason and questionability.

Certainly, for Gordon, Eurocentrism and colonial black racism are forms of bad faith. Bad faith, in Sartre's sense, is the refusal of our responsibility for the value judgments we make and the world we bring into being with such judgments. Bad faith in the most general sense is an attempt to hide one's freedom from oneself. Sartre uses the example of the sadist and the masochist as archetypes of bad faith. The sadist, in a deep sense, wants to play God, believing there are no others who can impose an ontological limit on their ontic creativity so as to make others and the world into an image of their own desire. Masochism, alternatively, tries to negate its subjectivity altogether by denying that it is a limit or a barrier to the imposition of the sadist on herself. Both forms of bad faith deny the freedom and limitation of subjectivity natural to a creature of finite embodiment. As we will see, Gordon considerably reworks Sartre's notion of bad faith within the context of black struggles for liberation and what it might mean after the seizure of state power. But, for now, we have to see that racism limits so seriously the options of black people that, for Fanon, armed struggle was the only way out for the black man who sought to live an authentic life. That such a move toward violence is the only way for a black man or woman to live an authentic life is tragic for Fanon, shows much sympathy for the call for armed struggle and even the inevitable murder of white colonialists.

For Fanon, in the armed struggle two important breaks in the phobogentic system of racism take place. The peculiar form of anonymity imposed on blacks is not claimed as a collective form of self-assertion that allows individuals to begin to fight back against the system of total demobilization. What was seen as a hopeless dilemma—either choose to be white and fail, or choose to accept the degraded position of a racially defined blackness—can now be overcome. The individual now finds himself or herself with other blacks, not in the bad infinite of one for the other but as comrades who collect their power and use it as a force to answer with guns and fists the devaluation that had imprisoned them in the claustrophobic world of phobogentic racism. By asserting that one is a part of a struggle with others who are now comrades is the only way an individual can fight back against the whole of racism imposed on a person. Fanon clarifies this point with important consideration, conveying:

> At the level of the individuals, violence is a cleansing force. It frees the native from his inferiority complex and from his despair and inaction; it makes him fearless and restores his self-respect. Even if the armed struggle has been symbolic and the nation is demobilized through a rapid movement of decolonization, the people have the time to see that the liberation has been the business of each and all and that the leader has no special merit. From thence comes that type of aggressive reticence with regard to the machinery of protocol which young governments quickly show. When the people have taken violent part in the national liberation they will allow no one to set themselves up as "liberators." They show themselves to be jealous of the results of their action and take good care not to place their future, their destiny, or the fate of their country in the hands of a living god. Yesterday they were completely irresponsible; today they mean to understand everything and make all decisions. Illuminated by violence, the consciousness of the people rebels against any pacification. From now on the demagogues, the opportunists, and the magicians have a difficult task. The action which has thrown them into a hand-to-hand struggle confers upon the masses a voracious taste for the concrete. The attempt at mystification becomes, in the long run, practically impossible.[14]

Fanon does not retreat from the conclusion that given the phobogentic aspect of racism some whites may have to die as a part of the process of decolonialization.

The killing of a white human being literalizes the dehumanization that has taken place and ends the fantasy that the white is a sadist, in Sartre's sense, untouchable through its delusion of divinity. This return to vulnerability of the oppressors at the hand of the gun is one of the tragic aspects of Manichean racism that does not allow symbolic disruption alone or nonviolence to end its rule. The answer for the black man or woman to the question of why one should live is the assertion of an effective power against degradation by uniting with others to end the colonial situation. Fanon was a great respecter of the movement of negritude and he always remained committed to the centrality of psychic and cultural transformation in any liberation effort. But as he reminds us in *Black Skin, White Masks* the symbolic assertion of the negritude movement could only go so far as long as the social reality of institutional repression remained. Fanon explains:

> A frequent mistake, and one which is moreover hardly justifiable, is to try to find cultural expressions for and to give new values to native culture within the framework of colonial domination. This is why we arrive at a proposition which at first sight seems paradoxical: the fact that in a colonized country the most elementary, most savage, and the most undifferentiated nationalism is the most fervent and efficient means of defending national culture. For culture is first the expression of a nation, the expression of its preferences, of its taboos and of its patterns. It is at every stage of the whole of society that other taboos, values, and patterns are formed. A national culture is the sum total of all these appraisals; it is the result of internal and external tensions exerted over society as a whole and also at every level of that society. In the colonial situation, culture, which is doubly deprived of the support of the nation and of the state, falls away and dies. The condition for its existence is therefore national liberation and the renaissance of the state.[15]

Yet, again as Gordon reminds us, even in his call for the armed struggle as necessary to break the black man or woman out of the phobogentic racist world in which they have been subjected, Fanon does so out of the recognition that this is a terrible tragedy brought on by a community that has systematically evaded its responsibility for the demotion of blacks. It is truly tragic that such an armed struggle is both progressive and regressive in that for the first time, the repressed individual becomes an objective limitation on the colonizer's sadist fantasy.

To get out of the slaughterhouse that has been so much of black life under colonial conditions, one must kill but knowing all of the while that the situation of the so-called gods demolished by the arms of the wretched of the earth can only justify itself if it seeks to truly restore justice. The powerful protagonist, in other words, must be shot not only because we must literalize the vulnerability of white people but also, more importantly, because by so doing justice can be restored. Otherwise, literalizing vulnerability without the aspiration for justice falls flatly into vengeance. It is this drive for justice, even in his most militant demands for armed struggle, which confirms the humanism in Fanon. Fanon saw no other way out. As Gordon tells us, even those who still hold on to the hope of radical transformation that does not involve armed struggle must face a fundamental truth:

> Nonviolent transformation boils down to none at all. Violence is broader than bullets, knives, and stones. Violence, fundamentally, is a form of taking that which has been or will not be willingly surrendered. Regardless of the perceived justice or injustice of the matter, regardless of the place of power in the matter, as long as someone is losing something that he currently has and wants to keep, there is violence.[16]

Thus, Fanon ends his classic study *Black Skin, White Mask*, which obviously builds toward the conclusion that the only way out is armed struggle, with a powerful prayer both to himself and to all others suggesting we still might restructure our world and live freely together:

> I do not have the duty to be this or that. . . .
> If the white man challenges my humanity, I will impose my whole weight as a man on his life and show him that I am not that "sho' good eatin'" that he persists in imagining.
> I find myself suddenly in the world and I recognize that I have one right alone: That of demanding human behavior from the other.
> One duty alone: That of not renouncing my freedom through my choices.
> I have no wish to be the victim of the *Fraud* of a black world.
> My life should not be devoted to drawing up the balance sheet of Negro values.
> There is no white world, there is no white ethic, any more than there is a white intelligence.
> There are in every part of the world men who search.
> I am not a prisoner of history. I should not seek there for the meaning of my destiny.
> I should constantly remind myself that the real *leap* consists in introducing invention into existence.
> In the world through which I travel, I am endlessly creating myself.[17]

For Fanon, the black struggle cannot by definition be the struggle of the black man or woman for the recognition of their humanity by white people.

Phenomenological symmetry is denied by the very designations of black and white in a racist system. What must happen for such symmetry to be reasserted is that white people must come fully to terms with the depth of their own bad faith and the loss of their own humanity.

Armed Struggle as Psychic and Cultural Transformation

Often, we hear of calls for recognition as if somehow things could just stay the same and we could include blacks as being human without questioning all the way down why such terms became designators in the first place. Fanon's argument about the armed struggle is that phenomenological symmetry and the promise of freedom have to be taken up and lived—never simply given by someone else. If we do not dare to restructure the world, then there will only be a continuation of what Gordon has called the bad faith of the denial of our intersubjective responsibility for the perpetuation of racism. But, for now, we at least have to remember that if there is some way out for the wretched of the earth other then armed struggle than it will demand political and social shifts on every level. For, as Fanon tells us, ethics starts with the Other as a limit to our subjectivity which is precisely what racism denies to people of color. Fanon's challenge is that in situations of colonialism there can be no ethical relation.

It is important to remember that for Fanon the armed struggle is the only possible way for blacks to seize their freedom, and without that freedom there is no way to overcome the trauma of colonialism. The humanist inspiration for the armed struggle lies precisely in its transformative possibilities. *Black Skin, White Masks* addresses the question of how one can be a human being and black. The ultimate answer is that there is no individual solution to the colonial situation that does not reinscribe black individuals into the original trauma of colonialism. At the heart of the struggle is not the devaluation of whites by exposing the obvious fact of their vulnerability; instead, the struggle is itself transformative of all of those who participate in it. It is through joining together and belonging together with others, and facing the trauma collectively, that the colonized find a way to meaningfully assert themselves as an epistemic limit to the imposition of white fantasy on who they can be in the world. Psychic transformation is ultimately what makes this struggle valuable.

For Fanon, then, the armed struggle always has a humanist justification and for the oppressor it brings them to justice, a justice that if they were fully human they would desire. For the oppressed it allows them to begin the effort to form, in Sylvia Wynter's words, a new *semioticbiogenesis*.[18] What does

Wynter mean by *semioticbiogenesis*? Wynter means both the symbolic reworking of the materials in which we make sense of our world and with it nothing less than new bodily forms that would allow us to truly move beyond racism. The struggle for development, in Wynter, is always teleological because at its core it has the ethical mandate that we must move beyond racism and colonialism if a different way of being human is to actually come into existence. So, the symbolic struggle is taken on in the name of developing and, indeed, living up to the promise of a new social genesis of our being human that is not scarred by the inscription of racism. Our bodies as well as our minds would have to change. Fanon was deeply sympathetic to the notion that in the armed struggle, and only there, could something like the beginnings of this semioticbiogenesis actually begin.

Famously, Fanon writes about the symbol of the veil. The veil has long, of course, been associated with Muslim fundamentalism. We need to note here that even for Muslim traditionalists there are many kinds of veils. Some of these practices of veiling do not demand that the entirety of the woman's body be veiled. However, the point Fanon makes is different. The veil in Fanon's analysis was imposed upon Muslim women by something external to them in the Muslim religion. But, in the course of the armed struggle Muslim women began to veil or unveil on the basis of the demands of the revolution. A Muslim woman took off her veil and dressed in European clothing so that she could pass into French areas that would otherwise be forbidden. A Muslim woman might instead put on the veil so she remains unnoticed and unthreatening, veiling nothing less than a bomb. In the course of her own struggle to come to terms with the veil as something which she either discards or puts on as necessary for the struggle, she begins to get a sense of her own choices and her own capacity for self-assertion. As we have seen, black philosophers of existence distinguish between choice and option. There is a sense in which we always are in the process of choosing and we are responsible for our choices. But, to make it clear that not all of us are able to choose equally in the sense of having the same sphere of options, black philosophers of existence, particularly Lewis Gordon, insist that the struggle is itself meant to open up options that were never before available and, in the space so opened, create the ability to reflect on how our seeming choices were formerly the result of having no other option.

The veil was an imposition, but by believing in the Muslim religion women could also choose to veil. However, since there was "no option to not veil," there was not any meaningful choice. Once the struggle began, the option to veil or not veil became available to women, at least according to Fanon's analysis, and these women are able to choose within a wider frame of options for their own self-assertion, allowing them to experience choice differently. Once the veil is consciously put into the field of choice, it is no longer a symbol of an imposed definition of woman. It becomes a symbol that has now been freed from its so-called traditional context, and we are all well reminded to note that the veil has always been a part of political struggle in the Arab world, since part of the choice to veil is not only about religious piety but also a means to avoid scrutinizing gaze from colonizers. It is, of course, naive of Western feminists as we trot around in our purportedly sexy outfits, endlessly trying to make ourselves into a perfect image of feminine desirability, to criticize such veiling without noting its many complications. For, what serious choices exist under the psychic force of a culture industry and its insidious methods of reminding us of the so-called necessity of plastic surgery—now often sold as a preventive measure for young girls—to stave off the unacceptable accouterments of old age? Are these really choices? In a deep sense they are choices in the meaning granted by black philosophers of existence. But, they are choices if in a different context of meaning that are constrained by symbolically imposed definitions of female ideality—and we might add the dictates of advanced capitalism that makes billions of dollars every year as women desperately try to live up to the demands of an ever more youthful, and imagined, female body.[19]

Feminism is always about expanding the options so women can reflect on choices and come to terms with the field of meaning and material reality that has limited their options and thus the field of possibility giving rise to their own images of themselves. To return to Fanon's point, the reworking of the body itself and bodily experiences becomes part and parcel of women's efforts to participate in the opening of the field of wider options. Fanon provides a complex dialectic about how the veil both protected women from the gaze of the European colonizer and, yet, when it was imposed served to limit her own sense that she was the source of her bodily integration:

> The shoulders of the unveiled Algerian woman are thrust back with ease and freedom. She walks with a graceful, measured stride, neither too fast nor too slow. Her legs are bare, not confined by the veil, given back to themselves, and her hips are free.
>
> The body of the young Algerian woman, in traditional society, is revealed to her by its coming to maturity and by the veil. The veil covers the body and disciplines it, tempers it, at the very time when it experiences its phase of greatest effervescence. The veil protects, reassures, isolates. One must have heard the confessions of the Algerian woman or have analyzed the dream

content of certain recently unveiled women to appreciate the importance of the veil for the body of the woman. Without the veil she has an impression of her body being cut up into bits, put adrift; the limbs seem to lengthen indefinitely. When the Algerian woman has to cross the street, for a long time she commits errors of judgment as to the exact distance to be negotiated. The unveiled body seems to escape, to dissolve. She has an impression of being improperly dressed, even of being naked. She experiences a sense of incompleteness with great intensity. She has the anxious feeling that something is unfinished, and along with this a frightful sensation of disintegrating. The absence of the veil distorts the Algerian woman's corporal pattern. She quickly has to invent new dimensions of her body, new means of muscular control. She has to create for herself an attitude of unveiled-woman-outside. She must overcome all timidity, all awkwardness (for she must pass for a European), and at the same time be careful not to overdo it, not to attract notice to herself. The Algerian woman who walks stark naked into the European city relearns her body, re-establishes it in a totally revolutionary fashion. This new dialectic of the body and of the world is primary in the case of one revolutionary woman.[20]

Here we see Fanon's analysis of how, to use the language of Gordon, the Algerian woman struggles to free herself from the bad faith of the masochistic position. Indeed, the colonizer, as Fanon tells us at the beginning of "Algeria Unveiled," makes the struggle to win the hearts and minds of colonists one of winning over the women of Algeria by insisting on their unveiling. This attempt to save women and justify colonialism through such imagined salvation obviously reinforced the strong belief in some women that resistance to imperialism began with the veil. Fanon tragically describes the violence within this dynamic between saving and veiling.

After each success, the authorities were strengthened in their conviction that the Algerian woman would support Western penetration into the native society. Every rejected veil disclosed to the eyes of the colonialists horizons until then forbidden, and revealed to them, piece by piece, the flesh of Algeria laid bare. The occupier's aggressiveness, and hence his hopes, multiplied ten-fold each time a new face was uncovered. Every new Algerian woman unveiled announced to the occupier an Algerian society whose systems of defense were in the process of dislocation, open and breached. Every veil that fell, every body that became liberated from the traditional embrace of the *haïk*, every face that offered itself to the bold and impatient glance of the occupier, was a negative expression of the fact that Algeria was beginning to deny herself and was accepting the rape of the colonizer. Algerian society with every abandoned veil seemed to express its willingness to attend the master's school and to decide to change its habits under the occupier's direction and patronage.[21]

Fanon's emphasis here is on the semioticbiogenesis in which the veil is both resymbolized as it becomes part of a woman's revolutionary self-assertion and also involves a profound difference in her lived body as she now claims her own choice to veil or unveil as the revolution and her part in it demands.

Recall that black philosophers of existence share with Sartre that we begin with three perspectives: the perspective of our embodiment, of being seen by others, and of seeing ourselves as being seen by others. For Fanon, the revolutionary woman who unveils herself or puts on the veil as she believes is necessary for her own revolutionary efforts reworks all three perspectives as she lives in her body differently. There is an important reminder for feminists in this analysis, suggesting that no matter how different our context may seem from the armed struggle in Algeria, women cannot rework these fundamental perspectives alone since they involve our embeddedness in a pregiven sociality by others. It is only by breaking off the forms of symbolic and social reality that have been taken for granted through their challenge in the armed struggle that women can collectively take up the reliving of their body as they assert themselves differently. A question, then, for the European white feminist remains: what are we doing when we attempt liberation by ourselves? Fanon's answer for all oppressed and traumatized people under symbolically imposed inscriptions on the flesh marking them as the degraded Other is always a move toward liberation made collectively.

Gordon's Reworking of Phenomenology

Such a steadfast commitment to liberation through collective action is, again, a contribution made by black philosophers of existence taking us beyond the existentialism of Sartre. Gordon has argued that what he offers is a phenomenological existentialism, or an exploration of "the implications and the possibility of studying the phenomenon of beings that are capable of questioning their ways of being."[22] In Sartre, although he, too, describes himself as a phenomenological existentialist, there is a deep problem because phenomenology always demands a reflection upon the "I" that is reflecting on the world. In phenomenology, which starts with Husserl, we begin our phenomenological reflection with the so-called natural attitude where we take objects as they seem to be given to us. But, any object only comes to us as we have invested an interest in it. To get to the objects themselves we must start by bracketing our interests and try to see things from different perspectives which not only involves bracketing but also the imaginative act of free variation.

We can perform such free variation in ordinary ways. I have an interest in my car and barely notice it. I get into the car to drive to work and go through the usual behaviors of driving automatically, as they are a part of my daily experience. But, I can bracket my interest and begin to see these objects called cars that allow human beings to move around the world in ways unimaginable a hundred years ago. I begin to imagine a world where there were no cars and yet know that cars exist today. I imagine the parts of the car, the way a motor works, and how with just the turn of the key we can ignite this incredible power. It is not surprising that free variation is often associated with wonder. For, as we bracket off our interest and imagine the object from different perspectives, even the perspective of a world where the object does not exist, we begin to see the object in a much richer and nuanced light. But, it will always be a light we cast on the object, which is a fundamental point for Husserl. We never truly get to the objects themselves because as we bracket the interest of our natural attitude and as we engage in free variation we run into something that is inevitably there: the "I" of directed or intentional consciousness. This "I" is indeed transcendental but not in sense meant by Kant, although much work needs to be done on the relationship between Kant and Husserl. It is transcendental in that it reflects on the constitution of our world as we recognize that all objects come to us in the light of consciousness.

An idea is subjective, for Husserl, in the sense that it premises itself in a shared capacity for transcendence in that consciousness is always conscious of "something else." A bracketed consciousness is bracketed precisely because it knows itself to be reflecting on objects through recognition of the process of bracketing and free variation. But, when consciousness returns to itself, or becomes aware of itself as consciousness, it is always transcendent for Husserl, who is suggesting that the "I" we run up against in bracketing and free variation is the "I" of intentionality. This "I" always points beyond itself since it can only "know" itself as consciousness of something. In a deep and profound sense, Kant and Husserl, although they come at this problem very differently, arrive at the notion that objective validity turns on the universal and necessary conditions for an idea. Such conditions are universal for us finite human creatures who make sense of their world. Again, Kant and Husserl are different in how they arrive at this idea but there is more that is shared here than has often been recognized and certainly more work should be done thinking through the complicated similarities and differences between each thinker. It is certainly not a coincidence that Husserl's great student Heidegger found an ally in Kant.

However, for our purposes we are interested in the way Gordon reworks Husserlian phenomenology by rightly pointing out that Sartre does not remain true to his promise to give us a phenomenological existentialism. In a certain sense, Sartre is trying to deny the transcendental presuppositions that seem to exist at the heart of Husserl's phenomenology. What we find in Sartre when we confront other people is the direct impact of their consciousness on us and this impact is an act of nihilation, as both consciousnesses are aware that this other is a threat and ultimately all objects, including other people, must yield to such nihilation if we are to own our own freedom. It is not that there is nothing there but our consciousness but that our consciousness of what is Other can only encounter another consciousness if we recognize our own freedom. However, for Sartre such a task is inseparable from our human imagination, which can literally render the world "no thing." No thing without us is ultimately Sartre's *nausea* since the things that we see are only the things of Husserl's natural attitude.

The ultimate gesture in Sartre is to have reflective consciousness reflect upon this natural attitude, or prereflective consciousness of objects, through a process of relentless negation. The sadist ultimately seeks to be God in that all prereflective things, including other people as things, are ultimately rendered only there for their own consciousness as it imposes its meaning on them. The masochist, in a sense, submits to the facticity that purportedly makes a human being only a thing for others. It seeks, paradoxically, through consciousness its own standing apart as consciousness. Bad faith is exemplified in both archetypes because both points of view deny freedom as the transcendence which inheres in consciousness itself. In the case of the sadist, one denies that there are others involved in the same struggle of nihilation that marks his own consciousness. In the case of the masochist, her consciousness is denied and marks her as a being who is also present as an epistemic limit only in the fantasies of the sadist. The serious sadist wants to deny that there are other points of view and the masochist wants to deny that she has a point of view. Gordon, in a brilliant move, takes out of Sartre the danger of psychologizing his analysis of sadism and masochism.

For Gordon, what is presupposed in his analysis of sadism and masochism is the beyond of intersubjectivity in which these two forms of bad faith operate. In a certain sense, then, Sartre denies that there is a transcendent intersubjectivity: a beyond that is presupposed, allowing us to make sense of sadism and masochism as modes of being in bad faith, which ultimately denies the truth of sociality. This is an extraordinary addition to Sartre because in a profound sense there is no way out for Sartre from sadism and masochism, leaving us caught in the bad infinite of nihilation. To recognize our sociality as something in which we partake, and which is always beyond us, is a step toward recognizing a common human world. Such acknowledged commonality can only grow out of our recognition that as embodied beings we will always speak to each other from different perspectives. To quote Gordon:

> That sociality could not be denied without contradiction is the message we gain from the analysis of bad faith. Sociality is so much at the heart of human relations—indeed, their relationality, through which emerges their historicity—that we might as well add another definition of bad faith. Bad faith is the denial of sociality. Since bad faith is also a lie to the self, then to lie about sociality is also a self-lie. What type of self could be such that it is at one with social reality? It is at last what we know as human reality. In denying our sociality we deny our humanity.[23]

One deep aspect of Gordon's work is to remind us of the humility that arises when we actually confront the truth that we must live in a field of sociality which both makes us who we are and is always beyond us. Such humility is an ethical attitude which, of course, demands that the sadist step down from the supposed throne of divinity and cease imposing fantasies and spurious claims of ontic creativity so as instead to become just another human being who must come to terms with other people as capable of transforming the world in accordance with their own perspective.

Gordon offers a profound political perspective which helps us begin to think about why Fanon's optimism about the actual struggles of Algerian women did not yield to what he thought it might: freed women in a freed Algeria. For Gordon, the simple seizure of state power cannot in and of itself overcome the invasion of our humanity that inheres in the bad faith explicit in our racist society. We must, instead, continuously confront the ways in which we are enabled to act by a sociality that is beyond us. And this struggle is one that is beyond the historical circumstances of colonialism. What Gordon is telling us is that racism is a form of existential exploitation which can remain long after state power is seized and the colonialists are literally overthrown. It is important to note here that Gordon is writing at a time when the seeming institutional support for racism has at least been weakened and yet racism remains virulent. Of course, Gordon agrees with Fanon that colonialism is the worst form of economic exploitation. But, in his onto-hermeneutics of antiblack racism Gordon is also reminding us that forms of racism have deeply embedded themselves in all social crevices, making themselves appear ontologically true. These semblances of determined presence provide such a deep sense of security to the oppressors and such a profound internalization of oppression in those who struggle against it that we can and must expect the traumas of antiblack racism to linger long after the actual seizure of power.

The Ongoing Vertical Drama

To use Paget Henry's analysis of Gordon, under this analysis of existential exploitation there is a recognition that the imagoes which have been limited by the *phobogentic* forces of colonialism can only begin to repair themselves through a constant struggle to turn thoughtless bad faith into critical good faith. Gordon, like other black philosophers of existence such as Wilson Harris, insists that there is a poetics of consciousness that both resists simple historicization and helps us to understand that the seizure of state power does not yield the new human being dreamed of in the revolutionary suggestions of Fanon. Harris suggests there is a *vertical drama* which demands that we use the power of poetics to open up a new semiosis for both redefining and reimagining identity.[24] This vertical drama both lingers after the seizure of state power and can help us understand how human beings caught in a phobogentic universe can find the creative resources to begin the struggle of restoring their own sense of self.

In Harris, Gordon, Henry, and Wynter, creativity lies in symbolic powers that resist the classical historicist claim that we only exist as we are constructed in history. The importance of such analysis lies in how the symbolic realm both constitutes us and also gives us our freedom, standing against theories of race through social construction which do us the disservice of eliminating a concept like race because it is not a scientific concept while all the while the world still continues to operate under racism. Gordon's argument has important political and ethical implications since the whole point Fanon attempts to make is that we can never create a new humanity as long as racism exists. Well-known thinkers like Anthony Appiah have argued that since race is not scientifically demonstrable, it is fictitious, and that ethically speaking it is a matter of impingement on free identification because it tells a person in advance who he or she is by ensnaring them in a truth of skin color that does not exist.[25] Gordon wisely remarks that Appiah's whole discourse turns on the assumption that race does not have any scientific validity and therefore reduces the reality of race to a simple dichotomy of postulation: either it is scientifically true or it is fictitious myth. However, as we have already seen in Cassirer, science itself is a symbolic form and scientific objects are themselves metaphoric constructs; thus, Appiah is relying on a pre-Kantian argument to make this simplistic reduction.

What needs to be remembered is that the denial of race as something that marks one in a form of bad faith and overplays the free play of identification ultimately undermines the phenomenological reality of a position. In *Between Women and Generations*, I distinguished between position, identity, and identification so as to underscore that there are realities to who we are and how we are positioned in the world, that there are identities and positions that can never be simply willed away.[26] In a racist and patriarchal world I am a white woman. Position, resonating purposefully with Marxism, suggests we are indeed positioned in hierarchies throughout advanced capitalist and racist society. But, we also have identities and these identities, although they are not necessarily reducible to material positions, are still not simply of our choosing. William Connolly offers a rather cogent definition of identity:

> My identity is what I am and how I am recognized rather than what I choose, want, or consent to. It is the dense self from which choosing, wanting, and consenting proceed. Without that density, these acts could not occur; with it, they are recognized to be mine. *Our* identity, in a similar way, is what we are and the basis from which we proceed.
>
> An identity is established in relation to a series of differences that have become socially recognized. These differences are essential to its being. If they did not coexist as differences, it would not exist in its distinctness and solidarity.[27]

The free play of identification is definitely associated with what Harris calls the vertical drama of our symbolic attempts to imagine and change the reality of our identity by posing different possible ways of presenting ourselves in the world not yet marred by the hierarchies that ensnare us as sunk into a density of determination that we cannot seemingly escape. The emphasis by Gordon and Harris on the vertical drama that must continue after the seizure of state power in no way denies the continuing reality of economic exploitation and, yet, ultimately offers us a profound moral image of freedom. To quote Gordon:

> Incantative forces need to be renewed and expanded in our humanistic search for our humanity. Many a thinker has called upon us to create new concepts, to set afoot new humanities, to engage the human struggle for significance. That struggle need not collapse into the nightmare of a boring world.[28]

What, then, can we who are professionals in the academy do to respond to the challenge of black philosophies of existence?

The Significance of Creolization

Henry has called us to an explicit process of creolization, defining it as "a process of semio-semantic hybridization that can occur between arguments, vocabularies, phonologies, or grammars of discourses within a culture or across cultures."[29] Creolization, of course, involves the inversion of a word from its negative meaning to something more affirmative.[30] But, it is also a call for white academics in the United States and Europe to retreat from bad faith toward a more critical, good faith. Again to quote Gordon:

> It presented itself this way while its incompleteness bled through its pores. The person of color, particularly the black, however, lived the contradictions of this self-deception continually through attempting to live this theodicy in good faith. This lived contradiction emerged for the black because a demand of this form of faith is that it be good without being *critical*. Critical consciousness challenges intrasystemic consistency by raising systemic critique.[31]

Of course, we never know and can never know that we are acting in good faith. But, it is our responsibility, nevertheless, to take up this process of creolization so that we actually meaningfully permit other points of view against the false positivity present in the ontologization of Europe. Certainly, it is not European ideas and culture that are being resisted in the battle against the dominance of Eurocentrism. Instead, it is a resistance against the attempt to turn an idealized Europe into the only cultural reality.

In a profound sense creolization reworks the familiar notion of hybridity. It has become commonplace to argue that the social, political, and cultural dimensions of our different lives are hybrid manifestations made up in the age of imperialism out of both colonial and indigenous elements. Henry often uses the Yoruba religion as a case in point, which came to the "new world" with the slave trade and was indeed Christianized. The great figures of the Orishas, like Yemaya and Oshun, were refigured as Christian saints, but in similar fashion the Christian religion was also refigured through the gods and goddesses of the Yoruba religion. Both religions changed, revealing that an important aspect of creolization is the revaluing and affirmation of indigenous values and ideals.

The call for creolization is both ethical and also a concrete demand that we rethink the basis of our disciplines, a problem which Gordon has defined as disciplinary decadence:

> The emergence of disciplines has often led to the forgetting of their impetus in living human subjects and their crucial role in both the maintenance and transformation of knowledge-producing practices. The results are special kinds of decadence. One such kind is disciplinary decadence. Disciplinary decadence is the ontologizing or reification of a discipline. In such an attitude, we treat our discipline as though it was never born and has always existed and will never change or, in some cases, die. More than immortal, it is eternal. Yet as something that came into being, it lives, in such an attitude, as a monstrosity, as an instance of a human creation that can never die. Such a perspective brings with it a special fallacy.[32]

The call to creolization should resonate with those of us in the academic world who still abide by lingering humanist influences in our study and our politics. Thus, at the heart of any project of creolization is a demand to academics, succinctly described by Jane Gordon:

> Creolization describes much larger and less controlled processes. And yet, just as we might be guided by certain other regulating norms and aspirations—to celebrate diversity, to seek a pure formalism, we might be galvanized and directed by an understanding of how genuine postcolonial thinking, which instead of a constellation of cultures, stresses the political natures of tenacious inequalities and thinks through the bottom.[33]

Thus, we can be committed to the best ideas of European philosophy and still equally committed to the struggle against Eurocentrism. More importantly, if we are to follow the black philosophers of existence then we must do so in the name of truth and in the name of the opening up of ethics. Nothing less is at stake here than the future of our humanity. Racism is always a denial of that shared humanity and of our inevitable sociality. Each one of us is responsible for how we take on this effort to fight against our own bad faith and with it to fight against what Amartya Sen has called the miniaturization of our human spirit.[34] For, we are not fated as whites to live out the superficial existence of denial that is premised by the refusal of our humility and our vulnerability. I am both an antiracist and a socialist due to my own understanding of why and how we must reconfigure our humanity in every aspect of our daily life if we are to seriously begin to bring forth anything like a more just world. What do white middle-class academics have to gain by the struggle for a better world free of racism and colonialization? What they have to gain is the chance of living up to their own humanity, which, as Benjamin reminds in the next chapter, is a debt that cannot be settled cheaply.

Notes

1. Lewis Gordon, *Existence in Black: An Anthology of Black Existential Philosophy* (New York: Routledge, 1997), 7.

2. Lewis Gordon, *Existentia Africana: Understanding Africana Existential Thought* (New York: Routledge, 2000), 65.

3. Gordon, *Existentia Africana*, 35.

4. Paget Henry, "Africana Phenomenology: Its Philosophical Implications," *CLR James Journal* 11, no. 1 (Summer, 2005).

5. Frantz Fanon, *Black Skin, White Masks* (New York: Grove Press, 1991), 35.

6. Fanon, *Black Skin, White Masks*, 38.

7. Lewis Gordon has argued that Jean Veneuse does not simply seek to escape from blackness through his love of Andree, a white woman, but also seeks to gain what Gordon calls words-of-whiteness (the "ticket, the "letter"). Gordon provocatively tells us that Veneuse and Capécia are both seeking recognition from the white man because there can be no object symmetry between black men and black women at the level of their objects of desire. See, for instance, Lewis Gordon, "Through the Zone of Nonbeing: A Reading of *Black Skin, White Masks* in Celebration of Fanon's Eightieth Birthday," *CLR James Journal* 11, no. 1 (Summer 2005).

8. Fanon, *Black Skin, White Masks*, 81.

9. Fanon, *Black Skin, White Masks*, 116.

10. Gordon, *Existence in Black*, 74.

11. Lewis Gordon, *Fanon and the Crisis of European Man: An Essay on Philosophy and the Human Sciences* (New York: Routledge, 1995), 41.

12. Gordon, *Existence in Black*, chapter 4.13.

13. Gordon, *Existence in Black*, 70.

14. Frantz Fanon, *The Wretched of the Earth* (New York: Grove Press, 1963), 94–95.

15. Fanon, *The Wretched of the Earth*, 244.

16. Gordon, *Fanon and the Crisis of European Man*, 79.

17. Fanon, *Black Skin, White Masks*, 229.

18. Gordon, *Existentia Africana*, 54.

19. This dynamic between choice and options is crucial to my own understanding of capabilities feminism which can be found in Drucilla Cornell, *Defending Ideals: War, Democracy, and Political Struggles* (New York: Routledge, 2004), chapter 4.

20. Frantz Fanon, *A Dying Colonialism* (New York: Grove Press, 1965), 58–59.

21. Fanon, *A Dying Colonialism*, 42.

22. Gordon, *Existentia Africana*, 119.

23. Gordon, *Existentia Africana*, 78.

24. William Harris, *History, Fable and Myth* (Wellesley, MA: Calaloux, 1995).

25. Anthony Appiah, *Color Conscious: The Political Morality of Race* (Princeton, NJ: Princeton University Press, 1998).

26. Drucilla Cornell, *Between Women and Generations: Legacies of Dignity* (New York: Rowman & Littlefield, 2005), 98.

27. William Connolly, *Identity/Difference: Democratic Negotiations of Political Paradox* (Minneapolis: University of Minnesota Press, 2002), 64.

28. Gordon, *Existentia Africana*, 179.

29. Paget Henry, *Caliban's Reason: Introducing Afro-Caribbean Philosophy* (New York: Routledge, 2000), 88.

30. See, for instance, an analysis of excitable speech and how the word *queer* was inverted in Judith Butler, *Excitable Speech: A Politics of the Performative* (New York: Routledge, 1997).

31. Gordon, *Existentia Africana*, 31.

32. Lewis Gordon, *Disciplinary Decadence: Living Thought in Trying Times* (Boulder, CO: Paradigm Publishers, 2006), chapter 1.

33. Jane Gordon, "Creolizing Rousseau" (paper presented at the annual meeting for the American Political Science Association, Philadelphia, PA, August 31 through September 3, 2006), 5.

34. Amartya Sen, *Identity and Violence: The Illusion of Destiny* (New York: W. W. Norton, 2006).

CHAPTER FIVE

Redemption in the Midst of Phantasmagoria: Dispelling the Fate of Socialism

I am, today, still a socialist. I write "still" because we have all encountered many commentaries on the supposed death of socialism. Over and over again throughout the 1990s we heard that the dream of a redeemed humanity, one that finally realizes the truth of its freedom in democratic control over the means of life and of death, had itself died. There is an obvious irony here in what it means to condemn a dream to death. After all, isn't a dream exactly what cannot be killed off because it does not have actual existence? The death of the dream, at least on the part of those determined to put it to death, clearly has an implicit, if not explicit, agenda to marginalize those who still identify themselves as socialists and as dreamers.

Particularly after 9/11, dreamers and idealists were condemned as being hopelessly out of touch with reality. The supposed reality of the post-9/11 world is one in which "we" are pitted against "them" and have to take all the steps "we" need to make sure that "we" contain "them" before "they" obliterate "us." But is this reality, or itself just a myth? Have we not heard over and over again about this reality from the Cold War until the present? Indeed, it is precisely the simple outlines of this recurring claim that this is a reality that Walter Benjamin would have called myth in the negative sense in which he used the word: to denote the fate of an eternal recurrence that wipes out the possibility of any meaningful moral agency where we have no choice but to go after "them" because this is the way the world must be. But Benjamin teaches us there is also, in even the most brutal reality, a dialectical opening that can illuminate another way of being in the world that allows us at least to have a glimpse of what a redeemed world might be like and, perhaps more importantly, what is our responsibility to those who have lived and died for it. As Benjamin reminds us:

> Fate is the guilt context of the living. It corresponds to the natural condition of the living, that illusion not yet wholly dispelled from which man is so far removed that, under its rule, he was never wholly immersed in it, but only invisible in his best part. It is not, therefore, really man who has a fate; rather, the subject of fate is indeterminable.... For fateful moments only exist in bad novels.[1]

Of course, the story of how we are fated to live in a post-9/11 world in which violence and war are inevitable counterparts of each other does not deny the terrible suffering of those who encounter the wrath of these two antagonisms. So many people have died in the wake of this needless suffering: thousands in the initial attacks and even more on both sides in the ongoing war in Iraq and in Afghanistan. But, what is particularly shameful, and perhaps dialectically startling, are the moments when people feel that there is seemingly no way out of the nightmare of advanced capitalism and its hierarchies of race, class, and gender. Even faith is not beyond of the reach of this nightmare, such as when we saw several young people become suicide bombers in England—something that perhaps only could be understood as a scene in a bad novel.

Expanding on this idea of living in a world that phantasmagorically seems to swallow up our deepest dreams of freedom in various capitalist nightmares of despair we can look to South Africa for further harrowing images of suffering that confront us with the brutal reality of life under apartheid. Many of those images have been kept alive in museums that have been built in the new South Africa. I am going to speak of only two such images, which in the language of Walter Benjamin I hope will give us the sort of dialectical jolt that might move us further into awakening and out of the nightmare-like slumber at hand.

First, there is a famous photograph taken during the Soweto uprising in which thousands upon thousands of children rebelled against being taught in what they saw as the language of the oppressor: Afrikaans. They were indeed children. Famously, the police gave no heed to that reality and shot into the crowd, leaving hundreds dead, more injured, and many who were never seen again after that tragic day. In a famous photo a young man, perhaps in his early teens, is carrying the dead, or dying, body of Hector Petersen. A young woman is running by his side. On both faces is a look of absolute horror. To this day, we do not know where that young man is, nor do we know where the young woman by his side is. What we have of these two children is this moment into which they have been forever frozen: a moment in which a child, rather than simply flee to save himself, picks up his dead or dying friend with the hope of saving him, or at least salvaging his then dead body from further brutalization by the police.

This image undoubtedly represents an act of salvation, of the young boy and girl salvaging what they can of what remained of Hector Petersen. Their companion is with them—grieving and terror-stricken—but with them still. This photograph can help us understand what Walter Benjamin means by a dialectical image. In the background we can see the township and the children who are rebelling against their oppressors. But they are running toward us. Who is this "us?" It is a generation that is beyond temporalization: a constellation of past, present, and future generations that are all being called to in equal force. As Walter Benjamin explains in "Theses on the Philosophy of History":

> The true picture of the past flits by. The past can be seized only as an image which flashes up at the instant when it can be recognized and is never seen again. "The truth will not run away from us": in the historical outlook of historicism these words of Gottfried Keller mark the exact point where historical materialism cuts through historicism. For every image of the past that is not recognized by the present, as one of its own concerns threatens to disappear irretrievably. (The good tidings which the historian of the past brings with throbbing heart may be lost in a void the very moment he opens his mouth).[2]

If Benjamin teaches us anything, then we should always remember that it is not a coincidence that "history" is best told in images. From the standpoint of those who had to endure apartheid such a lived brutality could be nothing other than senseless suffering. To give it meaning as a significant form of human social organization would already be a betrayal of those who had to live under its brutal disregard of their humanity.

As Benjamin also writes, "A dialectical image flashes up at a moment of danger,"[3] but it also illuminates a possible beyond. In that "possible beyond" we hear the call to justice of those children who had the daring and courage to shout out at their oppressors what their humanity demanded: "Justice! Noting more and nothing less." But we do not see a "risk manager" in this photograph. We see a young boy and girl, even in their terror, cherishing the body of their fallen comrade, and yet they are but children themselves. But we know that they not only saw something that took them out to the streets that day—perhaps a hope for a redeemed world beyond apartheid—but showed in their act of refusing to abandon Hector Petersen the depths of a humanity that would not bow down before the bullets and simply flee. They will never be gone to history, in Benjamin's sense, if we remember them. But, we can only remember them if we allow ourselves to see them. It is up to us to do it.

This is Benjamin's fundamental point when he calls us to anamnestic solidarity. As Benjamin writes:

> The past carries with it a temporal index by which it is referred to redemption. There is a secret agreement between past generations and the present one. Our coming was expected on earth. Like every generation that has preceded us, we have been endowed with a *weak* Messianic power, a power to which that past has a claim. That claim cannot be settled cheaply. Historical materialists are aware of that.[4]

What does it mean to "fan the spark of hope"[5] in the past if at the same time it demands that we look and force ourselves to see the terrible suffering inscribed forever on those children's faces as they confront the unbearable reality that another child has died, and that no matter what they do they will not be able to save him? For Benjamin, in this "call" we are made to face the figure of the one who refuses to stand still before the dialectical image. It is this call that, despite all odds, demands that we live up to such an image, one archetype of many, giving us a glimpse of the anamnestic solidarity with the dead we must bring into our own lives.

The dialectical image blows apart messages of good cheer and at the same time keeps open forms of experience in Benjamin's unique use of the word *Erfahrung*, which makes accessible the possibility of self-reflective passage through myth and with it the moral agency that insists such an experience is possible. In German the title of Benjamin's *Arcades Project* is *Passagen-Werk*, which we can at least translate as working through the passages of both history and myth. Thus, although Benjamin is critical of myth when it temporalizes the self as inevitably teaching a lesson that things will always be as they are now, this rebellion against historical compulsion still seeks to keep alive a horizon that does not relinquish the potential of myth to point to a different form of knowledge of the world around us. This *passageway*, and the rights of passage, between dreamful sleep and awakening is a phatasmagoric zone for Benjamin that in a deep sense breaks apart myth by its own means and thus salvages from it the possibility of a redeemed world of humanity despite our nightmarish surroundings. This fidelity before the threshold of another world that might yet be shows us that this passageway is open before us if we allow ourselves to move through mythical constraints so as to find the future under the ultimate myth of advanced capitalism, claiming that there is no truly different future but only the forever new that displaces one commodity for another commodity that is new only insofar as it is the same: a commodity.

Against what Benjamin thinks of as tired and fated truth he takes us through a passageway in which we can still be exposed to the *Wahrtraum*. Literally translated this word means "true dream," or to dream of what is true in the promise of the dialectical image itself: a humanity worthy of its own name. What is the trueness of the dream? How can a dream be true? It is true to what humanity might yet be when it is salvaged from the sameness of advanced capitalism. But we do not have to wait for that truth because, as we saw in the image of the young woman who runs away with the dead body of Hector Petersen, we have already glimpsed what it means to be a true human being (true here in the sense that it is true to an ideal that refuses to give in to the world-weariness of inaction).

In his endless effort to show us the reworking of symbols and allegory, we can still find a passageway that lights up the "tireless leap of action" Benjamin forever held onto as the truth of revolutionary courage. We find that courage in the act of the young man and woman. Yes, it is true that Benjamin tells us that the messiah might enter time at any minute. But, we are not fated to remain and wait as Benjamin tells us, "The Messiah comes not only as the redeemer, he comes as the subduer of antichrist. Only that historian will have the gift of fanning the spark of hope in the past who is firmly convinced that *even the dead* will not be safe from the enemy if he wins. And this enemy has not ceased to be victorious."[6] There is a sense in which we, the next generation with the weak messianic power, can subdue the antichrist. And it is only we who can do it. Benjamin never ceased calling us to action in the name of justice. As he tells us, "The past carries with it a temporal index by which it referred to redemption."[7] Perhaps the antichrist is our stillness before the dialectical image. For those of us in the United States, that we must subdue the antichrist should ring true indeed. For this antichrist comes very close to what Kant would have called the absolutely morally unfettered will, the *Willkur*, which can be expressed to us in the endless longing of the consumer for the false promises of empire that suggest we, and only we, are the ones, the chosen ones, who can drive Hummers.

But Benjamin's anamnestic solidarity itself keeps open the passageway between the living and the dead, but not in the historicist sense that we in any way belie the suffering of those who died by giving it a meaning as it were itself part of a context that already fated people to do what they did. We know that young man and woman as those who broke with apartheid and all of its claims upon them in that moment in which they are captured forever; we must heed their demand on us that we remain faithful to our own weak messianic power as the next generation is called to the struggle for a just world. Seeing the young man and woman gives us an image; heeding their call makes it dialectical.

In another photograph from South Africa, one of many that haunt me, a mother is speaking to the charred remains of her son. She is waving her hands gently over the body, coming as close as she can to stroking those charred remains. She cannot touch these remains, otherwise the body will dissolve. And she seeks to take her child home to the ancestors: the one place where this young man can finally rest in peace. Khulumani, an organization in South Africa, dedicates itself to those who continue to seek out the dead and the missing, and who by so doing keep open what Benjamin would call a passageway between the dead and the living. It is an ongoing work that is itself a remembrance of the horror under which so many died and a constant reminder of the ever-pressing danger which we are called to guard against. In a deep sense, the dead are allowed to speak to us.

Alongside the charred remains of the lost son is an AK-47 which for so many young people of my generation, and still in the world today, remains a symbol of empowerment even if it can only deliver vengeance. Again, we see the dialectical image before us in the sense Benjamin suggests to us. It is a deep ambiguity, this gun, because it represented, or became a kind of symbol loaded with the myth of, liberation, precisely in Benjamin's sense of the negative aspect of myth. In this figure liberation is reduced to a tragic necessity of violence—a tragic necessity that Benjamin believed in some circumstances we might be called to but may itself turn would-be liberators into shadows. In the movie *Lord of War*, a film in the "present," we also see young children proudly holding that same gun, which is now a popular item often sold by gunrunners. Benjamin teaches us how to unpack this simple thing, this gun, that promises what it itself cannot deliver, but only if we allegorize it through the lens of the despair that inheres in the belief that only in violence can we hope to save the dream of the better world.

Indeed, the very figure of the suicide bomber can be read as the figure who no longer believes that there can be meaningful action that could actually change the world. And, yet, still the call to act is necessary. In a deep sense, suicide bombing carries within it the recognition that any kind of killing must exact its retribution. But we are far here from the dream of armed struggle that could deliver us from the nightmare world of colonialism and, of course, advanced capitalism. The suicide bomber, in a profound sense, figures the moral basis for action as part of how we shape who we are as freedom fighters in the world (to use an old-fashioned phrase). The suicide bomber figures the moral basis for action precisely in the implicit acceptance of retribution as the result of killing. Suicide bombing is in a sense a last act, a last gasp that seeks to break out of the enclosure of a suffocating reality that buries the weak messianic power within us by turning us to death. Such a last gasp is the acceptance that to die is better than to live cut off from what is most meaningful in a human life: to transform ourselves together into who we might be in a better world, which would not silence the heed to the call of justice. It is the call to justice that echoes in the shattering blast of the suicide bomber that reminds us what was sought after was really a better world and not the obliteration of oneself in the fate turned character of killing.

This ethical basis for action was often lost in some of the Marxist-Leninist groups and parties, turning it into either a strategic necessity or the scientifically mandated end of capitalism. I was in many of those Marxist-Leninist groups in the late 1960s and early 1970s, and tried my best to defend then what I am defending here: the idea that socialism, as a better way of living together because it insists on mutual respect and responsibility for the world we make together, is always with each one of us now as a call to make ourselves the kind of people who in day-to-day actions in the present already promise the future. I know that may sound abstract. In my days as a union organizer—and a feminist union organizer at that—we did, of course, fight to bring an actual unions into the workplace. But we also did so by working together in union now. This being together "in union" was to be an experience in Benjamin's sense of the word *Erfahrung*.

Benjamin in his first published essay on experience writes against the so-called commonsense notion of experience. He writes:

> We, however, know something different, which experience can neither give to us or take away: that truth exists, even if all previous thought has been an error. Or: that fidelity shall be maintained, even if no one has done so yet. Such will cannot be taken from us by experience. Yet—are our elders, with their tired gestures and their superior hopelessness, right about *one* thing—namely, that what we experience will be sorrowful and that only in the inexperienceable can courage, hope, and meaning be given foundation? Then the spirit would be free. But again and again life would drag it down because life, the sum of experience, would be without solace.[8]

Benjamin is ironically commenting on how experience that points to hopelessness can never ground itself in the very idea of itself because experience is something we are always bringing into being. To return to my example about being in union, we were bringing into our day-to-day lives the experience of what, in Benjamin's sense, had been inexperienceable in the brutal workplaces where I organized: solidarity, comfort, solace, and support for each other in all of the actions we undertook together. It is not just that Lenin had it exactly wrong when he said the end justifies the means—although, of course, I believe he did—it is that the struggle for a better world is constantly bringing into our experience not only how we might shape that world, or what that world would look like, but how we ourselves become different as we try to actualize ethical relationships among ourselves. Sadly, it is only through bringing that experience into existence together, as so many of us did in the 1960s and 1970s, that we can retain a memory of different forms of solidarity and support: a memory that points us toward the future that many young people who do not have that "experience" refuse to struggle with today and see as beyond their reach. Ironically, it is the young now who before their time are world-weary, telling us that the fate of the world is such that the longing for socialism can only be utopian.

In his book *Specters of Marx*, Jacques Derrida argues that all of the metanarratives of "the end" run afoul of the mistake that inheres in Hegelian philosophical history. We read back the institutional structure of European modernity into all previous stages of history as if they were just incomplete precursors of it. Clearly, this kind of argumentation is circular at best and a self-congratulatory myth, in Benjamin's sense, at worst. For Benjamin, myth inheres in the sedimentation of what is our actual and ever-changing history in which all of the small challenges and resistances go unnoticed with the story of the victor claiming itself as truth. Derrida stands with Benjamin in that there is an undeconstructable experience of what he calls an "experience of the impossible" which marks the limits of history to finalize itself in the self-proclaimed inevitability of advanced capitalism as the only meaningful form of social organization. Derrida and Benjamin are using the word *experience* in a similar, if not identical, manner. But what both definitions of experience share is that any attempt to fully describe experience fails because it always points beyond itself to its own limit and how that limit opens up the space of the beyond.

In my book *The Philosophy of the Limit*, I renamed deconstruction the philosophy of the limit to bring out this integral connection between Benjamin's early writing on experience and Derrida's experience of the impossible. To quote Derrida:

> Well, what remains irreducible to any deconstruction, what remains undeconstructable as the possibility itself of deconstruction is, perhaps, a certain experience of the emancipatory promise; it is perhaps even the formality of a structural messianism, a messianism without religion, even a messianic without

messianism, an idea of justice—which we distinguish from law or right and even from human rights—and an idea of democracy—which we distinguish from its current concept and from its determined predicates today [permit me to refer here to "force of Law" and *The Other Heading*].[9]

For Derrida, it is only in this experience of the impossible limit that keeps the beyond, the beyond and the other as the other so that we can ethically respect and, indeed, heed the coming of the other and the other's demand on us. For Derrida, this "coming of the other" as the event, as the one who demands our hospitality, is a messianism without the messiah. If we are open to it then it can always pull us out of the supposed world of day-to-day experiences. An event for Derrida is only possible if it is indeed impossible in the commonsense notion of experience that Benjamin speaks of in his early essay. That world-weary experience predicts that everything will have to continue as it is now, but an event that could be described and predicted in all of its outlines would not be an event.

In 1992, I was writing against deconstructionists who interpreted Derrida's experience of the impossible as leaving us with another version of waiting for God to save us, or for a passivity before what might call us if we were to wait in silence. This reading of Derrida relies on his supposed alliance with Heideggerian pessimism, where we are fated to wait for God save us. I have always read Derrida against this pessimism. Derrida tells us again and again that ultimately we have a promise to the other and that as a promise we must seek its fulfillment. Toward the end of his life, Derrida argued that this promise actually calls us to institutional action now, or what he calls "the demand of negotiation." This demand for negotiation and institutionalization cannot, then, remain content with the "yes, yes" of a Nietzschean abstract affirmation. So, one must be patient but also organized. To quote Derrida:

> That is to say that in its self institutionalization in its very success threatens the movement of unconditional affirmation. And yet this needs to happen, for if the affirmation were content—how shall I say it—to wash its hands of the institution in order to remain at a distance, in order to say "I affirm, and then the rest is of no interest to me, the institution does not interest me . . . let the others take care of that," then the affirmation would deny itself.[10]

In a deep sense then the ethical call of this other demands that we risk "dirtying our hands." We risk knowing that any attempt to act in union might turn against itself precisely because we are struggling to move experience beyond itself as we shape a different way of being together. Although I cannot repeat that argument here, Derrida's experience of the impossible should never be read as knowledge of what is impossible, including the big dreams of socialism and justice. Indeed, the opposite is the case. Precisely because we cannot know what is impossible, precisely because every experience points beyond itself to its limit—which both defines the experience and yet marks it as limited—we are left with our own responsibility in whatever context we are in to struggle for justice. Derrida tried to make more and more explicit in his later writings that in the call for infinite responsibility to the other to this beyond we are never "off the hook" just because we can say it is no longer possible for us to live differently or for us to live well.

To return to Benjamin's essay on "Fate and Character," Benjamin reminds us that we cannot by definition be fated to have a particular character, nor can any previously ordained character be found to be the basis of our suffering. In the earlier quotation from Benjamin, he writes that "fate is the guilt context of the living" and he also reminds us that in notions of our fate what is best in us—our capacity for moral and ethical action—remains invisible. For Benjamin, our character is ultimately ethical, and in this of course he follows Immanuel Kant. But for our purposes Benjamin points to the ethical interests of those who are among the oppressors—all who live with all of the privileges of empire and the spoils of racism—in finding in themselves a source of responsibility that is not self-punishing but unfolds from an aspiration to be worthy of happiness.

To take us back to the example of Africa, Wole Soyinka argues that the beneficiaries of colonialism have a reason for accepting, and indeed demanding, of themselves reparations to all of the enslaved in Africa and, of course, those who were brought to the "new world." In broad brush strokes, Soyinka's argument was directed at a Truth and Reconciliation process, such as the one that was realized in South Africa, demanding it hold on to an idea of justice. Simply put, there can be no reconciliation without justice. But, I am in agreement with Soyinka that the challenge of South Africa is to be found in this struggle for justice, and that what justice demands—if it is not to be vengeance—has yet to be adequately addressed. But I want to return to the point by Benjamin which helps us to understand the profundity for each one of us as an individual of what it might mean to free ourselves from our so-called fated position as the beneficiaries of colonialism.

Instead, for Derrida the call for mourning and respect for what has gone before—and therefore constitutes us from within a relationality of debt—is ultimately inseparable from our mourning for actual ghosts: the ones who have gone before us, the ones who have suffered and died so that we may be. To quote Derrida again:

And all the grave stakes we have just named in a few words would come down to the question of what one understands, with Marx and after Marx, by effectivity, effect, operativity, work, labor [*Wirklichkeit, Wirkung,* work, operation], living work in their supposed opposition to the spectral logic that also governs the effects of virtuality, of simulacrum, of "mourning work," of ghost, *revenant,* and so forth. And of the justice that is their due. . . . Inscribing the possibility of the reference to the other, and thus of radical alterity and heterogeneity, of *différa*nce, of technicity, and of ideality in the very event of presence, in the presence of the present that it dis-joins a priori in order to make it possible [thus impossible in its identity or its contemporaneity with itself], it does not deprive itself of the means with which to take into account, or to render an account of, the effects of ghosts, of simulacra, of "synthetic images," or even, to put it in terms of the Marxist code, of ideologems, even if these take the novel forms to which modern technology will have given rise.[11]

There is a certain sense in which this openness to the other can keep us from bowing down to our fate as a colonizer: the privileged class who has joined the so-called victors of history. There is no apology for suffering except the action of redemption. As we have seen in Derrida, we must negotiate and pay back what can never be paid. Soyinka invites us all, as a hypothetical experiment in the imagination, to ask ourselves why there should not be a general levy imposed for such reconciliation, and defended in terms of reparations on the population of South Africa as part of their own struggle to free themselves from the imposed fate of the inevitable oppressor of the black population. To quote Soyinka:

> If, however, this attribution of self-redeeming possibilities within the psychology of guilt remains within the utopian imagination, and some external prodding proved necessary, the initiative could be taken up by someone of the nonestablishment stature of Archbishop Desmond Tutu. The respected cleric and mediator mounts his pulpit one day and addresses his compatriots on that very theme: "White brothers and sisters in the Lord, you have sinned, but we are willing to forgive. The scripture warns us that the wages of sin are death but, in your case, they seem to be wealth. If therefore you choose to shed a little of that sinful wealth as a first step to atonement . . . etc. etc.[12]

Benjamin would argue against the use of religious language of sin and atonement here and insist instead on the self-redeeming possibilities inherent in the unknowability of character, as we might yet become men and women of justice and begin to carve out a new pathway—one which would include the freedom that inheres not only in our acceptance but in our call for reparations for African slaves more generally. Soyinka is actually a part of a movement calling for reparations to Africa, but I am not speaking here about the programmatic efforts to make such a demand a reality. I want to stay with Benjamin's point about the self-redeeming possibilities of a character that does not submit to its fate to live out its life unjustly. I believe it is the insight of Benjamin that led Derrida to begin his book with the question: what does it finally mean to learn to live (and I would add "well")? If Benjamin teaches us anything, then it is that we cannot learn what it means to live well once and for all but we can seek to live up to its call and, indeed, do so in the name of our own freedom as well as that of others.

Benjamin's essay writes against the kind of discursive fate that gets frozen into bad idealizations of human nature. We all know of these static representations. For example, some say we are all utility maximizers and we can be no other way in this world. Or, we are all risk managers, and therefore incapable of something like true courage. But, these assumptions should be seen for what they are: myths propping up what we are fated to be in unjust world. And, yet, we know that millions upon millions of people in the twentieth century alone showed the falsity of such characterizations of fated nature by giving their lives for the fight for socialism. South Africa has become both a symbol and an allegory for many in the world today because the victorious struggle against apartheid ultimately took place in negotiations rather than through armed revolution that would have led to some system of government and law capitulating to the other in annihilation. In a certain sense the victory over apartheid is one of the most notable institutional state victories of a party that was once firmly committed to socialism. But the negotiations of course were only made feasible by wave after wave of rebellion and resistance as each next generation took on its own struggle against apartheid long after the leaders of the ANC (African National Congress) were in jail and the party in exile. Certainly, the ANC has wavered in its commitment, and some critics would argue capitulated to the demands of advanced capitalism. But, Benjamin and Derrida are suggesting to us that there is no end to what South Africa can become because of some metanarrative that dooms it in advance: to be eaten up by the machinery of capitalism.

Ironically, there is an ethical warning in Derrida about what it means to ascribe to such metanarratives because they allow us to get ourselves off the hook and ultimately fail to see that we are submitting to a fate as if it were necessary when our very submission was part of what it makes it seem as if it were inevitable. We may not be able to tell grand stories that will guarantee the ultimate success of socialism, but it is precisely because we cannot tell such grand stories that doom it to failure that leaves it up to us to make the "truth" of the ideal of socialism something that cannot be beaten out of this world. It is indeed up to us, and Benjamin gives us a complex answer as to why we might want to take up the challenge to live our lives in accordance with the call of justice rather than to submit to the fate of our utility-maximizing self-interest. For, it is in this struggle that we find our freedom, precisely because freedom is never something that is just there but in the slow work of forming a character that knows itself only in its endless effort to be other than its so-called fate. In this struggle we find our dignity; it is what we owe to ourselves and the dead.

Notes

1. Walter Benjamin, "Fate and Character," in *Reflections: Essays, Aphorisms, Autographical Writings*, ed. Peter Demetz, 308 (New York: Schocken Books, 1978).
2. Walter Benjamin, "Theses on the Philosophy of History," in *Walter Benjamin Illuminations: Essays and Reflections*, ed. Hannah Ared013, 255 (New York: Schocken Books, 1968).
3. Benjamin, "Theses on the Philosophy of History," 255
4. Benjamin, "Theses on the Philosophy of History," 254
5. Benjamin, "Theses on the Philosophy of History," 255
6. Benjamin, "Theses on the Philosophy of History," 255.
7. Benjamin, "Theses on the Philosophy of History," 254.
8. Walter Benjamin, *Walter Benjamin: Selected Writings: Volume 1, 1913–1926*, ed. Marcus Bullock (Cambridge, MA: Belknap Press, 2004), 1–5.
9. Jacques Derrida, *Specters of Marx: The State of Debt, the Work of Mourning, and the New International*, trans. Peggy Kamuf (New York: Routledge, 1994), 59.
10. Jacques Derrida, *Negotiations: Interventions and Interviews, 1971–2001*, trans. and ed. Elizabeth Rottenberg (Standford, CA: Stanford University Press, 2002), 25.
11. Derrida, *Specters of Marx*, 75.
12. Wole Soyinka, *The Burden of Memory, the Muse of Forgiveness* (New York: Oxford University Press, 1999), 25–26.

CONCLUSION

~

Heeding Piedade's Song: Toward a Transnational Feminist Solidarity

Can we aspire to transnational feminist alliances in a world devastated by war, the brutal legacy of colonialism, and the continued aggression of U.S. foreign policy? It is daunting, indeed, to envision how we might do so when the pull to the anonymity of our racialized world with the hierarchies it imposes is so great. Given the cemented meaning that fuels preconceived identities in the form of our "natural attitude" to one another, we can only do so by taking upon ourselves the vertical drama of a new poetics of consciousness given to us as a challenge in chapter 4 by Harris. A new poetics allows us to see each other differently and possibly create new ways of belonging together. In this chapter, I will offer a reading of Toni Morrison's *Paradise* through a lens using the Kantian interpretation of the sublime. We will thus be returned to some of the key features of my discussion in chapter 1 on the various roles of the imagination in Kant's critical philosophy.

Aesthetic Judgment and Sublime Affinity

Let me review, briefly, the difference between the use of the imagination in cognition and its deployment in reflective and aesthetic judgment. The ground of our knowledge is the transcendental imagination in which we intuit our world as always already in space and time. Remember, the transcendental imagination gives us the world of presentation and with it, all things that can be known. The cognition of objects, which is for Kant what constitutes determinate judgment as such in the first *Critique*, is carried out through a mediation in which the judgment consists in matching up the categories of the understanding with the raw material supplied by sensibility. Kant famously argues that this determination demands a schematization of the objects to be subsumed under the categories carried out by the imagination. The schema is a mediating representation that, to use Kant's words, is "homogenous with the category, on the one hand, and with the appearance, on the other, and that thus makes possible the application of the category to the appearance."[1] We need to be able to imagine the abstract content of a concept so that we can adequately apply it to its various manifestations that, despite seeming differences, instantiate the concept. Kant provides the following example:

> The concept of dog signifies a rule whereby my imagination can trace the shape of such a four-footed animal in a general way, i.e., without being limited to any single and determinate shape offered to me by experience, or even to all possible images that I can exhibit in concreto.[2]

Kant refers to this schematic representation of a dog as a template, or as he sometimes calls it, a monogram, for dog-hood, that links the concept to our sensible images of such an animal. In this case, understanding delimits the role that imagination can play. In other words, the cognition of objects serves a mediating role central to determinative judgment, in that its schemata make possible the subsumption of particulars under concepts, that is, dogs under dog-hood. Understanding legislates the form of representation, and the schematizing aims of imagination are limited by the aims of cognition. Although this may seem abstract and far from feminist struggles, we can begin to deepen the profound suspicion that some feminists have of knowledge through concepts, including any concept of woman or even of women, because the imagination, in order to cognize the group, will inherently schematize and idealize the factors that are to be given substantiality in the concept itself. In other words, if we had a concept of woman, we would limit our imagination in terms of how and who we might be through the reimagining and resymbolization of the feminine within sexual difference. If feminism is ultimately to concern itself with women as subjects, then there is a deep sense in which we do not want to seek in advance concepts that would limit the imagination in its portrayal of the richness of that subjectivity.

Aesthetic reflection in Kant, in both the beautiful and the sublime, alternatively does not ascribe objective properties to things as determinate judgment does, but rather cultivates a subjective relationship between imagination and its object. Although I will not spend much time on the aesthetic judgment of taste in this conclusion, I do want to emphasize that the difference between the judgment of taste and the judgment of the sublime does implicate a different role for the imagination. There is a specific sense in which the formalism of Kant's idea of aesthetic judgment in taste limits the imagination. Apprehending and reflecting on an object's form will necessarily involve exploring the temporal and spatial relations among its various parts, since the transcendental imagination is in the end what gives us our world. If the spatial and temporal form of an object spontaneously accords with the faculty of concepts, which is inevitably dependent on the form of space and time, then that form gives pleasure in the sense that we spontaneously feel the unity of our faculties. Concepts, it is important to note, are not brought to bear directly on aesthetic judgment; instead the imagination freely plays over the object so as to feel the harmony of cognition with sensibility, the harmony between the free imagination and the lawfulness of understanding, which takes us back to the attribution to a beautiful object of a purposiveness. This purposiveness is ultimately produced as a new way to regard the object as a formal unity that invents the harmony we seek out. It does so by creating in us a feeling that we can freely reach an accord between our faculties by allowing an imagination not properly determined by any concept, yet one that must still synchronize with the limits of the understanding if the object is to please us as we sink in the possibility that our understanding does not need to alienate us from our sensibility. On this reading, Kant's famous appeal to a *sensus communis*, so as to confirm the intersubjective validity of aesthetic judgments, does not take us to any established community or communities. Instead, it appeals to a possibility that is available to all of us, precisely because we are rational creatures that think through the ground of the transcendental imagination, and therefore the feeling of pleasure we get from the harmony of our cognitive powers can be agreeable to all such creatures because it points to a cognitive relation common to all.

A judgment of the sublime, in contrast to beauty, is generated in us when an object defies the imagination's effort, an effort required because of its relationship to reason to present our world as a whole and the objects in it as comprehensible. Here we need to briefly review why affinity has transcendental purchase in Kant. Kant asks how particular instances are made possible by the preconceptual work of productive imagination. His answer is as follows: "The basis for the possibility of the manifold's association, insofar as this basis lies in the object, is called the manifold's affinity."[3] The imagination proceeds through three principles of synthesis. These three principles are apprehension, reproduction, and recognition. The synthesis of reproduction provides the possibility that presentations are associable and comparable as such. In other words, if we did not reproduce an image that differentiates between dog-hood and cat-hood, we would not know the actual difference between dogs and cats. As a result, we could not recognize this specificity and difference between the two creatures. We need reproduction in order to get the recognition we need to organize what we apprehend under categories. Affinity is the preconceptual relationship that we imagine as there between diverse objects so that we can not only know objects, but also know the relationships between them. But the transcendental purpose of affinity is that it gives us a world in which objects are in relation to one another, and it is precisely the conceptually undetermined relationships that take us back to imagined connections of the relata to which we now give a nonconceptual and new and different sense. But this "whole," precisely because its basis is preconceptual, can never itself be fully conceptualized. Reason reaches the limits of its aspiration exactly as it attempts to encompass all the faculties, and ultimately to find its way to fully rationalize the schemata. Sublime imagination and reason ultimately confront each other as what is unbounded by comprehensibility. In the mathematical sublime, the failure of the imagination to comprehend what is being presented to it turns on its inability to retain an ever-growing volume of apprehension. Apprehension explodes comprehensibility, and the imagination falters before what it is asked to take in. Under the breakdown of the imagination, we find ourselves instead confronted with an overwhelming, indeterminate multitude of connotation. The meanings that sublime reflection ascribes both to artworks and to aesthetic ideas more generally must remain indeterminate and open-ended, precisely because they can never be schematized or even harmonized as the imagination invents an object that seems to us as one with our understanding and our sensibility. If the judgment of taste links, but does not fully determine, imagination's relationship to the understanding, sublime reflection links the imagination to the ideas of reason, ideas which presume a totality that Kant's whole critical work demands that we apprehend as beyond the reach of the understanding, precisely because the understanding itself is grounded in intuitions that give us a preconceptual world which is at the same time the basis for all conception.

Sublime reflection produces uncanny relations among phenomenan that seem to have no obvious connection, and by so doing, opens us to a differential affinity of relata, an affinity that denies schematization or determination by any definite concept. In the sublime, everyday concepts fail us and we must struggle to make a different kind of sense of the uncanny. The imagination necessarily fails us in sublime reflection, and as we have seen, reason ultimately has to appeal to the imagination in its aspiration to totality, therefore we can only trace out the meaning of the ideas of reason through aesthetic ideas that can at best represent them, but never capture them. In Kant, it is the tension between reason's aspirations, imagination's failure of comprehension, and our respect for both that yields the feeling of sublimity. In determinate judgment, we subsume particulars under universally valid concepts, universally valid for creatures who have to think through the world in terms of time and space, and whose cognitive faculties are inevitably divided in the tasks they serve under the rubric of the understanding. In the case of aesthetic judgment, however, there are no concepts under which to place particulars. I need to stress this, because some commentators have suggested that aesthetic reflection broadens our mind, and indeed broadens our concepts. But a broad concept would still be a concept in Kant, and it is precisely not the task of aesthetic judgment to generate concepts.

It is this uncanny sense of ourselves and the affinity of our affective relationships that I believe is a crucial aspect of feminism. Ethical feminism, as I have defined it, inverts the relationship between the positive and the ethical in this sense. Ethical feminism promotes the recognition that who and how we have been as women who make our own histories will always slip beyond the grasp of our current conceptual knowledge precisely because of the way in which hegemonic patriarchal conceptions of women make the imagination of us as those subjects next to impossible.[4] What I mean by the ethical, here, is precisely the demand put on us, and particularly those of us who are white women in the rich countries of the north, to recognize that when we seek to "understand" women, and this so easily happens when we try to "comprehend" women of other cultures, we fall all too easily into the inherent objectifying tendency in a modernity that always understands others as objects of our knowledge, and judges them by the categories and concepts through which we grasp our world.[5] Ethical feminism is, for me, an ethical, aesthetic imperative which demands that we take seriously the *vertical drama* suggested by Harris as well as accept our responsibility to constantly question our habits, to spin new extensions of webs of meaning, and to respect the open efflorescence of significance given in such a rich field of ontic orientations that we now face in our world. Can we dream that the overwhelming complexity of the divergent ways in which human beings "world their world" and still aspire to another dream, that of a reconciled humanity that aspires to the idea of Kant's ultimate idea of reason, the idea of humanity itself is possible? Perhaps we can, if we dare to dream of paradise.

Toni Morrison's *Paradise*

In Toni Morrison's novel *Paradise*, a diverse group of women, Mavis, Gigi, Seneca, and Pallas, find their way to a former religious school once under the leadership of Mary Magna. As the novel begins, Mary Magna is still alive, although fading under the burnout of extreme old age, the flame of her life fanned by her devoted friend Connie. Connie was a "stray" child found by Mary Magna in Brazil and brought to this country to serve with her in her religion school. The women who wend their way to the convent are running away from the past, a world in which they were ensnared in patterns of abuse and neglect. They do not share anything in common other than that they are runaways. We know from the first sentence of the novel that one is white; later on, we are told that Connie is Brazilian. The convent is made up of women who literally straggle in, and after Mary Magna's death, Connie retreats into her basement, only rarely engaging the women who have set up their home under her roof. The convent is outside a town called Ruby formed by a devoted group of black men, devoted to their God and to each other as "8-rocks," whose almost blue-black color is read by them as a symbol of their racial purity. An illegitimate affair between Connie and one of the founders of Ruby is not the only contact that the convent has with the town. Women from Ruby find solace and female treatment there. And indeed Connie first comes to terms with the extent of her spiritual power in raising from the dead one of the young men who had driven out along the road beside the convent.

Ultimately, as we will see, Morrison is contrasting two very different views of identity. The men of Ruby can clearly not conceive of these women as other than a threat to their identity, their God, and their town. For them to maintain their identity, the women must be driven out, if not simply killed. But under the spiritual rituals led by Connie, who renames herself Consolata Sosa, the women find a way to a different identification with each other, an identification other to strays and runaways, now transformed by what it demanded, or more accurately did not demand, of them. The women gaze at Consolata as she calls them into the ritual space that will "reform" them as belonging to a new covenant in the convent. The women are drawn in, even as they question Connie:

> What is she talking about, this ideal parent, friend, companion in whose company they were safe from harm? What is she thinking, this perfect landlord who charged nothing and welcomed anybody; this granny goose who could be

confided in or ignored, lied to or suborned; this play mother who could be hugged or walked out on depending on the whim of the child?[6]

In her tales, Consolata Sosa remembers the world of African religion, and more specifically of the Candomble houses out of which she came and allows herself to return to by claiming her own spiritual power and the traditions in which it is rooted.

> Then, in words clearer than her introductory speech (which none of them understood), she told them of a place where white sidewalks met the sea and fish the color of plums swam alongside children. She spoke of fruit that tasted the way sapphires look and boys using rubies for dice. Of scented cathedrals made of gold where gods and goddesses sat in the pews with the congregation. Of carnations tall as trees. Dwarfs with diamonds for teeth. Snakes aroused by poetry and bells. Then she told them of a woman named Piedade, who sang but never said a word.[7]

For those unfamiliar with the rituals of Candomble, Consolata takes her "children" that are in disarray into an embrace that can hold them all by allowing them to return to the site of their trauma and to reimagine themselves apart from it. Morrison's symbolism here is that Consolata is the daughter of Yemoja who is, in the Yoruba pantheon, both the goddess of the ocean and the patron orisa of the Gelede Society. The Gelede Society, in the original Yoruba religion that comes from Nigeria, celebrates the powerful women witches of the world, who had both the power to help build society and the power to destroy it. Yemoja is the ultimate manifestation of female spiritual power, and therefore metaphorically at least, she is the "greatest witch of all."

Consolata's first command to the women is that they draw a template of themselves. As we have seen in Kant, a template or a monogram is a schematization of what is shared in common by the objects of the manifold so that it can be intuited as things within the conceptual unity. But here the template is where the women will draw what does not yet exist, and what cannot be conceptualized. In current psychoanalytic language, each woman has suffered a severe wound to the imagined image of herself through profound trauma. In the template, they will draw out a new self, one no longer hunted and haunted; but they cannot do this without being returned to the self before the trauma which is, at least psychoanalytically conceived, the no-self. This imagined no-self, this chance to go it again and become a person differently, and perhaps a person at all for the first time, is what Morrison describes in the undergoing of each woman of a shared ritual. The first step in that ritual is the loud dreaming in which their identifications blend with one another.

> That is how the loud dreaming began. How the stories rose in that place. Half-tales and the never-dreamed escaped from their lips to soar high above guttering candles, shifting dust from crates and bottles. And it was never important to know who said the dream or whether it had meaning. In spite of or because their bodies ache, they step easily into the dreamer's tale. They enter the heat in the Cadillac, feel the smack of cold air in the Higgledy Piggledy. They know their tennis shoes are unlaced and that a bra strap annoys each time it slips from the shoulder. The Armour package is sticky. They inhale the perfume of sleeping infants and feel parent-cozy although they notice one's head is turned awkwardly.[8]

But the loud dreaming is ultimately a call to draw out a different self from within the ritualistic connection that now supports them in a new promise of who they can be. They turned their templates into artworks in which their reimagined body is now reinterpreted by the others as giving expression to a history and to an experience that had no capacity to make itself into their world before they drew it and then explained it.

> Life, real and intense, shifted to down there in limited pools of light, in air smoky from kerosene lamps and candle wax. The templates drew them like magnets. It was Pallas who insisted they shop for tubes of paint, sticks of colored chalk. Paint thinner and chamois cloth. They understood and began to begin. First with natural features: breasts and pudenda, toes, ears, and head hair. Seneca duplicated in robin's egg blue one of her more elegant scars, one drop of red at its tip. Later on, when she had the hunger to slice her inner thigh, she chose instead to mark the open body lying on the cellar floor. They spoke to each other about what had been dreamed and what had been drawn. Are you sure she was your sister? Maybe she was your mother. Why? Because a mother might, but no sister would do such a thing. Seneca capped her tube. Gigi drew a heart locket around her body's throat, and when Mavis asked her about it, she said it was a gift from her father which she had thrown into the Gulf of Mexico. Were there pictures inside? asked Pallas. Yeah. two. Whose? Gigi didn't answer.[9]

In her initial opening to the ritual that forms the new covenant in which each woman's personhood is supported, Consolata appeals to a unity of the good and bad mother, a unity again which was the sublime affinity, not a concept, of what these figures are or even should be in some limited moral sense. "Here me, listen. Never break me in two."[10] This imagined affinity of the "good and bad," Eve as Mary's mother and Mary as the daughter of Eve, symbolizes the bringing together of parts of themselves buried in self-blame that each woman had buried in order to survive her traumatic past. Described at the end of the ritual, the women are returned to a kind of joy in their relationship to the great waters, rivers, and oceans that Consolata invokes in her ritual. These dancing women have found themselves in a reimagined covenant in which each is returned through ritual to an originary rebirth out of the water that first contained them.

> Consolata started it; the rest were quick to join her. There are great rivers in the world and on their banks and the edges of oceans children thrill to water. In places where rain is light the thrill is almost erotic. But those sensations bow to the rapture of holy women dancing in hot sweet rain. They would have laughed, had enchantment not been so deep. If there were any recollections of a recent warning or intimations of harm, the irresistible rain washed them away. Seneca embraced and finally let go of a dark morning in state housing. Grace witnessed the successful cleansing of a white shirt that never should have been stained. Mavis moved in the shudder of rose of Sharon petals tickling her skin. Pallas, delivered of a delicate son, held him close while the rain rinsed away a scary woman on an escalator and all fear of black water. Consolata, fully housed by the god who sought her out in the garden, was the more furious dancer, Mavis the most elegant. Seneca and Grace danced together, then parted to skip through fresh mud. Pallas, smoothing raindrops from her baby's head, swayed like a frond.[11]

Morrison evokes the possible viewer who might have stopped by the convent during the ritual and seen the women in the magnificence of their freedom. The viewer would have been puzzled by what she saw; so uncanny and so unfamiliar would be the sight of these women who were at peace with each other and with themselves, and with the rain. As Morrison writes, maybe this visitor would have had the flash of an insight that the convent women were no longer "haunted." The viewer confronts the sublimity of these women now imagined to be free and as she does so, confronts what is most unfamiliar—a covenant based not on restrictive identities who have to abject what is unlike themselves but on the promise of a reconciled life with each other and with nature, and what is promised in the sublimity of that imagined reconciliation if not paradise.

This covenant worked out in ritual certainly does not proceed under the concept of woman. Yet the ritual itself explicitly turns on the "material" of the feminine imaginary. Famously, Jacques Lacan defined the feminine imaginary as what was pushed under by the symbolic order, leaving only the residue of the psychical fantasy of woman in the place of the ultimate object of desire, the mother-Other which is always there for the subject. The fantasy split off into "good" and "bad" woman so as to tame that unbearable desire, is exactly what Consolota puts into play at the beginning of her ritual. Her reminder, Eve as Mary's mother, Mary as the daughter of Eve, is to seek to reclaim both good and bad woman in the process of reimagining the significance of both. Simple identification along the lines of good and bad is as a result broken up, and the women can then own up to, and live differently with, the "bad" girl they have always abjected in themselves. Lacan, of course, would not have believed that such a ritual could heal, nor that women could ever live beyond being haunted by the inexpressibility of their feminine sexual difference, and hunted by men if they try to break up the symbolic order, so as to alter themselves in a new field of desire and significance.[12] Yet, of course, Lacan had no experiences with the rituals of the Yoruba-based religion, or more specifically, of the Candomble traditions and practices of Brazil. Morrison invites us to imagine such a ritual in all its sublimity. And yet it is not just the ritual and loud dreaming that is sublime; it is the full acknowledgment of each woman by every other of the intensity of her suffering that is itself sublime. Time itself is lost as the women engage in the reworkings of their feminine imaginary. As Morrison writes:

> January folded. February too. By March, days passed uncut from night as careful etchings of body parts and memorabilia occupied them. Yellow barrettes, red peonies, a green cross on a field of white. A majestic penis pierced with a Cupid's bow. Rose of Sharon petals, Lorna Doones. A bright orange couple making steady love under a childish sun.[13]

Sublime reflection allows us to explode the sedimented meanings we associate with the name *woman*, and even with the name *women*. In a deep sense, what matters is the singularity of each woman's past; and yet that past only comes to mean for each woman as she reimagines herself through turning her template, her idealized person, into something she now shapes.

Does race and ethnicity play out in this reidentification? We know that not all the women are black. So if there is race and ethnicity in the convent, it remains as the marks on the flesh which themselves have to be reimagined, in the remaking of who they are, together. If we wanted to use psychoanalytic terminology here, the women are remaking themselves through their sexual and racial difference and not despite it. I have distinguished elsewhere between identity, position, and identification.[14] In ritual, these women explicitly play with the meaning of the identification "woman" as it comes to them in all the bits and pieces of the images of the feminine imaginary. But they also have an identity for the men in the town as women. They are positioned as the ultimate bad women, who dare witchcraft and threaten with the power of their orisas, the phallic-identified stability of the town. This convent, with the fear and awe it inspires, had to be a woman's convent. It was only such a convent that could threaten the men of Ruby, precisely because their covenant, their paradise, is incompatible with the safe and stern phallic home the men have identified as their only hope for redemption from a racist world. Their terror of the women explodes in the meeting the men held to take the decision that these women had to be hunted down and removed of all their contaminating influence, so that the town could once again be in its purity.

> It was a secret meeting, but the rumors had been whispered for more than a year. Outrages that had been accumulating all along took shape as evidence. A mother was knocked down the stairs by her cold-eyed daughter. Four damaged infants were born in one family. Daughters refused to get out of bed. Brides disappeared on their honeymoons. Two brothers shot each other on New Year's Day. Trips to Demby for VD shots common. And what went on at the Oven these days was not to be believed. So when nine men decided to meet there, they had to run everybody off the place with shotguns before they could sit in the beams of their flashlights to take matters into their own hands. The proof they had been collecting since the terrible discovery in the spring could not be denied: the one thing that connected all these catastrophes was in the Convent. And in the Convent were those women.[15]

The specificity of these women's lives is neither reducible to some overarching concept of woman, but nor is it based in a simple notion of their difference. Difference, in other words, is not a spelled-out, marked, feminine difference that can be used as a standpoint of critique for universalist humanist notions, or even as the basis of some attempt to ascribe universality to the concept woman. As Adam Thurschwell and I wrote in 1987,

> In a related manner, the gynocentric critique of universalist feminism is a critique of the identity category that (mistakenly) accepts this category for what it claims to be. We fully share the motivations that inspired this critique, but have attempted to show that understood properly, the stark choice between universality and absolute difference is a misrepresentation of the interlocking interplay of sameness and difference. Furthermore, it is a false choice: the gynocentric response reinscribes itself in the same repressive logic of identity that it criticizes in universalist feminism. We condemn a reified gender differentiation

not in the name of some "universal human nature," but because it would confine us to certain socially designated personality structures, and because it misrepresents the self-difference of the gendered subject. It restricts the play of difference that marks every attempt to confirm identity.[16]

We have seen that for Kant, aesthetic ideas seek to express what can never be conceptualized, including the ideas of reason themselves. In Morrison's novel, paradise evokes a number of aesthetic ideas that force us towards new insights and visions which defy total comprehension. These insights push us toward drawing out new networks of affinity, including the affinity the women find in their being-together in their dance in the rain. But Paradise, in the most profound sense, is itself an aesthetic idea. Its promise is clearly beyond any notion of it. But it is just such a promise that Morrison evokes as always a possible new covenant, a new way of relating to nature, and a different, ethically altered humanity. Paradise, as itself an aesthetic idea, can only be brought into shape as ultimately what denies the very process of shaping itself. Imagination falters before what it most seeks to envision. And so as we strive to evoke Paradise as an aesthetic idea, we also have to acknowledge that all such expressions are imperfect, that they break down under the very demand of what the aesthetic idea longs for but cannot realize in any form of knowledge. Paradise is even irreducible to the great Kantian ideal of humanity, which regulates us as moral creatures as we aspire to live together in the kingdom of ends. For in this beyond, we not only find the magnificent sternness of the moral law, a sternness that the men of Ruby believe themselves to ever try to live by; we find the happiness of the rain dance, we find what Adam Thurshwell and I defined as reconciliation: the coincidence of love and freedom. This is a promise that Consolata envisioned with Piedade's songs. Piedade's song and Consolata's insight allows her to ascend to the practice of healing, and even of breathing life back in to what appears to be dead. For in a sense, is that not what the ritual gave to the women? Another vision of who they might be together, and with the world around them? As an aesthetic idea, always incomplete in its imagined affinity that leaves human beings at peace with all that is, paradise undermines the very shapes it seeks to actualize.

Was paradise ever there? Did the story happen? Was Consolata really a witch who could raise the dead? I ask you to imagine with me, if you can, that other space of our being-together, through an affirmation of our sexual difference that itself never claims to be anything other than a vision that as it glimmers, necessarily fades if we try to hold on to it too strongly. If we listen hard enough, can we hear Piedade's songs, even if there is no actual sound that goes with them? When Richard Misner, the politically inspired minister of Ruby, returns to the convent with Anna to see what is left, they find nothing there. Consolata was shot; so was the "white woman." The others supposedly ran into the garden. Anna and Richard take some eggs from the henhouse and then they see it, or rather sense it. Anna said she heard a door close; Richard saw a window. On the way home, they laugh about who is the pessimist, who the optimist. But both "knew" that for a minute they had had insight, and that insight led them to the sublime questions that they, and of course we, rarely want to confront. "Whether through a door needing to be opened or a beckoning window already raised, what would happen if you entered? What would be on the other side? What on earth would it be? What on earth?"[17] Perhaps paradise. Do you dare to open that window? Can you bear to hear Piedade's song? Morrison herself has dared to open that window, returning us to an initial imaging of Piedade, Yemoja, and her circle in the Gelede Society, Osun and her enchanted waters, which always allow us to see ourselves differently. Did this initial imagining force the story on the writer? Does it make us confront unbearable hope and dread as we open the window or shut the door? Do we dare to try to imagine the sublimity of that story of paradise, told through figures of women of overwhelming power? If we do so dare, then it will be our story, our imagining, and our struggle. And if we do dare, then there is hope because for a moment at least, we have insight into the full force of the promise of paradise. I leave Morrison with the last word:

> In ocean hush a woman black as firewood is singing. Next to her is a younger woman whose head rests on the singing woman's lap. Ruined fingers troll the tea brown hair. All the colors of seashells—wheat, roses, pearl—fuse in the younger woman's face. Her emerald eyes adore the black framed in cerulean blue. Around them on the beach, sea trash gleams. Discarded bottle caps sparkle near a broken sandal. A small dead radio plays the quiet surf.
>
> There is nothing to beat this solace which is what Piedade's song is about, although the words evoke memories neither one has ever had: or reaching age in the company of the other; of speech shared and divided bread smoking from the fire; the unambivalent bliss of going home to be at home—the ease of coming back to love begun.
>
> When the ocean heaves sending rhythms of water ashore, Piedade looks to see what has come. Another ship, perhaps, but different, heading to port, crew and passengers, lost and saved, atremble, for they have been disconsolate for some time. Now they will rest before shouldering the endless work they were created to do down here in paradise.[18]

Notes

1. Immanuel Kant, *Critique of Pure Reason*, trans. and ed. Paul Guyer and Allen Wood (Cambridge: Cambridge University Press, 1998), A138/B177.
2. Kant, *Critique of Pure Reason*, A131/B180.
3. Kant, *Critique of Pure Reason*, A113.
4. Drucilla Cornell, *Beyond Accommodation: Ethical Feminism, Deconstruction, and the Law* (New York: Routledge, 1991).
5. Dipesh Chakrabarty, *Provincializing Europe: Postcolonial Thought and Historical Difference* (Princeton, NJ: Princeton University Press, 2000).
6. Toni Morrison, *Paradise* (New York: Plume, 1999), 262.
7. Morrison, *Paradise*, 262–263.
8. Morrison, *Paradise*, 264.
9. Morrison, *Paradise*, 265.
10. Morrison, *Paradise*, 263.
11. Morrison, *Paradise*, 283.
12. Jacques Lacan, *On Feminine Sexuality: The Limits of Love and Knowledge*. The Seminar of Jacques Lacan, book 20 (New York: Encore, 1998).
13. Morrison, *Paradise*, 265.
14. Drucilla Cornell, *Between Women and Generations: Legacies of Dignity* (New York: Palgrave, 2002), 98–100.
15. Morrison, *Paradise*, 11.
16. Drucilla Cornell and Adam Thurschwell, "Feminism, Negativity, Intersubjectivity," in *Feminism as Critique: Essays on the Politics of Gender in Late-Capitalist Societies*, ed. Drucilla Cornell and Seyla Benhabib, 160–161 (Minneapolis: University of Minnesota Press, 1996).
17. Morrison, *Paradise*, 305.
18. Morrison, *Paradise*, 318.

Bibliography

Adorno, Theodor. *Minima Moralia: Reflections on a Damaged Life*. New York: Verso, 1978.
Appiah, Anthony. *Color Conscious: The Political Morality of Race*. Princeton, NJ: Princeton University Press, 1998.
Arendt, Hannah, *Lectures on Kant's Political Philosophy*, Ronald Beiner ed. (Chicago: Chicago University Press: 1992).
Benjamin, Walter. "Fate and Character." In *Reflections: Essays, Aphorisms, Autographical Writings*, ed. Peter Demetz, 304–11. New York: Schocken Books, 1978.
———. "Theses on the Philosophy of History." In *Illuminations* ed. Hannah Aredmt, 253–64. New York: Schocken Books, 1968.
———. *Selected Writings: Volume 1, 1913–1926*. Ed. Marcus Bullock. Cambridge, MA: Belknap Press, 2004.
———. *Selected Writings: Volume 2*, Michael Jennings, eds. (Cambridge, MA: Harvard University Press, 1999).
———. *Selected Writings: Volume 3*, Howard Eiland and Michael Jennings, eds. (Cambridge, MA: Harvard University Press, 2002).
———. *Selected Writings: Volume 4*, Howard Eiland and Michael Jennings, eds. (Cambridge, MA: Harvard University Press, 2003).
Brown, Wendy. *States of Injury: Power and Freedom in Late Modernity*. Princeton, NJ: Princeton University Press, 1995.
Butler, Judith. *Excitable Speech: A Politics of the Performative*. New York: Routledge, 1997.
———. *Gender Trouble: Feminism and the Subversion of Identity*. New York: Routledge, 1999.
Cassirer, Ernst. *An Essay on Man*. New Haven, CT: Yale University Press, 1972.

———. *The Philosophy of Symbolic Forms*, vol. 1, *Language*. New Haven, CT: Yale University Press, 1955.
———. *The Philosophy of Symbolic Forms*, vol. 2, *Mythical Thought*. New Haven, CT: Yale University Press, 1955.
———. *The Philosophy of Symbolic Forms*, vol. 3, *The Phenomenology of Knowledge*. New Haven, CT: Yale University Press, 1957.
———. *The Philosophy of Symbolic Forms*, vol. 4, *The Metaphysics of Symbolic Forms*. New Haven, CT: Yale University Press, 1996.
Chakrabarty, Dipesh. *Provincializing Europe: Postcolonial Thought and Historical Difference*. Princeton, NJ: Princeton University Press, 2000.
Cohen, Hermann. *Kants Theorie der Erfahrung*, 2nd ed. Berlin: Dimmler, 1885.
Connolly, William. *Identity/Difference: Democratic Negotiations of Political Paradox*. Minneapolis: University of Minnesota Press, 2002.
Cornell, Drucilla. *Between Women and Generations: Legacies of Dignity*. New York: Palgrave, 2002.
———. *Beyond Accommodation: Ethical Feminism, Deconstruction, and the Law*. New York: Routledge, 1991.
———. *Defending Ideals: War, Democracy, and Political Struggles*. New York: Routledge, 2004.
———. *The Imaginary Domain*: Abortion, Pornography, and Sexual Harassment (New York: Routledge, 1995).
———. *The Philosophy of the Limit*. New York: Routledge, 1992.
Cornell, Drucilla, and Adam Thurschwell. "Feminism, Negativity, Intersubjectivity." In *Feminism as Critique: Essays on the Politics of Gender in Late-Capitalist Societies*, ed. Drucilla Cornell and Seyla Benhabib, 143–62. Minneapolis: University of Minnesota Press, 1996.
Derrida, Jacques. *Acts of Religion*. Ed. Gil Anidjar. New York: Routledge, 2002.
———. "Choreographies. An Interview with Jacques Derrida and Christie McDonald." *Diacritics* 12, no. 2 (1982): 66–76.
———. "Différance." In *Margins of Philosophy*. Trans. Alan Bass, 1–28. Chicago: University of Chicago Press, 1982.
———. *Negotiations: Interventions and Interviews, 1971–2001*. Trans. and ed. Elizabeth Rottenberg. Stanford, CA: Stanford University Press, 2002.
———. *Specters of Marx: The State of Debt, The Work of Mourning, and the New International*. Trans. Peggy Kamuf. New York: Routledge, 1994.
Fanon, Frantz. *Black Skin, White Masks*. New York: Grove Press, 1991.
———. *A Dying Colonialism*. New York: Grove Press, 1965.
———. *The Wretched of the Earth*. New York: Grove Press, 1963.
Fukuyama, Francis. *The End of History and the Last Man*. New York: The Free Press, 1993.
Gordon, Jane. "Creolizing Rousseau." Paper presented at the annual meeting for the American Political Science Association, Philadelphia, PA, August 31 through September 3, 2006.

Gordon, Lewis. *Disciplinary Decadence: Living Thought in Trying Times.* Boulder, CO: Paradigm Publishers, 2006.

———. *Existence in Black: An Anthology of Black Existential Philosophy.* New York: Routledge, 1997.

———. *Existentia Africana: Understanding Africana Existential Thought.* New York: Routledge, 2000.

———. *Fanon and the Crisis of European Man: An Essay on Philosophy and the Human Sciences.* New York: Routledge, 1995.

———. "Through the Zone of Nonbeing: A Reading of *Black Skin, White Masks* in Celebration of Fanon's Eightieth Birthday." *CLR James Journal* 11, no. 1, (Summer 2005): 1–43.

Guyer, Paul. *Kant's System of Nature and Freedom: Selected Essays.* Oxford: Oxford University Press, 2005.

Harris, William. *History, Fable and Myth.* Wellesley, MA: Calaloux, 1995.

Heidegger, Martin. *Kant and the Problem of Metaphysics,* 5th ed. Trans. Richard Taft. Bloomington: Indiana University Press, 1997.

———. "Letter on Humanism." In *Martin Heidegger: Basic Writings,* ed. David Krell, 213–66. San Francisco: Harper Collins, 1993.

———. "The Question Concerning Technology." In *Martin Heidegger: Basic Writings,* ed. David Krell, 307–42. San Francisco: Harper Collins, 1993.

———. *What Is a Thing?* Trans. W. B. Barton and Vera Deutsch. South Bend, IN: Gateway Editions, 1967.

Henrich, Dieter. *Aesthetic Judgment and the Moral Image of the World: Studies in Kant.* Stanford, CA: Stanford University Press, 1992.

Henry, Paget. "Africana Phenomenology: Its Philosophical Implications." *CLR James Journal* 11, no. 1 (Summer, 2005).

———. *Caliban's Reason: Introducing Afro-Caribbean Philosophy.* New York: Routledge, 2000.

Kant, Immanuel, *Critique of Pure Reason.* Trans. and ed. Paul Guyer and Allen Wood. Cambridge: Cambridge University Press, 1998.

———. *Critique of the Power of Judgment.* Cambridge: Cambridge University Press, 2001.

———. *Kant: Anthropology from a Pragmatic Point of View,* Robert Louden & Manfred Kuehn, eds. (Cambridge: Cambridge University Press, 2006).

———. *Prolegomena to Any Future Metaphysics That Will Be Able to Come Forward as Science.* Trans. and ed. Gary Hatfield. Cambridge: Cambridge University Press, 1997.

———. "Toward Perpetual Peace." In *Practical Philosophy,* trans. Mary Gregor, 311–52. (Cambridge: Cambridge University Press, 1996.

Karatani, Kojin. *Transcritique: On Kant and Marx.* Trans. Sabu Kohso. Cambridge, MA: MIT Press, 2005.

Kearney, Richard. *Poetics of Imagining: Modern and Postmodern.* New York: Fordham University Press, 1998.

Lacan, Jacques. *On Feminine Sexuality: The Limits of Love and Knowledge*. The Seminar of Jacques Lacan, book 20. New York: Encore, 1998.

Levinas, Emmanuel. *Humanism of the Other*. Chicago: University of Chicago Press, 1972.

Makkreel, Rudolf, *Imagination and Interpretation in Kant: The Hermeneutical Import of the Critique of Judgment* (Chicago: University of Chicago Press, 1995).

Marx, Karl. "A Contribution to the Critique of Hegel's Philosophy of Law: Introduction" [1844]. In *Collected Works*, vol. 3, Karl Marx and Friedrich Engels. New York: International Publishers, 1976.

Morrison, Toni. *Paradise*. New York: Plume, 1999.

Pillow, Kirk, *Sublime Understanding: Aesthetic Reflection in Kant and Hegel* (Cambridge, MA: The MIT Press, 2003).

Rawls, John. *Collected Papers*. Cambridge, MA: Harvard University Press, 1999.

———. *Political Liberalism*. New York: Columbia University Press, 1996.

———. *A Theory of Justice*. Cambridge, MA: Harvard University Press, 1999.

Rose, Jacqueline. *States of Fantasy*. Oxford: Oxford University Press, 1998.

Schiller, Friedrich. *Essays*. Ed. Walter Hinderer and Daniel Dahlstrom. New York: Continuum, 1993.

Sen, Amartya. *Identity and Violence: The Illusion of Destiny*. New York: W. W. Norton, 2006.

Soyinka, Wole. *The Burden of Memory, the Muse of Forgiveness*. New York: Oxford University Press, 1999.

Index

academia, 132, 134; racism, 114
Adorno, Theodor, 8; background, 1–2
aesthetics, 6, 17–21, 23–24, 153–54; Kantian, 11; misconceptions, 7. *See also* art
Africa, 146–48
African National Congress (ANC), 148
Afrikaans, 138
anonymity, 113–14, 116
anthropology, 88
Anthropology from a Pragmatic Point of View (Kant), 31
anti-Americanism, accusations of, 2–3
antichrist, 141
apartheid, 69, 139, 141–42, 148
Appiah, Anthony, 130–31
a priori judgments, 40, 51
Arcades Project (Benjamin), 140
archetypes, 23–24
Arendt, Hannah, 29–30
Aristotle, 53
armed struggle, 142; vs. negotiation, 148

art, 87, 89, 154, 158; commodification, 2; and self, 92
Auschwitz, 69

bad faith, 118, 122, 128, 132
beauty, 21, 23–24; and morality, 24–25. *See also* aesthetics
Being, 54–55, 57–60, 64, 67
Being and Time (Heidegger), 45–46, 52, 63, 99; influences on, 39, 46, 49
Benjamin, Walter, 134, 137–38, 139–43; on character, 147–48; on experience, 144–45; on fate, 146; on justice, 149; on myth, 144. *See also Arcades Project*; "Fate and Character"; "Theses on the Philosophy of History"
Berkeley, George, 43
Berlin Wall, fall, 2, 32
Between Women and Generations (Cornell), 131
Beyond Accommodation (Cornell), 7
blackness, 119
blacks, in the white imaginary, 115

Black Skin, White Masks (Fanon), 109, 120–22
body, 122–25
Bringing Down the House, 117
Butler, Judith, 15. *See also Gender Trouble*

Capécia, Mayotte, 112
Capital (Marx), 7
capitalism, 32; Adorno on, 8; inequality, 1; as myth, 140–41
Cassirer, Ernst, 76–82; on *Dasein*, 97; at Davos, 45, 47, 96, 100; essays, 93–94; and Fanon, 109; and Heidegger, 95, 99; on humanity, 4–5, 105; and Kant, 30, 82–84, 86, 92; on language, 85, 88–91; on science, 130–31. *See also Essay on Man*; *The Philosophy of Symbolic Forms*
categorical imperative, 7, 27, 62
categorization, 114
choice. *See* rational choice theory
Christianity, 132
civil rights, 115
Civil Rights Act (1965), 11
civil rights law, 11–12
colonialism, 113, 120, 122; and academia, 106; aftereffects, 129; background, 5; effects, 151; implication in, 146; and race, 106, 110; teleology, 123
commodities, fetishization, 81–82
common sense, 21–22
Connolly, William, 131
conservatism, extreme, 3
constitutional democracy, 2
consumerism, 8–9; ill effects, 2
Copernican revolution, 102
courage, 148
creativity, 130
creolization, 132–33
criminality, 118. *See also* violence

critical theory, teleological, 31–33
Critique of Judgment (Kant), 34, 92, 95; on humanity, 32, 82; politics, 29; *sensus communis*, 21–22; on symbolic form, 76
Critique of Practical Reason (Kant), 30, 47–48
Critique of Pure Reason (Kant), 20, 21, 41, 82

darstellen, 5, 17–18, 26
Dasein, 76, 82, 92; definition, 47, 49–50; eccentric character, 102; and freedom, 96–97; Heidegger on, 55–57, 59, 61–62; objectification, 98
Davos, 47, 95–96, 100
de Beauvoir, Simone, 5
decadence, disciplinary, 133
deconstruction, 3, 6, 72, 145; Derridean, 63–64; names for, 144. *See also* philosophy of the limit, as term
degradation prohibition, 13–14
democracy, constitutional, 2
Derrida, Jacques, 3, 5–7, 36, 63, 144; on colonialism, 146–47; on guilt, 69–70; and Heidegger, 63–65; on the impossible, 144–46; and Kant, 67; play, 15; on the unknowable, 35. *See also Specters of Marx*
Descartes, Rene, 43
despair, postwar, 1–2
destiny, 59, 61
dialectical image, 138–42
différance, 7–8, 64–65
divinatory memory, 31
divine knowledge, 82
divinity, 120, 129
double consciousness, 105
dualism, 48, 58, 93
Du Bois, W. E. B., 105–6, 108–9

empathy, under oppression, 115
empiricism, 80, 118
empowerment, 142
Eskimos, 80
Essay on Man (Cassirer), 93–94
ethics, 93–95; responsibility, 8
Eurocentrism, 5, 76, 118, 132–33; idealism, 7
"European Man," 76–77
existentialism, black, 105–7, 126
experience, 144

faith, 138
faith, bad. *See* bad faith
Fanon, Frantz, 90, 105, 108–9; on armed struggle, 120–23; and Cassirer, 109; on colonialism, 125–26; humanism, 106, 121; on race, 111–14, 116, 119–20, 122, 129
"Fate and Character" (Benjamin), 146
feminism, 14; ethical basis, 155; history, 5; and ideality, 124; inequality, 32–33; quandaries of, 11–12; transnational alliances, 151. *See also* Butler, Judith; queer theory; women
Finding Forrester, 115–16, 117
Frankfurt School, history, 1, 3
freedom: of consumerism, 2; in *Dasein*, 96–97; definition, 60–62; naturalistic ideas, 6; somatic, 13–17, 32
Freud, Sigmund, 15; on sexual norms, 13–14

Galileo Galilei, 89–90
Gegenstand, 51, 52
Gender Trouble (Butler), 15
genealogy, 6
Ginsburg, Ruth Bader, 12
God, Kantian, 82
Gordon, Jane, 133
Gordon, Lewis, 126, 128–30; on anonymity, 114, 116–18; on decadence, 133; on Fanon, 106–7, 120–23; on humanity, 129; on vertical drama, 131–32
government, 3. *See also* U.S. government
Groundwork on the Metaphysics of Morals (Kant), 30
Guyer, Paul, 31, 32

Habermas, Jürgen, 67, 70
Harris, Wilson, 130, 151, 155; on vertical drama, 131
Hegel, G. W. F., 5, 31, 56; on freedom, 34; philosophical history, 144
Heidegger, Martin, 40, 93, 96; and Cassirer, 95, 99; on *Dasein*, 97; at Davos, 96; and Derrida, 5, 7, 63–65; on ethics, 59–60, 75; on hospitality, 71; on humanity, 57–59, 61, 98; on imagination, 47–48; influences on writings, 39, 49–51; and Kant, 4, 41–46, 54, 76; on knowability, 35–36, 52; pessimism, 9; on thought, 51, 53–55. *See also Being and Time; Kant and the Problem of Metaphysics;* "Letter on Humanism"
Henrich, Dieter, 31, 33–35
Henry, Paget, 106, 108; on creolization, 131–32; on Gordon, 130
historical materialism, 56. *See also* capitalism
history, and images, 138–40
Holocaust, 1
homosexuality, 11–12, 32–33
hope, 34–36
Horkheimer, Max, background, 1–2
hospitality, 67–68, 71
humanism, 106, 122
humanity, 56–57, 68, 98, 105–6; Cassirer on, 79; and history, 31–32; Kantian, 75; and race, 133–34
Husserl, Edmund, 4–5, 126–27

hybridization, 132
hypotyposis, 26

ideal, definition, 21
idealism, 43; critical, 52, 66; death of, 137; German, 7
ideality, 93
ideals, 2; universal, 5
identification. *See* identity
identity, 106–7; feminine, 158–62; free play, 131; Morrison's view, 156–59, 160–63. *See also* blackness
imaginary domain, 11, 14–15, 18; sexuality, 15
The Imaginary Domain (Cornell), 32
imagination, 26; ambivalence about, 30; arguments against, 95; feminine, 159–60; Heidegger on, 4; hypothetical, 27; Kantian, 6, 11, 43; mediational role, 41–42; role of, 11, 28; and taste, 152–53; and thought, 151–52; transcendental, 39–40, 44
imperialism, 67
interchangeability of people, 114, 116–17
interiority. *See* subjectivity
interracial relationships, 111–12
invisibility, 113
Irigaray, Luce, 68
Iraq War, 138
Islam. *See* Muslims

judgments, a priori, 40, 51
justice, 100; naturalistic ideas, 6; as self-fulfillment, 28
"Justice as Fairness" (Rawls), 28

Kant, Immanuel, 3–4, 6, 128; aesthetics, 16, 162; on beauty, 17–22; and Cassirer, 82; common sense, 22; on concepts, 155; dualism, 30; and Heidegger, 39, 41–42, 44–46, 50–51; on holiness, 62; on hospitality, 67; on humanity, 98; imagination, 11, 14, 19–21, 30–31; on knowledge, 52, 54; on moral agency, 58; on nature, 89; readings of, 96; schemas, 82–84, 86, 151–52; subjectivity, 8; on the sublime, 25–26; transcendental, 127; on understanding, 154. *See also Anthropology from a Pragmatic Point of View*; *Critique of Judgment*; *Critique of Practical Reason*; *Critique of Pure Reason*; *Groundwork on the Metaphysics of Morals*; "Toward Perpetual Peace"
Kant and the Problem of Metaphysics (Heidegger), 47
Kearney, Richard, 46
Keller, Helen, 79
Khulumani, 142
knowledge, 45–46; knowability, 49–51; transcendental, 40

Lacan, Jacques, 159–60
language, 84; architectonicity, 80–81; diversity, 88–89; flexibility, 79–80; and knowledge, 89–90; of the oppressed, 110; and self, 92; transformative, 90–91. *See also* Cassirer, Ernst; symbolic formation
Lenin, Vladimir Ilyich, 144
Leninism, 143–44
"Letter on Humanism" (Heidegger), 56, 76
Levinas, Emmanuel, 62, 68, 94–96, 102; on meaning, 100–102
liberation: human, 107; of violence, 142
limitation, 3, 77; embodiment, 4; on European philosophy, 5; knowability, 5–6. *See also* philosophy of the limit, as term
Lord of War, 142

Makkreel, Rudolt, 21, 25
Mandela, Nelson, 21, 31–32
Manicheism, 107
Marburg school, 95
Marcuse, Herbert, background, 1–2
Marx, Karl, 6–7, 31, 56; on capital, 81; on freedom, 34. *See also Capital*
Marxism: effects, 1; ethical basis, 143–44; materialist, 90; practical, 7; and technology, 63
masochism, 118, 128–29
materialism, historical, 56
mathematics, 25, 53–54, 86–89
messianism, 17, 141–42
metanarratives, 148–49
metaphysics, 40, 52
morality: and beauty, 24–25; European, 35; Kantian, 75; and the sublime, 25
Morrison, Toni, 151, 156, 159–63. *See also Paradise*
multiculturalism, 77–78
murder, 121; of whites, 120
Muslim Circle of North America, 70
Muslims, 70, 123–24
myth, 87–88, 99–100, 137; of capitalism, 141; of history, 144; self-reflective, 140

naming, 79–80
national security, 2
naturalism, 6
nature, definition, 89
Nazis, 95
negrification, 106, 120
neo-Kantianism, 77–78
Newton, Isaac, 52–54
Nietzsche, Friedrich, 2, 6, 145
nihilism, 35, 61–62
9/11 attacks, 2, 137–38
norms, 22. *See also* sexuality
nothingness, 98

objectification, 155
objectivity, 92, 94–95
O'Connor, Sandra Day, 12
ontology, 102, 107, 132; critiques, 59, 93; definition, 65–66
oppression, 110–11; definition, 114–15; internalization, 129–30
Orishas, 132
overdetermination, 113, 115

Palestine, 69
Paradise (Morrison), 151, 156–59, 160–63
Parks, Rosa, 114–15
passivity, 145
pessimism: pitfalls, 3, 6; reasons for, 100; universalism, 8; varieties, 8–9
Petersen, Hector, 138–40
phenomenology, 105, 115; black, 106, 108, 122; definition, 108
philosophy: basis of, 4; black, 105–8; political, 14
Philosophy of Symbolic Forms (Cassirer), 77–78, 83, 95
philosophy of the limit, as term, 3. *See also* limitation
Philosophy of the Limit, The (book), 3, 63, 72, 144, 101–2
phobogenticism, 119
Pillow, Kirk, 22–23
pluralism, 5
politics, 3
populism, 3
positivism, 6
postcolonialism, 102
postmodernism, 3; and aesthetic ideas, 7
pragmatism, 60
psychoanalysis, 12, 160–61

Queen Latifah, 117
queer theory, 12. *See also* homosexuality; sexuality

race: and armed struggle, 119–23; fictitious nature, 130; and relationships, 111–13
racism, 107, 110–11, 120; colonial, 118; definition, 133; as existential exploitation, 129; and humanity, 130; teleology, 123
rational choice theory, 6
Rawls, John, 27–28, 47, 90. *See also* "Justice as Fairness"; *A Theory of Justice*
reason, theoretical vs. practical, 48
redemption, 70; via dialecticism, 137–38
reductionism, 3
reflectiveness, 128; second level, 33
relativism, 76; problematic, 5
religion, threats to, 123–24
reparations, 147–48
reproduction, in synthesis, 153–54. *See also* schemas
responsibility, ethical, 8
rhetoric, 2–3
risk management, 6, 148
Rose, Jacqueline, 12–13, 15
Rousseau, Jean-Jacques, 34, 90
Rwanda, 69

sadism, 118, 120, 128–29. *See also* violence
Sartre, Jean-Paul, 48, 109, 118, 126
schemas, 82–84, 86, 152, 154; limits of, 157
Schiller, Friedrich, aesthetic play, 15–16, 17
Schutz, Alfred, 114
science, 86–87, 89–90; experimentation, 52–53; objectification, 4; and race, 130–31; and self, 92. *See also* technology

scientific law, 3–4
security, 2
self: autonomous, 29; noumenal, 28; perception of, 45–46
self-esteem, 28
semioticbiogenesis, 126; definition, 122–23
Sen, Amartya, 33, 94, 133
sensation, 51, 83–84
September 11, 2001 attacks, 2, 137–38
sexuality: aesthetic play, 16; Kantian, 32; norms, 12, 14, 15. *See also* feminism; homosexuality; queer theory
signs vs. symbols, 78
socialism: continued existence, 137; ideal, 1; metanarratives, 148–49; utopian, 144. *See also* Marx, Karl
sociality, 129
Soweto Uprising, 111, 138–40
Soyinka, Wole, 146–48
spatialization, 65, 79–80
Specters of Marx (Derrida), 144
stereotypes, 117. *See also* racism
subjectivism, 59
subjectivity, 2, 4, 9, 118
sublime, 153–55, 160–61
suicide, Kant on, 32
suicide bombers, 138, 142–43. *See also* September 11, 2001 attacks; violence
Supreme Court, 12
symbolic formation, 26, 76, 78–81; diversity, 89; multiplicity, 99–102; objectivity, 92; oppressed, 110; plurality, 86–87, 94–95; and race, 112–13. *See also* language
symbolization, 85. *See also* symbolic formation
symbols vs. signs, 78
synthesis, 40, 44–45, 153–54

Take Back the Future, 70
taste, 152–54
technology, 60, 63–64
temporalization, 65, 79–80, 83; limits of, 139
terrorism: effects, 138; fear of, 137
theology, negative, 70
A Theory of Justice (Rawls), 27
"Theses on the Philosophy of History" (Benjamin), 139
thinking, axiomatic, 51
Thurschwell, Adam, 161–62
"Toward Perpetual Peace" (Kant), 67
transcendence, 98
transgendering, 11–12. *See also* queer theory

uncanny. *See* sublime
U.S. government, 3
U.S. Supreme Court, 12
universalism, 5, 76

universalization, 79–81
universities, racism in, 114

veiling, 123–26
veil of ignorance, 27–28, 30, 90
vertical drama, 130–31, 155
violence, 119–21: and empowerment, 142; and race, 119. *See also* criminality; suicide bombers
vorstellen, 5

Wittgenstein, Ludwig, 5–6, 85, 88
women: morality, 15; workplace issues, 11. *See also* feminism
Woolf, Virginia, 13
words, 84–85. *See also* language; symbolic formation
World War II, 1; origins, 3
Wynter, Sylvia, 2, 122–23, 130

Yoruba, 132, 157, 160–61

About the Author

Drucilla Cornell received her B.A. in philosophy and mathematics from Antioch College in 1978, and her J.D. from UCLA Law School in 1981. She is professor of political science, women's studies, and comparative literature at Rutgers University, and she has recently accepted an appointment as a chaired professor with the faculty of law and philosophy at the University of Cape Town.

www.ingramcontent.com/pod-product-compliance
Lightning Source LLC
Chambersburg PA
CBHW020802160426
43192CB00006B/407